RECONCILIATION IN A MICHIGAN WATERSHED

RECONCILIATION IN A MICHIGAN WATERSHED

Restoring Ken-O-Sha

Gail Gunst Heffner
David P. Warners

MICHIGAN STATE UNIVERSITY PRESS | *East Lansing*

The Calvin Center for Christian Scholarship provided funding for workshops, research assistance, and publishing.

Michigan State University Press
East Lansing, Michigan 48823-5245

Library of Congress Cataloging-in-Publication Data
Names: Heffner, Gail Gunst, author. | Warners, David P., author.
Title: Reconciliation in a Michigan watershed : restoring Ken-O-Sha / Gail Gunst Heffner, David P. Warners.
Description: East Lansing : Michigan State University Press, [2024] | Includes bibliographical references and index.
Identifiers: LCCN 2023032385 | ISBN 9781611864939 (paperback) | ISBN 9781609177621 | ISBN 9781628955231
Subjects: LCSH: Plaster Creek (Kent County, Mich.) | Plaster Creek Watershed (Kent County, Mich.) | Watersheds—Michigan—Kent County—History. | Watershed restoration—Michigan—Kent County—Citizen participation. | Ottawa Indians—Michigan—Kent County—History. | Environmental justice—Michigan—Kent County. | Reconciliation—Michigan—Kent County. | Kent County (Mich.)—Environmental conditions.
Classification: LCC GB991.M54 H45 2024 | DDC 577.6/270977455—dc23/eng/20230817
LC record available at https://lccn.loc.gov/2023032385

Book and cover design by Anastasia Wraight
Cover art: Beautiful waterfall with colorful stones in autumn forest, digital painting, by Grandfailure

Visit Michigan State University Press at www.msupress.org

Contents

THIS IS WHERE

we meet the Great Spirit
swallowtails on the spice bush

waters of the walleye
gypsum cliffs

oil slick of the blackbird
buckthorn, purple-berried

prickly pear & lobelia
deer scat

the culms of beak grass
mandibles of beetles

spider wort
the kingdom of screeches

bluebells (if
the Milky Way (if

Indiana bats in the shagbark hickory
pawpaw & riverbank rye

(where there is no walleye)
(where there is no gypsum)

stream laced with snuffbox mussels
the oriental bittersweet

milkweed & sideoats grama
rod-shaped bacteria

wings that stridulate
anthers of wild ginger

wild onion
the phylum of peepers

you can hear them)
you can heed it)

—*Lewis S. Klatt*

Preface

We live in a world of beauty and of wounds. Some days we awaken to bird song and a glorious sunrise. Some days we awaken to sirens and the fear of harm—from injury, flood, wildfire, or cancer. No matter where we live, we see beauty and we see brokenness. This book tells a story of splendor and provision while also revealing a story of disorder and degradation. Ken-O-Sha, now known as Plaster Creek, is an urban waterway in West Michigan that carries a complicated history—one that is both delightful and discouraging. Over time this waterway has been both life-giving and life-threatening. While still mirroring its natural beauty, Plaster Creek also reveals a past of neglect and abandonment. And as in other places throughout North America, brokenness exists between groups of people who have lived here for centuries. A story told about early interactions between Native people and European missionaries is revealing.

In the 1830s, not long after the first missionaries had settled near the long-standing Ottawa village at the rapids of O-wash-ta-nong ("Faraway water," today known as the Grand River), one of the elders was a man named Mack-a-de-pe-nessy (Chief Blackbird).[1] A skilled orator and strong leader, he distrusted white people because of past interactions, including an incident when he had been abandoned on a remote island and left there to die by trappers whom he thought were his friends.[2]

In 1926 Charles Belknap, who moved with his family to the Grand Rapids area in the mid-1800s, recorded his father's story about Chief Blackbird's resistance to evangelism.[3] He was unconvinced by the religious teaching that to learn about

God one must read about God in a book. The Ottawa experienced the Great Spirit by 'reading' the natural world in which they lived. He was also perplexed by the notion that to worship God one must move into a building on one particular day each week; his people practiced spirituality constantly and ideally outdoors.

These ideological differences led to an ongoing debate between the missionaries and Chief Blackbird. At one point, as the story goes, the Ottawa leader took one of the missionaries in his canoe down the Grand River to where "Kee-No-Shay" (Water of the Walleye) emptied into O-wash-ta-nong. The two men paddled up the smaller creek for about one mile to a waterfall that cascaded over a rocky outcrop and poured into the wide Grand River floodplain. The milky, orange-colored rock on this exposed, west-facing ledge glowed in the late afternoon sun. It must have made for a spectacular scene in this gentle West Michigan landscape, dominated by rounded hills and gradual slopes. Chief Blackbird explained to the missionary that this was a special, sacred space where his people encountered and worshipped the Great Spirit.

The missionary collected a sample of the curious, orange-colored rock and sent it to Detroit for analysis. The report came back that the rock was high-quality gypsum. In those days Americans imported gypsum from as far away as Nova Scotia. Once ground into a powder, it was spread onto farm fields as a fertilizer or used to make stucco and plaster for buildings. The first gypsum mine in the Grand Rapids area was established in 1841 at this very site.

Ken-O-Sha Becomes Plaster Creek

Although European immigrants may have viewed the discovery of high-quality gypsum in West Michigan as fortuitous while they were setting up farms and constructing new buildings, it had a harmful impact on the Ottawa. Surface mining of gypsum had a disastrous effect on the landscape and on the quality of this stream, and soon the walleye stopped coming up the creek to spawn. The moment in history when the missionary discovered gypsum marked the beginning of a steady and precipitous decline in the health of this waterway, and Ken-O-Sha was renamed Plaster Creek.

The name change reveals a significant worldview shift that was taking place in the mid-nineteenth century. Ken-O-Sha identifies the creek by a living creature that resided within it. Plaster Creek identifies this water by a non-living resource

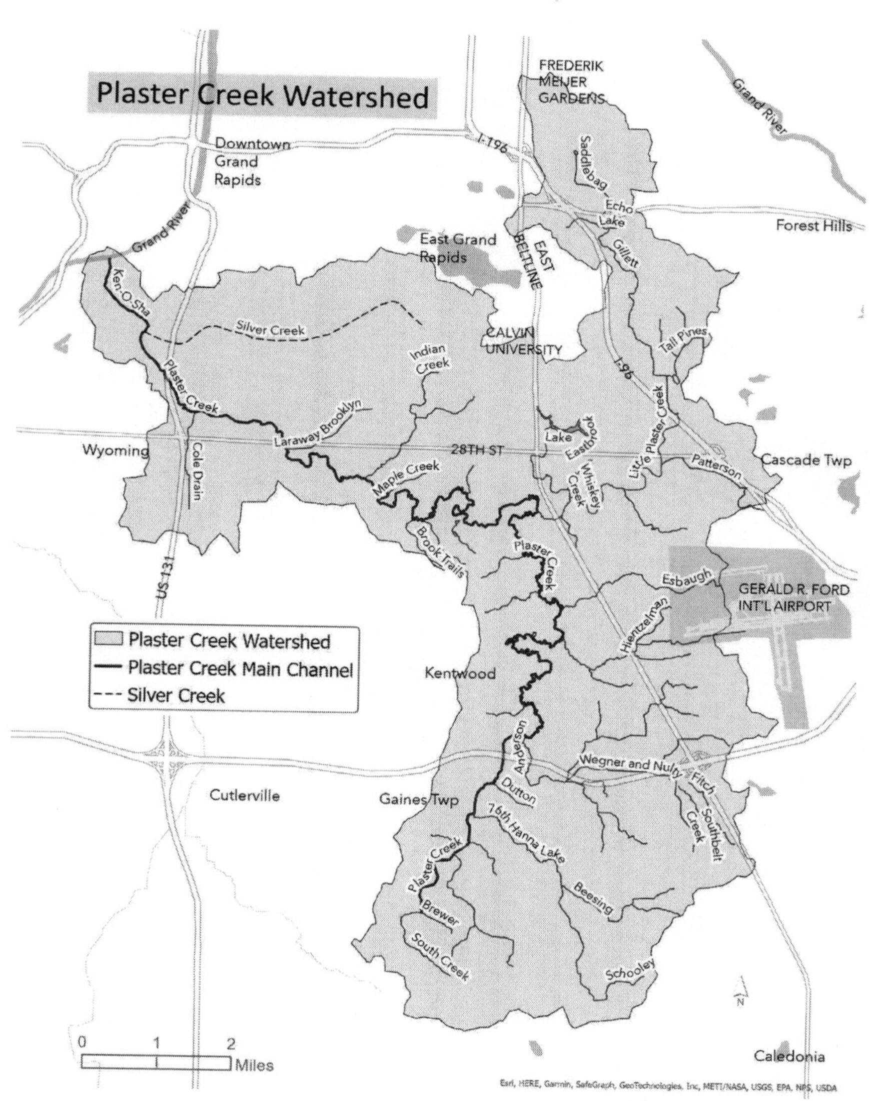

MAP 1. Plaster Creek watershed with its main tributaries and municipalities.

CREATED BY NELLIE ANDERSON-WRIGHT.

that was mined from its banks. Ken-O-Sha provided food while Plaster Creek provided financial wealth, at least for a time. Ken-O-Sha included a sacred space for worship; Plaster Creek became a convenient garbage conduit. Ken-O-Sha was life-giving; today Plaster Creek is life-threatening.

Plaster Creek is important locally to the city of Grand Rapids, Michigan, and to the Great Lakes region, which contains more than 20 percent of all the freshwater in the world. Fresh drinking water is not only a global issue but also a concern for cities in the United States. Lake Michigan itself is the main source of drinking water for more than 6.6 million people and a recreational destination for countless others. And Lake Michigan doesn't just magically contain water. It is constantly being filled by rivers that are fed by smaller creeks and streams, such as Plaster Creek, which drains into the Grand River one mile south of downtown Grand Rapids. The Grand River meanders forty miles downstream to Grand Haven, where it flows into Lake Michigan. What happens in small streams like Plaster Creek has an impact on larger rivers and on all the Great Lakes. Plaster Creek has been monitored for high levels of bacterial contamination for several decades now and has the unfortunate reputation of being the most contaminated urban waterway in West Michigan.

In the early 2000s two faculty members from Calvin University, a Christian liberal arts university in Grand Rapids, began hearing of the problems with water quality in the community. Gail Gunst Heffner, a social scientist with a background in urban studies and community development, and David Warners, a botanist and restoration ecologist, began attending meetings to learn more about local water issues. We joined with others to raise awareness of the problems with Plaster Creek and to galvanize residents to take action. Our early combined efforts as part of a broad Plaster Creek Working Group coalesced and intensified with the formal emergence of Plaster Creek Stewards (PCS), a watershed restoration initiative launched by Calvin in 2009.

Unhealthy Water Reveals Unhealthy Relationships

Everyone lives in a watershed, an area of land that drains to a common point. So becoming familiar with a particular watershed is one good way to start noticing the relationship between humans and the natural world. Water is also a great metric for assessing the health of both social and environmental relationships. Healthy water connotes healthy relationships. Contaminated water signals brokenness. John Wesley Powell, an explorer of western North America, understood this very well: "A watershed is that area of land, a bounded hydrologic system, within which all living things are inextricably linked by their common water source and where, as humans settled, simple logic demanded that they become part of a community."[4] Everyone who lives in a common watershed is in relationship with everyone else in that watershed, including the non-human creatures. Watersheds connect communities.

Watersheds are naturally delineated features of the landscape within which a strong sense of community can be built, but also within which inequalities often exist. Watershed advocate Ched Myers writes,

> *All* human life is watershed-placed, without exception . . . Watershed consciousness is not just an ecological orientation, but a way of looking at the world . . . Most watersheds on the planet bear the marks of modern human oppression and degradation. Social disparity, exclusion, and violence—historic and current—can and should be mapped and engaged at the watershed level . . . [requiring] a constructive reimagining of economic, political, and social lifeways.[5]

As we have tried to understand how our local watershed has changed over time, we have learned much about the events, attitudes, and practices that have coalesced to produce today's dangerously contaminated Plaster Creek. There is evidence that Plaster Creek has been worsening decade by decade for more than 150 years. How did this creek become so polluted? How extensive is the problem? What does this mean for the neighborhoods through which the creek flows? What, if anything, can be done? One question has led to another, and to another.

For the past twenty years we have taken a multidisciplinary approach to answer these questions and to understand how people have come to accept this contaminated creek flowing through rural parks and urban neighborhoods. Over time we realized that our task was not simply to clean up a polluted stream. If we successfully cleaned up Plaster Creek without changing the underlying causes, then ongoing degradation would advance as before. Instead of decontaminating the creek, we came to realize our focus should address the reasons why this creek has become so contaminated.

To do that, we needed to understand the history of this watershed: the ecological, social, spiritual, and economic histories that have played out over time in this fifty-eight-square-mile portion of the West Michigan landscape.[6] We needed to better understand the worldview that has allowed—and at times even promoted—the degradations to which this creek has been subjected. A life-supporting, self-sustaining ecosystem has been mistreated and mismanaged such that today, instead of the blessing it was in former days, it presents an imminent threat to many of its watershed inhabitants.

Healing Our Waters

As our work has unfolded, we have come to realize that our efforts to restore this waterway best fit into the emerging field of reconciliation ecology. Reconciliation ecology is the science of restoring, creating, and maintaining habitats and conserving biodiversity in the places where people live, work, or play.[7] The goal is to re-invent the human presence to better accommodate, affirm, and fit into the landscape of biodiversity that surrounds us.[8] The research, education, and restoration work of PCS is an ongoing attempt to put reconciliation ecology into practice. To begin, we knew we had to educate people about what a watershed is and about how their daily choices contribute either to the health of their watershed or to its demise.

Human beings are fundamentally ecological and social creatures, and how we interact with one another will also influence the environment within which we exist. Broken relationships between people often result in degradation and damage to the earth because of the interconnectedness of all of life. Our watershed work has taught us that reconciliation ecology needs to focus not only on the damaged human—creation relationship, but also on the damaged relationships between groups of people. Brokenness in all these relationships has resulted in the interconnected social and ecological problems we face today.

The PCS's efforts that we have been involved in for the past two decades in one small area of North America have taught us that simply working to change water quality in the short term will not have lasting impact. These problems have origins far back in history, and as we have learned more about the history of our place, we have become deeply troubled. But we have also been inspired to refuse to accept the outcomes of this history in the form of pervasive environmental disregard, inattention to watershed neighbors, environmental injustices, severely reduced biological diversity, and a contaminated creek unfit for children to play in. We are working to change the future story that will be told in this watershed by addressing the broken relationships at the root of these problems. How we engage in reconciliation ecology in the Plaster Creek watershed provides hopeful ideas for doing reconciliation work in other places.

This book is the result of shifting our attention beyond research and teaching, community meetings, and grant proposal writing to tell the big story of this watershed, to explain how Plaster Creek became so contaminated, and to highlight the efforts underway to restore it to a safe and life-supporting stream once again. This is a story that has broken our hearts repeatedly, but also one in which we have found hope and inspiration. We have been humbled to see that when people come together to care for their common place, divisions of politics, religion, culture, and class can fade. New relationships can be forged, and diversity in all its beauty can begin to flourish once again.

Learning from History

As teachers and researchers, we have learned the importance of understanding the context within which we do our work. Part of this understanding was to realize there are rich lessons to learn from history—sometimes distressing, sometimes inspiring. To understand the history of this watershed, we have consulted archival documents and the insights of geologists, archaeologists, sociologists, anthropologists, theologians, and historians. And uniquely we have also listened to community voices, hearing from long-term residents who have told us compelling stories of what Plaster Creek was like when they first encountered it years ago. We conducted more than eighty-five formal oral history interviews with residents of all ages within the watershed. These conversation partners have informed the telling of this story.[9] Mothers and fathers, grandparents and children, teachers and pastors, government officials and community organizers, the powerful and the marginalized tell the history of their relationship with the creek. These interviews have helped us better understand who has been blessed by the creek's presence over time and who has been most harmed. Historically faith groups have not been actively involved in environmental work and have often been overlooked as partners in ecological restoration. Yet spirituality has been and continues to be an important motivator for many people, including Indigenous people, to care for the earth.

For history to inform, accuracy is important. Biases in the telling of history are unavoidable, because typically the voices of those in power are the most heeded. Yaa Gyasi in her stunning novel *Homegoing* makes this important point: "when you study history, you must always ask yourself, whose story am I missing? Whose voice was suppressed so that this voice could come forth? Once you have figured that out, you must find that story too. From there, you begin to get a clearer, yet still imperfect, picture."[10] As white academics, we understand that we have interpreted our own experiences and perceptions through our whiteness and through our socioeconomic and educational backgrounds. Our understanding has also been clouded by the stories we have been told by other white people who have occupied positions of power as we participate in the dominant cultural group. However, in telling the story of Plaster Creek, we have done our best to recognize these limitations, to discern biases in the historical accounts, and to include marginalized voices with ours. We are attempting to decolonize our worldview. These stories—some frightening and some exhilarating—reveal how important water is to the human story. "Wherever there is a river [or creek], somehow that's at the very heart of our being, even if we don't know it."[11] Through careful listening to these stories, the community itself and its complex past emerge as a rich resource for learning how to live better into the future.

Because we come from different disciplinary backgrounds and life experiences, we weave together theoretical perspectives, scientific explanations, historical accounts, and personal stories. Gail supervised the social research of data collection and analysis of the Plaster Creek Oral History Project, and Dave supervised the ecological research. Where appropriate, we identify which of us is speaking to help the reader understand perspective.

In the introduction we set the context of the story of Plaster Creek, provide a brief overview, and introduce reconciliation ecology. This book is then organized into three major parts, each of which addresses steps in a process of reconciliation. In the first part, we bring the problems we encountered into clearer focus and show how these problems arose. We examine the geologic and natural history of West Michigan and compare a healthy watershed with the Plaster Creek watershed today. We then explore how the Native people in this place, particularly the Anishinaabeg, lived in and cared for the land and water prior to European settlement. Recognizing the problem—both the broken relationships among people and the broken relationships between people and the natural world—is the necessary first step before reconciliation can begin.

In the second part, we explore how the arrival of European immigrants, starting in the early 1800s, transformed the landscape in dramatic and destructive ways, acknowledging the colonists' complicity in the harm that was done to the land and to the Indigenous people who lived here. We also turn our attention to the urbanization in West Michigan in the late nineteenth and early twentieth centuries and the impact that it has had on water. We contrast the worldviews of the new settler colonists with Indigenous worldviews. In telling the larger story of Plaster Creek, we hope readers will develop eyes to see what has transpired in the last couple hundred years and will have courage to acknowledge human complicity in the ongoing degradation. This part of the reconciliation process is difficult and is cause for lament. Acknowledging our complicity in the broken relationships among people and between people and the natural world is the second necessary step before reconciliation can begin.

In the last part, we highlight how recognition of the problem and acknowledgment of complicity can motivate restorative action, and we explore ways to enact the work of reconciliation ecology—to repair and restore. We describe how PCS emerged and how priorities were identified as a response to a pressing community need. We highlight six strategies that have helped us put reconciliation ecology into practice: place-based education, applied research, on-the-ground restoration, promoting environmental justice, engaging faith communities, and shaping future environmental leaders. As we took initial action steps, we began to develop new eyes to see and understand past and current problems. We began asking different kinds of questions and began to see the need for honest community dialogue and decolonizing action. Stories and ideas shared through the Plaster Creek Oral History Project (PCOHP) helped us envision and begin to implement concrete ways to build restored relationships among people and between people and the natural world. The beauty and tragedy of Plaster Creek is not unique to our place but can be seen again and again in watersheds throughout the United States. The final chapter describes key lessons learned and their broad applicability for readers interested in promoting reconciliation ecology in their own places. What we are learning in the Plaster Creek watershed has implications that stretch far beyond West Michigan. The story of Plaster Creek offers a microcosm of the story of life on earth for us all.

Acknowledgments

First, we want to thank our parents, siblings, and extended families who introduced us to the natural world when we were very young and instilled in us a love for creation. Walks in the woods, fun days at the beach, camping and backpacking, or road trips to national parks, all created opportunities for us to begin learning about the world and our place in it.

We are particularly indebted to the Indigenous people who cared for the land and water long before we arrived, and we're grateful for those still here from whom we have much to learn.

We are grateful to fellow Plaster Creek Stewards (PCS) coworkers who have been terrific colleagues through thick and thin for the past fourteen years. The team started out small but continues to expand, and we remember with gratitude all those who have labored alongside us for a season or for years before moving on to graduate school or other vocational adventures. Thank you, Peter Hiskes, Nate Haan, Mike Ryskamp, Deanna Geelhoed, Ana Singh, and Araceli Eikenberry. And to those who are carrying this work forward, Julie Wildschut, Benji Steenwyk, Haley Weesies, Betty Gronsman, and Matt Hubers, we love your commitment. This work happens because of your dedicated hearts, minds, and bodies!

Special shout-out to Andrea Lubberts, who started as an amazing volunteer, then became an interviewer for the Plaster Creek Oral History Project, then an administrative assistant, and now serves full time as the program manager for PCS. Andrea brings joy to whatever task she engages. We have been blessed to work alongside her, and we are grateful for her many contributions.

We remember with gratitude more than 120 student research assistants and interns who have contributed their skills, stamina, and hard work to assist us in so many different areas: social sciences, engineering, restoration ecology, microbiology, plant physiology, water chemistry, and geographic information systems (GIS). Particular thanks to Katie Van Dyke who helped with early drafts of the manuscript, especially searching out details for notes and bibliography.

Several amazing people have taken our vision for involving high school students and turned it into an award-winning program. So much thanks to Gary Warners, Nichol DeMol, Georgia Donovan, Jamie Vaughn, Rachel Warners, and Jia Luchs. We are also grateful for the many college students who have served as mentors, and the over 150 high school Green Team participants over the years, many of whom have endeared themselves to us as they've grown into young adults.

Right from the beginning Calvin University has supported this work as legitimate for faculty involvement. Provost Claudia Beversluis and Biology Department chair Randy Van Dragt provided tangible support and encouragement in the early years. We're grateful for initial funding from the Calvin Center for Christian Scholarship (CCCS) for our first workshop to invite congregations into the Plaster Creek initiative. CCCS also provided ongoing funding for research assistance, a writing co-op, and publishing. Faculty from departments across the campus have become involved in creative ways: Biology, Chemistry, Engineering, History, Sociology, English, Art, Geology, Geography, and Environmental Studies. Beth Dykstra from the Calvin Grants Office has been a genius in helping us secure grants. Special kudos to Nellie Anderson-Wright who created new GIS maps for inclusion in this publication despite a quick turnaround. DataWise (formerly the Calvin Center for Social Research) has helped us gauge the educational impact of our work through community surveys and data analysis. The Calvin Ecosystem Preserve and Native Gardens has been a partner all along, modeling what careful tending of upstream habitats should look like.

Special thanks to Diana Toledo (with River Network) and Ann-Marie Mitroff (formerly with Groundwork USA) who provided the first grant PCS ever received back in 2011 as part of the inaugural group of the Urban Waters Learning Network. Your vision for building our organizational capacity by supporting the Plaster Creek Oral History Project came at the perfect time. And you helped us extend our reach by introducing us to river champions all over the country. We wouldn't be where we are today without your visionary leadership, wisdom, and guidance.

There are so many funding partners who provided financial support for various aspects of our work that enabled us to go farther than we ever dreamed possible. We're especially grateful for the amazing staff from the Michigan Department of Environmental Quality (now known as the Department of Environment, Great Lakes, and Energy) who patiently helped us learn, assisting us every step of the way, and provided significant financial support for many restoration projects. We're grateful for the U.S. Environmental Protection Agency (EPA) who provided workshops, technical assistance, and important funding for strategic projects that extended our impact. Funding from the Great Lakes Restoration Initiative and the National Fish and Wildlife Foundation enabled us to install multiple green infrastructure projects in the watershed. We're grateful for local funding from the Bosch Community Fund, the Wege Foundation, and the anonymous donor who provided funding to hire our first program coordinator. Recent funding from the USDA/Forest Service, Michigan Sea Grant, and Michigan Space Grant has enabled us to hire summer students to study important research questions, enabling this work in watershed restoration to broaden and deepen.

Learning and working together to improve local, regional, and national watersheds has been facilitated by the amazing partnerships and collaborations from which we have benefited: City of Grand Rapids, Lower Grand River Organization of Watersheds (LGROW), Trout Unlimited/Rogue River Watershed, West Michigan Environmental Action Council (WMEAC), Friends of Grand Rapids Parks, Grand River Bands of Ottawa Indians, National Wildlife Federation's Sacred Grounds, River Network, Kent Conservation District, Kent County Drain Commission, Kent County Parks, and many neighborhood associations and community organizations.

Working alongside community volunteers, some who have been supporting us consistently for over a decade, has been a rich blessing. Your thoughtful conversations, sweat equity, and joyful spirits have made the hard times easier and the good times better. Many community members have also become financial donors, and we acknowledge and appreciate all the many ways you have helped the work of watershed restoration to deepen.

The staff at Michigan State University Press has been amazing. Catherine Cocks helped us move early drafts of this book into a publishable manuscript. Caitlin Tyler-Richards patiently guided us through the acquisitions process.

Anastasia Wraight was the project editor who carried this project over the finish line. As managing editor, Kristine Blakeslee handled myriads of details during production, and Nicole Utter helped with marketing plans. We appreciate all the ways MSU Press has shepherded this project to completion and encouraged us along the way. We also benefited from three anonymous peer reviewers whose insightful comments greatly improved the manuscript.

Throughout the years of working on this book, life has happened. Our friends and families have kept us going amid major changes: family births and deaths, a global pandemic, personal health challenges, and life transitions. Both of us gain so much from our children, who inspire and model for us a more hopeful future. So special thanks to Andrew and Morgan, Daniel and Janelle, Elisabeth and Zach, Micah and Eryn, Rachel, and Ana Li. Our beloved spouses, Ken and Teri, have been particularly integral in keeping us grounded through all the changes, and it is to them that we dedicate this book.

Introduction

It started with a simple rain garden in a rural part of the watershed, a hand-dug depression we planned to populate with native plants to catch stormwater that was running off a parking lot at Kent County's Dutton Shadyside Park. This old parking lot had been constructed right next to the creek with cemented runways to usher the water quickly off the asphalt directly into the stream. But our ideas were met with skepticism when we showed the site to a stream ecologist from the Michigan Department of Environmental Quality (MDEQ). He worried that the volume of water from the parking lot would overwhelm a rain garden, saturate the entire site, and result in a large blowout of soil into the creek. Instead, he looked over the entire park property and told us he thought we should be thinking bigger.

With his help and help from several other experts, we developed a much larger plan to restore the natural floodplain. At that time, the section of Plaster Creek running through the park was surrounded by lawn, and the streambanks were collapsing because of severe erosion by stormwater runoff upstream. Many large old trees had already fallen into the creek. Although lawn grasses are good for frisbee and soccer, their shallow root systems are not helpful in protecting streambanks. With the help of a Kent County engineer and a Kent County Parks landscape architect, we developed a detailed plan. This would be a large project, covering twelve acres and requiring heavy excavating equipment, a new bridge for park visitors, over two hundred trees, and seventy thousand plugs of native plants. After careful review of the plan by experts at the state level, Plaster Creek Stewards (PCS) secured $600,000 in federal funding for the project from MDEQ.

FIGURE 1. Extreme erosion at Shadyside Park before restoration project.
PHOTOGRAPH BY DAVID P. WARNERS.

By the time PCS was ready to announce the approved plans for Shadyside Park in the spring of 2016, we had already been deliberating about this project for five years, and we were learning step by step the requirements for implementing such a large project. To receive a state permit to begin construction, a project of this size requires notifying the public and providing an opportunity for feedback. So we distributed a public announcement, and that's when the rumbling started. A few neighbors read the proposed plans and misunderstood them. PCS held several open-house meetings at the park pavilion to explain the plans, but very few people attended. Instead, the upset neighbors began circulating flyers claiming the proposed plans would cause upstream flooding and would ruin their beloved park.

With guidance from MDEQ, PCS scheduled a public hearing, thinking that once people understood what was being proposed, they would welcome the park improvements. In honesty we were naïve about the intensity of resistance. As word spread about the public hearing, we began to receive threatening messages on social media warning that we would be physically harmed if this project were undertaken. We were advised to have law enforcement present at the public hearing to guarantee our safety.

On the evening of the public hearing, held at a local library in July 2016, I (Gail) stood at the door shaking hands and welcoming people. An older couple approached me, and as I put out my hand to welcome them, the man defiantly crossed his arms, shook his head, and said, "Why should I shake your hand?" Caught off-guard, I weakly replied, "Well, um, thank you for coming. I just wanted to welcome you to the meeting." Thus began a very contentious forum.

Facilitated by state officials, the meeting began with PCS staff introducing the project, a Kent County engineer describing the engineering plans, and a state geologist explaining the hydrological improvements. Then came time for public feedback. Of the seventy-five people in attendance, only a few expressed support. Person after person got up to denounce the project, accusing us of intending to destroy the park, and challenging each aspect of the plan. One community member said vehemently, "I don't like the government getting involved in our community, I don't like higher education, and I don't trust your science." The project had government funding, a college was administering it, and several scientists had explained the plans!

We were completely blindsided by the public outcry and by the subtle and not-so-subtle threats of violence. Three resistant neighbors subsequently filed an appeal with MDEQ, which was responsible for issuing the permit, and a judge was assigned to review the case. This appeal process took two additional years before the case was settled. After all these deliberations, the project was finally granted a permit, and we were given a green light to proceed.

Throughout this process, we learned so much. As we were trying to address brokenness between people and the creek, we encountered brokenness among different groups in the watershed—rural residents who are suspicious of the government, downstream residents who blame upstream neighbors for causing problems, and farmers who distrust academics. We now understand our naïveté. We assumed everyone would recognize the benefits of the project for the park and its surrounding neighborhood once they learned the details. We assumed upstream residents would be glad to know these improvements would benefit their downstream neighbors. We failed to recognize the magnitude of worldview

FIGURE 2. Plaster Creek Stewards volunteers of diverse ages and backgrounds planting a newly restored floodplain at Shadyside Park.
PHOTOGRAPH BY GAIL GUNST HEFFNER

differences and how they can be a stumbling block when trying to work on a public project. We realized that we hadn't worked hard enough to develop a community listening process. We were guilty of not developing relationships of trust with community members first, before beginning the project planning.

In the end we made significant adjustments to the plan to honor some of the concerns expressed by park users. As a result, when construction finally began, hundreds of volunteers stepped forward to help with planting trees and native plants in the floodplain corridor. Some local residents were supportive and became involved. Others remained vocally skeptical. But in the end, this large installation to connect Plaster Creek with a newly contoured floodplain in the upstream reach of the watershed was hugely successful. This project captures stormwater, allowing it to percolate slowly into the ground rather than rushing quickly through the deeply channelized stream. From a community perspective, too, the project eventually garnered support from local residents: teachers brought their students

FIGURE 3. Restored native floodplain habitat at Shadyside Park.
PHOTOGRAPH BY DAVID P. WARNERS.

to help plant, businesses provided opportunities for their staff to volunteer, and some of the originally resistant neighbors had a change of heart.

Writing this story of the Shadyside Park project evoked painful memories of our early missteps, despite the eventual positive outcomes. On the very day we finished our first draft of this story, we were happily surprised to receive an email from a local resident, someone we had not met before, and she agreed to allow us to include parts of her message here. Amy B. wrote, "I had many concerns along with my neighbors when I first heard that changes were being considered to our beloved park and creek. Many residents thought that the rain garden would look overgrown, unkempt, and that enlarging the creek would just make a breeding ground for mosquitoes and cause flooding in the Spring to neighboring properties. We didn't want to see our majestic old trees removed either." But over time, her views changed. "Now that the project is complete, I can see the great improvement to the park. Thank you! . . . I hope you will keep this letter and others like it when you share with other communities about your upcoming plans. I hope that my story will be an encouragement to people that your plans are made thoughtfully and carried out successfully." Her email was an unexpected affirmation of the hard, committed work this project required. It underscores the connection between ecological and social reconciliation.

Reconciliation is a process that takes honest and committed engagement. It requires concerted effort and time; it is hard work. Reconciliation involves justice, but it goes beyond justice. Justice seeks to separate the offender from the victim, making the offender suffer consequences for their unjust action. Reconciliation, by contrast, works to bring the offender and the victim back together again to restore the relationship that had become broken. Reconciliation works to heal, to rebuild, and to allow the two entities a chance to try again and to move forward together into a new and more hopeful future. It is never easy, but when done well, reconciliation can result in meaningful and lasting change.

As our watershed work has progressed, we see again and again that the reconciliation needed between people and the natural world is similar to the reconciliation process needed between groups of people. The first published attempt to extend the concept of reconciliation to the human–creation relationship was by Dr. Michael Rosenzweig in his 2003 book, *Win-Win Ecology*. Rosenzweig describes reconciliation ecology as the branch of ecology that works to alter human behavior in human-dominated ecosystems in order to welcome greater biodiversity.[1] His work broadens other approaches in ecology including preservation (setting land aside) and restoration (improving degraded ecosystems). Both preservation and restoration ecology are often carried out in areas where people themselves are not living. In fact, the preservation efforts that resulted in our national park system involved removing people, first Native Americans and later white landowners, from places where they had been living, sometimes for generations.[2] Preservation and restoration efforts work to protect and improve nonhuman ecological relationships, but protecting or improving human relationships typically falls outside their scope.

By contrast, reconciliation ecology is practiced intentionally in the places where people live, work, play, or worship.[3] This approach embraces people who are in these places and encourages them to modify their existence so that human-dominated landscapes can become more environmentally friendly and biodiverse. The focus is not so much on ramping nature up, but on dialing humans down. Humans are recognized as important agents in nature, but not as a separate entity altogether, and human flourishing depends on the health of the land.[4]

Proponents of reconciliation ecology point out that much of the earth's land surfaces have become dedicated to the ongoing support of one species, *Homo sapiens*, while much less land has been dedicated to supporting all other species. Instead of assuming that land is for either people or nature, a reconciliation ecology approach integrates these two, focusing on re-creating the human presence in ways that invite other species to return and coexist with people. However, the current literature on reconciliation ecology fails to outline specific strategies that are needed to engage a genuine and successful reconciliation process.

In thinking about how to enact reconciliation ecology in the Plaster Creek watershed, we have learned important principles from reconciliation efforts undertaken in South Africa after apartheid. Under apartheid from 1948 until 1994, Black South Africans were denied basic civil rights and suffered greatly at the hands of white South Africans. In 1994, South Africans held their first democratic election, and Nelson Mandela was elected president. Then South Africa faced a reckoning because of the devastation and deep suffering Black South Africans endured under apartheid. Mandela recognized that a process for reconciliation and societal healing was needed if there was any hope for their future. So, he charged Archbishop Desmond Tutu to establish a Truth and Reconciliation Commission, outlining a process to foster genuine reconciliation.[5]

The South African Truth and Reconciliation Commission provides a model of what is possible when people are willing to face their past as a necessary component of moving forward into a transformed future. Reconciliation begins with an honest recognition of the wrong that has been perpetrated. Tutu writes, "True reconciliation exposes the awfulness, the abuse, the pain, the degradation, the truth. . . . It is a risky undertaking, but in the end, it is worthwhile, because in the end dealing with the real situation helps to bring real healing."[6] Recognizing the wrong often causes remorse, leading the offender to admit the wrong that has been done and to ask for forgiveness. Forgiveness does not mean condoning what has been done. It means taking what happened seriously and not minimizing it.[7] Lastly and most importantly, there needs to be some form of tangible restoration or reparation for the victim. A successful outcome is never guaranteed, yet this process offers a hopeful example of what is possible.

The same steps of the reconciliation process described by Archbishop Tutu can be implemented in efforts to reconcile the human–creation relationship. The first step in a reconciliation ecology process is to honestly examine current conditions and recognize what damage has been done. Second, the offenders need to acknowledge and lament their own role in causing the harm, whether their complicity is from direct action that caused injury or indirect carelessness and neglect. The honest acknowledgment of our role in causing the damage opens the door to an opportunity for restored relationships. The final step is to repair and restore the damaged relationship. This step involves a commitment to doing no further harm and working to heal past brokenness. When relationships are broken the land suffers, but when relationships are repaired the land can regain its ability to support life in all its complexity and beauty. Each of these three steps is described in more detail below.

Recognizing Things Are Not as They Should Be

One of our conversation partners in the Plaster Creek Oral History Project (PCOHP) succinctly described the problems we are facing in the Plaster Creek watershed, many of which are unknown to the average resident: "We have tremendous amounts of erosion, there's hardly any fish diversity, there's no recreational access, there's no interaction between Plaster Creek and the residents of this [watershed]—I think it's an incredible loss to them."[8]

As we began to recognize the ecological problems, we also sensed the disconnect between residents and the creek. We realized the people who lived in the Plaster Creek watershed and the land through which Plaster Creek flowed had almost no relationship with it. Most people were living in the land without any knowledge of its history, ecology, or beauty. And there was virtually no interaction between the different groups of people who live upstream and downstream within this watershed. Early on we knew we needed to center our work on fostering healthy relationships.

Recognizing that something is wrong can, at times, be a difficult step. For people who represent the majority subculture, or those who have power and privilege, it may be easy to think nothing is seriously amiss. Social and environmental problems are easy to deny or overlook as long as privileged people are isolated both from the problems and from those who are most impacted.

Much of our PCS work is to sound the alarm: "Grand Rapids, we have a problem!" Given how fundamentally important water is for life, the fact that a dangerously contaminated stream can flow right through a city without wide recognition that anything is wrong is remarkable. Until people realize things are not the way they are supposed to be, they will not be motivated to work toward reconciliation. Educational outreach, awareness building, water-quality data, and actual visits to see the creek are important ways to convince watershed residents that something is decidedly wrong. As Nobel Prize winner Wangari Maathai has argued, "If you are going to do anything for the environment, you have to *see* what has been disconnected" (emphasis added).[9]

Fred Bahnson and Norman Wirzba argue further that environmental degradation happens when people's lives are insulated from the impacts of their lifestyle choices:

> Massive ecological destruction becomes more likely when people are not in a position to see the effects of their decisions. When the location of increasingly insular and urban living shields us from the harmful effects of our consumer preferences, we are more likely to destroy what we clearly depend on: clean water, healthy forests, and vibrant mountain communities.[10]

Perhaps because water is ubiquitous in Michigan and many other places, people fail to notice it and too often take it for granted. What we fail to notice we cannot possibly develop affection for, and what we fail to have affection for, we will not take care of.[11] Affection for Plaster Creek has eroded over time, contributing to the problems it poses today. Our challenge is to motivate and inspire people to pay attention to their place, accurately recognize present problems, and cultivate an affection for the land, water, and species that are present here. This is the first step in a reconciliation ecology process.

Acknowledging Past Wounds and Lamenting Our Complicity

Simply recognizing that a problem exists is not sufficient for addressing that problem. We must also understand what happened in the past that caused the problem. We need to move beyond recognition to acknowledge human responsibility and our personal complicity. Many factors have contributed to our degraded creek; some are recent and relatively obvious, but others stretch far back in time. To address the challenge of living sustainably, whether in a watershed or on the planet, we need to understand the underlying causes of the current situation and acknowledge our involvement in the degradation that has occurred.

There was a time, just prior to the arrival of Christopher Columbus in 1492, when the presence of human beings in the Americas did not have a decidedly negative impact on the land. Indigenous people were essentially living sustainably in the landscape before Europeans began immigrating to this continent. One might assume this was because there were so few people on the continent during that time. Yet, when Columbus arrived, there was approximately the same number of people in North America as in Europe, suggesting that a large number of people living in a particular place does not necessarily lead to environmental degradation. Another possible explanation is that a large number of people have minimal impact if they are living impoverished lives, and that as the quality of life goes up, the quality of the landscape must necessarily go down. But many historians have claimed that the quality of life in fifteenth-century America was higher than in Europe, where the natural environment had been largely sacrificed, classism created widespread unrest, and human health was severely compromised by violence, unsanitary living conditions, and disease.[12]

When European immigrants became the dominant human presence in North America, the prevailing worldview in this continent was significantly altered. Over the course of about three hundred years (1600–1900), Indigenous people were largely displaced by western European immigrants with an Enlightenment-influenced worldview. Worldviews are not simply abstract ideas that occupy peoples' minds; they are enacted in real time and in real places. Worldviews influence the behaviors of embodied people, and those behaviors will undoubtedly impact the ecosystems in which the people reside. The new worldview introduced with European colonization displaced Indigenous ways of living and resulted in a significantly altered North American landscape.[13]

European worldviews differed in at least four profound ways from Indigenous worldviews. First, Europeans brought a sense of landownership that was foreign to Indigenous people who understood themselves to be part of the land.[14] Second, Indigenous people understood themselves as being in relationship with the creatures with whom they coexisted; the concept of relationship for Europeans was only ascribed to other people. Third, Europeans viewed the North American landscape as comprised of resources that could be converted into capital instead of filled with gifts that provided for the flourishing of all creatures, humans included.[15] Fourth, many Europeans came with a religious conviction that they were God's chosen people, mandated to conquer and control this new land and its inhabitants.[16] Most European immigrants perceived themselves and their own ways of thinking as superior to other people. This attitude resulted in the dehumanization of Native Americans and widespread human rights violations culminating in genocide and forced migration.[17] The expansion of European colonists westward had devastating effects on the people and the places they encountered. It is important for those of us with European ancestry to acknowledge the damage that was done by our forebearers and to admit that many of us in the United States today have greatly benefited from the mistreatment of people and land that occurred.

How do we begin to address the worldview that has caused so much harm? Is it possible to undo the damage that has been done to the land and its people? How do we admit our complicity and honestly come to terms with what has happened? When past harms are brought to light, opportunities for healing become possible. But without learning the often-painful details of the past, without listening to stories of those harmed, without careful examination of the soil or the water or the air, the more privileged among us will live under the illusion that everything is fine, which only perpetuates the problems. Theologian Willie Jennings emphasizes the need to learn about the history of our places, to take seriously who has lived there in the past in order for us to live ethically in that place into the future. If people move to a place and only "extract from it, take and move on . . . then at the deepest level of life, we are living a lie."[18] We have a moral responsibility to cultivate a geographic sensibility to effectively promote human and nonhuman flourishing.

Wendell Berry also emphasizes the importance of place in recognizing and mitigating harm: "Land abuse, I know, is pretty much a global phenomenon. But it is not happening in the whole world as climate change happens in the whole sky. It is happening, because it can happen, only locally, in small places, where the people who commit the abuses also live." He goes on to ask, "How can humans willingly turn against the earth, of which they are made, from which they live? . . . What is wrong with the way we are keeping house, the way we make our living, the way we live?" And considering the way we live raises an even deeper question: "What is happening to our souls?"[19]

To produce lasting improvements in the social and ecological health of a place, the worldview that has contributed to damaged relationships needs to be acknowledged and examined. Daniel Wildcat writes, "The first peoples of this land understood something scientists and policy makers need to understand—sustainability requires the recognition and restoration of reciprocal relationships between people and places."[20] Acknowledging our destructive behaviors and our need to work toward reciprocity in our relationship with the natural world can lead us to better ways of honoring our ecological and social relationships.

Committing to Restoration and Reparations

Humans have the ability to think and act, reflect and change our behaviors. Our daily decisions and actions contribute either positively or negatively to the communities in which we reside. This process of reflection and action upon the world with the purpose of transforming it is known as praxis.[21] Praxis involves ongoing critical thinking, which leads to certain actions, followed by further reflection. Paulo Freire has written, "apart from inquiry, apart from the praxis, individuals cannot be truly human. Knowledge emerges only through invention and re-invention, through the restless, impatient, continuing, hopeful inquiry human beings pursue in the world, with the world, and with each other."[22]

A healthy relationship between a person and a place will be characterized by reciprocity: a balance of giving and taking. These behaviors are influenced by our thinking, and our thinking is influenced by our behaviors. The starting point must be a present, concrete situation in which people recognize a problem that requires a response, not just on an intellectual level, but at the level of action.[23] In the case of the Plaster Creek watershed, we became aware of a degraded waterway threatening the public health of our community, which led to focused action.

Our ways of thought and action in the Plaster Creek watershed need ongoing careful reassessment and redesign. New relationships are possible for watershed residents. The reconciliation steps of recognition, acknowledgement, and restoration are there in front of us, inviting our engagement. We are not beholden to live in ways that continue to damage the creek or the land that supports us.[24]

The story of reconciliation ecology in the Plaster Creek watershed offers concrete examples of hope and inspiration for people everywhere who want to find new, more sustainable ways to live on the earth. To do this we must work for reconciliation, and it starts with telling the truth. We cannot get to reconciliation in the future without confronting the reality of what has happened in the past.

PART 1

DISCOVERED IGNORANCE

RECOGNIZING THE PROBLEM

CHAPTER 1

Ken-O-Sha's Geologic Past and the Plaster Creek Watershed Today

In the spring of 2013 rainfall throughout the midwestern United States was unusually high. In Grand Rapids we experienced two full weeks of heavy rainfall, and the ground became saturated. Total rainfall exceeded eleven inches in the month of April. All the tributaries to the Grand River spilled over their banks in what was called a one-hundred-year flood, and the rise was dramatic.

The Grand River crested at 21.85 feet (3.85 feet above the eighteen-foot flood level) on April 21, 2013. Thousands were forced to evacuate their homes, and the mayor declared a state of emergency. At the Grand Rapids wastewater treatment facility, partially treated wastewater overflowed despite efforts to prevent this from happening. Plaster Creek overflowed its banks flooding downstream neighborhoods.

A flood of this magnitude was frightening, yet we were heartened to see people throughout the Grand Rapids community rally to help. Thousands of residents volunteered to fill more than one hundred thousand sandbags. Near Plaster Creek, where the Grand Rapids wastewater facility is situated, a 1.25-mile wall of sandbags was built. Later as the flood waters receded, Plaster Creek residents came out to assist with the clean-up, and hundreds of bags of trash and debris were collected and removed. This flood revealed how vulnerable we actually are and how the way we have altered the land has heightened that vulnerability.[1]

Some of the current challenges we face as a society are clear and undeniable; others are less obvious. Recognizing the problem—both the broken relationships among people and the broken relationships between people and the natural

FIGURE 4. Extensive flooding in downtown Grand Rapids following a one-hundred-year storm of 2013.

PHOTOGRAPH BY GAIL GUNST HEFFNER

world—is the necessary first step before reconciliation can begin. The problems we encountered in the Plaster Creek watershed were, to us at first, subtle and hard to identify. As we gained understanding, we realized the problems had been there for decades. In this process of discovering our ignorance,[2] we wondered how this could have happened without us knowing about it. We began to recognize the *roots* of the problems.

What Is a Watershed?

As rain falls or snow melts, it flows downslope across the landscape to lower and lower contours. The collective area that drains to one common point is referred to as a watershed. Every home, school, business, church, workplace—everything exists within a particular watershed. Smaller watersheds are nested within larger watersheds. For example, the campus of our school, Calvin University, is drained by a small stream known locally as Whiskey Creek. Therefore, we are situated in the

Whiskey Creek watershed. But after leaving our campus, Whiskey Creek winds its way north and flows into Little Plaster Creek. So Calvin is also in the Little Plaster Creek Watershed. Little Plaster Creek then flows west and joins Plaster Creek, so it is also accurate to say that our campus is situated in the Plaster Creek watershed.

Watersheds integrate communities. In many places, rural residents live within the same watershed as urban residents, and wealthy residents share the same watershed as those who live in poverty. Often individuals from these disparate groups don't know each other or even think about how their behaviors influence one another, but what happens in the upper reaches will influence those who live downstream. When an upstream section receives contaminants (e.g., manure from agricultural fields, fertilizers from suburban lawns, or chemicals dripping from vehicles), those contaminants will have an impact on the downstream sections. In fact, contaminants can become increasingly concentrated as they move through a watershed, resulting in heightened danger to downstream communities. The quality of water flowing out of a watershed reflects the way people are living within that watershed. Because of the way human settlements arose along major rivers in the United States, many urban areas today are in downstream sections of watersheds and have suffered serious ecological degradation. Contaminated streams illuminate the need to develop new ways of living. And the way people live is based on the worldview they hold.

To fully understand the condition of any given waterway, it is important to learn about the activities happening in its surrounding watershed. It is also critical to learn about the watershed's history, both physical and social. Becoming familiar with the history of a place will help shed light on the current problems, which in turn can lead to more lasting solutions. Though Plaster Creek faces similar challenges as many other urban waterways, every watershed has unique aspects. No other stream on the planet is like Plaster Creek, and Plaster Creek is the way it is today both because of the way people are living in the watershed now and because of its history.

Early Geological Forces that Shaped the Plaster Creek Landscape

Historical descriptions of West Michigan often begin with the white men who first explored this region or those who set up the earliest trading post or mission.

Sometimes historical accounts will mention the long-standing and expansive Ottawa villages that were located at the rapids of the Grand River and other local villages such as the one at the convergence of the Thornapple and Grand Rivers. Less frequently a historical treatment of West Michigan will reach back to the Hopewell people who predated the Ottawa in this landscape by centuries. Stretching further into history brings recognition of the archaic Paleo-Indians who tracked the receding glaciers northward and hunted Pleistocene mammals in West Michigan beginning about eleven thousand years ago. Ultimately such historical musings bring us to the most recent glacier that covered the West Michigan region until about twelve thousand to fourteen thousand years ago. Yet that glacier occurred only during the most recent ice age (called the Wisconsin), which was the fifth in a sequence of glaciations, the first of which occurred approximately two million years ago.

But what happened long before this series of ice ages has also contributed to the condition of Plaster Creek today. Although hard to imagine, over the period of 230–600 million years ago inland saltwater seas existed in today's midwestern United States and Great Plains. These seas, like the glaciers, expanded and dried repeatedly (at least six times).[3] As these oceans receded and evaporated, mineral deposits were laid down. During the fifth or Mississippian period, vast deposits of a mineral composed of calcium and sulfate were formed in the area subsequently designated as the Michigan Basin. By the time the last glaciers had receded from West Michigan, these layers typically lay six to eight feet below the soil and gravel deposited by the glaciers. But at certain spots, especially along waterways, these deposits were visible, and their orange milky appearance attracted attention.[4] When trying to understand how Plaster Creek became so degraded, we need to go back 350 million years to when this peculiar rock known as gypsum was formed.

A relatively soft rock, gypsum is composed of calcium, sulfate, hydrogen, and oxygen. Because it was formed when the inland seas dried up, it is called an evaporative mineral.[5] Although formed long before people were present, gypsum has an enduring relationship with humans. A particularly fine-grained form of gypsum called alabaster was used to create sculptures in ancient Egypt, Mesopotamia, and Rome. In the mid-eighteenth century, a German Reformed clergyman and experimental agriculturalist named Johann Friderich Mayer was the first to espouse the benefits of gypsum when ground up and used as a fertilizer.[6] In the early 1800s English botanist Richard Weston elaborated on Mayer's findings and instructed people on how to grind and apply the mineral on farm fields.[7] Gypsum

FIGURE 5. During a stream profile survey, a remnant piece of gypsum is discovered. A surprising find these days!
PHOTOGRAPH BY GAIL GUNST HEFFNER.

became widely used by farmers in Europe because it was cheaper and easier to transport than animal manure. These features also made it an especially valuable product for poor immigrant farmers who were relocating to North America, as we will see.

The Influence of Glaciers on the Plaster Creek Watershed

As the glaciers worked and reworked the West Michigan region, they distributed a mixture of soils across the land. The character of these soils strongly influenced vegetation patterns, as well as subsequent human activities. The lower regions of the Plaster Creek watershed had sandy soils and became covered with oak, chestnut, and hickory forests. More open savanna habitats and small pockets of prairie emerged on many of the south- and west-facing slopes. These soils were easily excavated, and their well-drained character made them ideal for building sites during the early development of Grand Rapids. The upper headwater reaches of the watershed were covered with clays and loams, and the forests that populated these areas were mostly sugar maple, hemlock, and beech. The level aspect and fertile soils in these areas made them more attractive to farmers. Low-lying basins of swampland were mostly dominated by black ash, white cedar, swamp white oak, and silver maple. Floodplain forests along the sides of the creek supported sycamores, tulip poplar, chestnut oak, bur oak, and other tall, canopy-forming trees. Orchids grew abundantly in the Saddlebag Swamp, an expansive wetland in the northeastern part of the watershed along Little Plaster Creek, and early settlers often collected blueberries here.[8] This swampland, as well as most of the floodplain forests, was drained for early agricultural purposes and later filled in for urban expansion.[9]

Watershed Services Provided by Forests

By appreciating the characteristics of a healthy landscape, we can more clearly recognize the symptoms of an unhealthy one, and it is difficult to overstate the importance of trees to the ecological health of the Great Lakes region. The Great Plains had their prairies, the southwest its deserts, but the upper Midwest was home to vast acreages of stately forests. Occasionally, forests would thin and transition into savannahs and prairie openings (in exceptionally dry locations) or sunny marshes (in the wettest places), but the ecological theme of forest held sway as the dominant habitat of this region. The contributions made by all these trees to healthy land and water can be separated into categories of nutrients, insulation, water retention, and flood control.

Trees manufacture nutrients for the soil by discarding leaves, twigs, bark, and roots that are decomposed by fungi, microbes, and soil invertebrates. And when trees die, their trunks provide slow-release fertilizer for decades. It may be obvious—but still worth mentioning—that no one ever needs to spread fertilizer into a woodland to promote growth. All the dead things in a forest support an amazing assemblage of living soil organisms that turn the dead biomass into available nutrients to further support other life forms.[10] When European settlers first started clearing the forests to begin farming, they were amazed by the soil's fertility. Yet, after a few years of growing crops, fertility declined, and it became clear that ongoing agriculture would require fertilizers.[11] This makes perfect ecological sense because the cycle of nutrient sustainability that allows forests to indefinitely perpetuate themselves was abruptly disrupted when the nutrient sources—the trees themselves—were removed from the system.

By contrast, the Ottawa practiced agriculture by clearing small forest patches, cultivating them for a few years, and then abandoning them to be returned to forest habitat once again.[12] The temporary forest openings in which the Ottawa grew their crops allowed sunlight to reach the ground, which was essential for growing maize, beans, and squash. And yet, the small size of these patches also allowed nearby trees to keep adding nutrients via their leaves and twigs. Furthermore, the short period of farming did not exhaust the soil's fertility, and when the patches were abandoned, the trees grew back and joined the surrounding forest once again. Indigenous agriculture fit into the natural cycles of life, death, decomposition, and renewed life. At the same time, the forest was utilized in ways that contributed to the well-being of humans by supplying agricultural crops as well as many other useful products.

Similarly to how trees add nutrients to the soil, trees that arch over waterways also deposit nutrient-rich organic material directly into the water. Leaf packs and twigs in streams accumulate behind rocks and downed branches, as well as along stream banks where water moves more slowly. These clusters of biomass become sites for the first wave of aquatic decomposers—the shredders—who begin breaking the debris into smaller pieces. Another group of aquatic insects—the collectors—grab these smaller pieces for further processing as they are carried downstream. Woody debris, as it does on terrestrial surfaces, provides a slow-release nutrient source while also creating microhabitats of currents, light, and substrate that enhance stream diversity. All of these small stream organisms not only break down organic material, but also provide food for larger predatory aquatic insects who in turn are eaten by fish, some of whom are eaten by larger fish and terrestrial mammals and birds. Taking away leaves and twigs completely disrupts this healthy, diverse stream ecosystem and significantly compromises the ability of a stream to be the wellspring of biodiversity it is intended to be.

When autumn leaves from forest trees are left where they fall on the land, they also provide benefits for nearby waterways. The collection of leaves on a forest floor insulates the soil, protecting it from drying out. In spring, snow in woodlands melts more slowly than on open ground, and the snow itself provides an added layer of insulation that protects the soil beneath it. As a result, the frost layer stays shallow under trees, and the soil retains more moisture, good news for the all-important soil microbes. In addition, the persistence of snow under trees means that spring meltwater is released more gradually compared to the surges of meltwater that come off open land. This is one reason why streams that flow through forests are more steady and fluctuate less dramatically than streams moving through cleared land.

The trees that grow along the edge of waterways provide another important insulating benefit, especially to small creeks. Forest shade keeps the water cool. In the absence of this canopy, creeks and the rainwater that flows into them (runoff) are much warmer because of exposure to direct sunlight. This unusually warm volume of runoff, especially exacerbated when sheeting off large parking lots or roadways in the summer, is referred to as "thermal pollution." Summer thunderstorms in watersheds with lots of rooftops and pavement will produce a large slug of warm water that moves into and through a stream like Plaster Creek and may harm many aquatic creatures.[13]

Besides providing nutrients and insulation, trees are important in modifying the dynamics of peak flow. Peak flow is the maximum rate of water moving through a stream after a rainfall. Tree roots slow down runoff by their physical presence, allowing more rainwater to percolate into the ground. But tree roots are also like straws, taking water from the ground and passing it upward inside stems and branches and out through tiny pores called stomata on leaf surfaces. This process, known as transpiration, moves large volumes of water from the soil into the air as the tree is growing. A mature deciduous tree will generate approximately one hundred thousand leaves, approximately the same number as hairs found on a human head. On average, each of those leaves has three hundred microscopic stomata *per square millimeter*, which means each tree has the capacity to move huge volumes of water. In fact, scientists have calculated that one mature silver maple tree transpires sixty gallons of water every hour—that's over five hundred gallons of water moved from the soil into the air by a single tree each day![14] With a healthy forest growing all along the banks of a creek, tree roots intercept a great deal of stormwater before it can make its way into a creek, significantly moderating peak flow.

But why is peak flow a problem? Doesn't a creek need to have water in order to be a creek? Water to a stream is indeed a necessary ingredient, but too much of a good thing can become a problem. Without forest cover, much more water enters a stream or river over a shorter period of time, bringing with it whatever it collected from the land. When waterways swell, they gain power and exacerbate erosion, which adds more particulate matter to the water. Cloudy, chocolate-milk-looking water full of sediment is problematic for most aquatic creatures. So the loss of trees translates into more runoff and more erosion, decreasing water quality and stream biodiversity.

In this way, clearing the landscape of trees will increase the potential for flooding. Undisturbed creeks and rivers have an associated floodplain—the adjoining low-lying land that receives water when a stream or river swells above its banks. Natural floodplains are vegetated with trees and other plants that help slow the floodwater. Slower water has less energy and cannot carry as much sediment, so particulate matter drops out, effectively cleaning the water. Additionally, much of the flood water infiltrates the soil and is pumped back into the air by floodplain plants, especially the trees. Healthy floodplains are like giant sponges. They play a critical role in moderating stream flow and keeping the water clean.

Within a floodplain, a waterway will occasionally shift its main channel laterally. A straight-flowing stream accumulates speed and energy that will lead to significant erosion at the next bend. By contrast, every time a meandering stream forms a bend within the contours of a broad floodplain, the energy it carries dissipates, water slows, and the potential for downstream erosion declines. Curved stream banks that are populated by trees and other floodplain plants act as shock absorbers to high-energy water as it makes its way from higher to lower places across the landscape.[15]

We have focused so far on the chemical and physical contributions that trees make to the health of a watershed. But it is also important to recognize that trees themselves are absolute wellsprings of biodiversity. Insects feast on trees, and birds feast on insects. Trees also harbor pathogens, serving as hosts to myriad microbial, fungal, and parasitic insects that in their own way also feed off trees. While occasionally diseases become problematic, normally a pathogen lives off a tree but doesn't kill it. Oak trees are especially known to carry a very high pathogen load. Similar to leaf-chewing insects, these pathogens also provide food for larger creatures. When trees are removed, the land supports far less biodiversity than it did when the trees were present. In summary, the loss of trees creates a negative feedback loop, resulting in an overall loss of environmental health and a decline in biodiversity. But when trees are added back into a landscape, the multitude of positive influences they provide can return, in a steadily recovering positive feedback loop.

Changes in Plaster Creek from Forest Clearing and Gypsum Mining

Forest clear-cutting and gypsum mining initiated a decline in the health of Plaster Creek. Extensive deforestation began in West Michigan in the early 1800s. At the time, the mindset of colonists was that a forested landscape was wild and in need of "improvement," which meant removing the trees. European settlers seeking an independent farming life first practiced clear-cutting on a small scale, and lumber barons built incredible financial wealth later by doing it on a much larger scale. The forests they cleared were not like most forests we know today. More than 75 percent of those early forests were old growth, with tree trunks four to five feet wide and canopies easily surpassing one hundred feet tall.[16] By comparison, far less than 1 percent of Michigan old-growth forest remains. The largest trees today have grown up in the aftermath of those early logging days and are at most three feet wide and seventy feet tall. One place where mature old-growth forest can still be appreciated is Hartwick Pines State Park near Grayling, Michigan. Encountering this forty-nine-acre ecosystem, and picturing forests like this all across Michigan, reveals the tragedy of how completely altered this land became.

Deforestation itself certainly amplified extreme flow cycles, but when those deforested lands were capped with impervious surfaces like rooftops, roads, and parking lots, the problems intensified. In 1910 Charles Garfield, who grew up in the Plaster Creek watershed and became the first president of Michigan's Forestry Commission, wrote:

> [Plaster Creek] has almost nothing now in the way of tree growth from its source to its confluence with the Grand River, and instead of being the beautiful even-flowing stream throughout the year, as in my childhood, it is now a most fitful affair, full to the brim and running over at times, yet most of the year it is only a trickling rill.[17]

Trees were also cleared to create the open spaces and transportation routes needed for gypsum mining activities. In 1838, Michigan's first state geologist, Douglass Houghton, visited West Michigan to investigate the potential for salt mining. His findings were less than promising for salt, but while in the Grand Rapids area he was impressed by the presence of high-quality gypsum outcrops (also referred to back then as "land plaster").[18] Further research showed that gypsum deposits underlay much of the area, and three years later, in 1841, Warren Granger and Daniel Ball established the first gypsum mine at the site, sacred to the Ottawa, where Plaster Creek flowed over an exposed gypsum ledge into the Grand River floodplain.[19] During these early mining days the area along Plaster Creek was known as "Happy Valley," and an 1841 press release captures some of the mine owners' excitement:

> PLASTER! PLASTER! The subscribers have now completed their Plaster Mill on Plaster Creek . . . which is now in operation. They respectfully inform the public that they have on hand at the mill or at either of their stores at Ionia or this place a constant supply. As the quality of the Grand Rapids Plaster is not equaled by any in the United States, they hope to receive a share of patronage as the price is less than it can be obtained for at any place in Michigan. Wheat, pork, and most kinds of produce received in payment.[20]

The discovery and processing of gypsum was an early boon to the Grand Rapids economy; by 1850 the company was producing sixty tons a day. However, this economic windfall had a devastating effect on the ecology and water quality of Plaster Creek. The waterfall was completely obliterated, and the route of the creek was repositioned and channelized. The creek was dammed to form a pond to provide water used in the mining.[21] Once the Granger and Ball mine began operations, runoff from surface mining so degraded the downstream sections that walleye stopped coming up Plaster Creek to spawn.

In 1860 several quarries combined to form the Grand Rapids Plaster Company. The mills close to Plaster Creek used water diverted from the creek to power the grinding stones.[22] At peak production there were thirteen separate gypsum mine operators in the area, and by 1890 the gypsum industry was recognized as adding "inexhaustible wealth to our city."[23] In these early days there was no shortage of demand for gypsum. By 1900 it was also being used to make stucco for exterior walls and plaster (and later drywall) for interior walls. Even after large quantities of gypsum had been extracted, in 1904 geologist G. P. Grimsley wrote,

> There are approximately six square miles of gypsum area near Grand Rapids, with an average thickness of 10 feet. . . . This quantity would supply the whole United States for 170 years or more at the present rate of consumption.[24]

Gypsum was particularly important as a fertilizer—it was called "soil sweetener"—because clear-cutting had decreased the fertility of the soil. For this reason, nineteenth-century settlers in New England and the Great Lakes region were eager to buy it. Gypsum from Grand Rapids was shipped down the Grand River and northward through the Straits of Mackinac to Detroit and into surrounding territories throughout the Great Lakes and was even exported westward by railroad cars all the way to California.

Unhealthy Waters

Because of forest clearing and the proliferation of impermeable surfaces in the watershed, Plaster Creek today receives far too much water when it rains, which causes a multitude of problems. And today that water carries with it all kinds of contaminants: heavy metals, visible garbage, microplastics, hydrocarbons, oils, excess fertilizers, and road salts. Another contributor to pollution in Plaster Creek is animal feces, which introduce bacterial contamination, resulting in elevated levels of microbes that are harmful to human health. Some level of fecal contamination has been present since the days of mammoths and mastodons, but *E. coli* levels are dangerously high today because too much animal waste is being washed into the stream.

To evaluate how contaminated a stream is with fecal pathogens, one of those pathogens, *E. coli*, is used as an indicator. Michigan's standard for full body contact (safe for swimming) is set at a thirty-day mean of 130 *E. coli* colonies per 100 ml of water. For partial body contact (safe for touching) it's 1,000 *E. coli* colonies per 100 ml.[25] In Plaster Creek, *E. coli* levels always increase after a rainfall because rain washes fecal material into the creek. We have documented *E. coli* levels higher than 25,000 colonies per 100 ml of water. Levels this high pose significant health risks for people and animals who come into contact with the creek—and of course for the many organisms that live in the water. Our research has helped identify the tributaries that carry higher levels of *E. coli* than others, and we've been able to discern the likely animal sources, including geese on golf courses, cattle in feedlots, dogs enjoying the dog park, and humans with leaky sewer lines or septic systems.

Michigan has received official documentation of the problems experienced by Plaster Creek. The Clean Water Act of 1972 instructed states to evaluate the ability of each of its waterways to safely support the kind of activities normally expected there. After years of assessment, in 2002 the Michigan Department of Environmental Quality (now known as the Department of Environment, Great Lakes, and Energy or EGLE) concluded that two such activities were severely impaired in Plaster Creek. First, it supports significantly less aquatic life than it should. And second, its bacteria levels are consistently too high, rendering the creek a human health hazard. In government language, Plaster Creek has two official impairments or TMDLs—meaning that it exceeds safe levels in two categories of "Total Maximum Daily Loads." A TMDL establishes the maximum amount of a pollutant allowed in a water body and serves as the starting point for restoring water quality.[26] In this way, TMDLs help to officially recognize the problems associated with waterways like Plaster Creek, which is the critical first step in reconciliation ecology.

Plaster Creek's Recent Degradation

For most of the life span of Plaster Creek, it was a thriving and life-supporting waterway. However, today it suffers from many problems experienced by other urban waterways throughout the country. The extent and intensity of symptoms in Plaster Creek have earned it a reputation as West Michigan's most contaminated waterway. The activities that take place in the watershed today are not guided by a balance between use and protection, to our own detriment. Forests have been replaced by land uses that move water into the creek as quickly as possible. Floodplain trees were removed right up to the stream banks, and multiple sections of the main creek bed were straightened (or put underground) so that the stream would not take up so much space. The significant changes we have imposed upon this landscape have resulted in a seriously unhealthy stream. Plaster Creek's degraded condition also seems to invite additional negative attitudes and behaviors, illustrated by the tendency of some people to use it as a dumping ground for old tires, shopping carts, worn out appliances, old furniture, and more (we actually found a discarded toilet in the creek back in 2014). It is heartbreaking to recognize that Plaster Creek is far from the life-giving stream it once was.

After giving presentations to community groups, we are often asked how long it will take to clean up the creek. Our response is that the creek has become increasingly degraded for nearly two hundred years now, and we will likely need several decades of concerted effort before we begin to see improvements. But from a geomorphological perspective two hundred years is a tiny portion of the life span of Plaster Creek. Only during this most recent history has the waterway become a public health hazard. Realizing that the problems associated with this creek are so recent, and that they have resulted completely from human action and neglect, gives us hope. If humans are capable of causing such degradation, then humans are also capable of repairing the damage and returning health and beauty to the creek.

And yet the challenge of cleaning up a degraded waterway like Plaster Creek involves so much more than picking up trash, eliminating the inputs of toxic chemicals, or identifying the sources of bacterial contamination. Something deep down is not right in the way many of us are living and the way we think about ourselves in relation to the natural world, evidenced by perfectly acceptable behaviors that destroy the places where we live. To gain a better understanding of this problem, we need to take a closer look at the different groups of our own species, *Homo sapiens*, who have occupied this land. Historian William Cronon points out, "Changes in the way people create and re-create their livelihood must be analyzed in terms of changes not only in their *social* relations, but in their *ecological* ones as well."[27]

CHAPTER 2

Earliest Watershed Inhabitants and the Arrival of the Ottawa

It had rained overnight, and the morning vegetation was dripping with moisture. The soil, as well as the air itself, was laden with wetness. Although the rain had stopped, after only a few steps into the forest my boots and jeans were saturated. It was a cool morning in late September 2020, and I (Dave) had come for a visit to the Norton Mound complex, better known locally as the Indian Mounds.

While doing research for this book, I had been reading a lot about the Hopewell people in West Michigan. I thought it only appropriate, since the Norton Mound complex is the largest group of Hopewell Mounds remaining in the state and only nine miles from my house, to pay them a visit. The previous evening, I found Hopewell Indian Mounds Park on Google Maps. But if I hadn't intentionally gone looking for it, I would have never known where this remarkable collection of mounds was located. To get there, I turned north off 28th Street onto Indian Mounds Drive just before the overpass for the Grand River. Where a bicycle bridge extends westward over the river, I pulled my car off onto the right-hand shoulder. This was where the map said the mounds were. But there was no signage, nor any apparent entry point, and I certainly didn't see any mounds. All that was here was a beat-up looking forest and a lightly worn footpath leading along a section of tall fencing, away from the road.

I took the path. Looking through the chain links I noticed that the forest floor was covered with several species of plants that thrive in disturbed sites—clearweed, poison ivy, nettles, jumpseed, and stickseed. Some of these plants were growing in medieval Europe when the Hopewell occupied this landscape. After following a deer trail for a bit, I found a spot where a fallen box elder tree had leveled the fence, and I was able to make my way through the rubble and step down into the floodplain forest.

According to written accounts, the mounds seemed to be located further back, nestled between the interstate highway buzzing with morning traffic and a large ponded borrow pit, left in the wake of highway construction. I worked my way through brambles, buckthorn, and nettles, frequently ducking under grapevine thickets that when bumped greeted me with cold rain droplets down the back of my neck. I often had to step high over large fallen white ash trees, casualties of the emerald ash borer, another element of our environment that the Hopewell never had to experience. The air smelled like oil, most likely from the active wells I saw along the road just before parking my car. It struck me how different this landscape is today compared to when the Hopewell inhabited these woods.

Eventually the mounds came into view. These landscape features are so different in their shape, symmetry, and contours than anything else in the vicinity. They slope gently upward and then down, circularly symmetrical, like large goosebumps on the land. Some very old trees were standing guard. Although certainly not old enough to date back to the Hopewell, I wondered if these trees could be offspring of great grandparents present at the time the mounds were being constructed. The site gave me a feeling similar to the respect and awe I sense when looking at a centuries-old bonsai plant, except that this was an entire landscape. I slowed down, moved with caution, and couldn't stop looking at the mounds. They were captivating. Something significantly meaningful happened here that calls for acknowledgement, admiration, and a serious attempt at understanding.

Early European immigrants described the esteem that the Ottawa (who arrived centuries after the Hopewell) had for the mounds, even though they were unaware of who constructed them.[1] The Ottawa considered these sites sacred and treated them with honor and reverence. In fact, they often used the Hopewell mounds as burial sites themselves, adding bones of their deceased above those of their predecessors, which for a time confused early archaeologists.[2] Today, we know more than the early Ottawa knew about who made these mounds, how old they are, and their ceremonial significance. And much of what we know comes from excavations and the removal of human remains and funerary goods, activities Indigenous people regard as sacrilegious and exploitative. Yet our passive response to these mounds today is not out of respect but neglect, symbolized in weedy brambles, oil wells, and a constant roar from the adjacent interstate, which during its construction obliterated half of the mound complex. As I left the site and started my walk out of the woods, I felt a heavy sense of sadness. There is so much here to be honored, revered, and learned. But those of us with a more recent West Michigan origin have been ignoring this place and missing important lessons that could be gleaned by paying attention to those who lived and thrived in this land long before we arrived.

Human Presence in West Michigan

The human presence in this region over time involved arrivals, expansions, movements, retreats, mergers, and displacements. The earliest Indigenous inhabitants were Paleo-Indians who followed the melting glaciers north, while the most recent were the Ottawa, who were a subgrouping of the larger Anishinaabe people, and the group who were present here when Europeans first started arriving. And yet, this is not a history that can be conveyed by a single-file ordering of one group followed by another. Instead, it is much more complex because the Indigenous groups did not come to West Michigan to set up camp indefinitely, as the European immigrants intended to do. From the Paleo-Indians to the Ottawa, Native Americans interacted with the landscape while moving around in it. Sometimes the movements were rapid as they traversed the land while hunting or relocating, sometimes they were seasonal, and sometimes they occurred slowly, over a period of years. But occupying specific coordinates on a map and calling that place home was simply not something Native Peoples did. While some understanding of these cultures can be gained by investigating specific encampments and sacred spaces, the impact of early inhabitants was dispersed lightly over broad reaches of the landscape.

Therefore, the history of people in West Michigan is dynamic, often with blurred boundary lines that sometimes overlapped, but at other times didn't. It is a history of shifting cultures and worldviews that have each influenced the land in different ways. And although much remains undiscovered, a good deal is known, especially about the more recent beliefs and practices of the Anishinaabeg—knowledge that deserves to be more notably brought to light.[3] Twenty-first-century North Americans have much to gain by carefully considering earlier groups of people who were accomplished in the very challenge that faces our global community today—living sustainably in the land.

Paleo-Indians

The diversity of habitats created by glaciers in West Michigan yielded a diversity of foods and other provisions for the animals and the Native Peoples who moved into this recently glaciated region about twelve thousand years ago. In addition, the climate of West Michigan was tempered by Lake Michigan with winters less frigid and summers more mild than nearby areas of northern Illinois and eastern Wisconsin. It is understood that the Paleo-Indians were descendants of groups who initially made their way to North America across the Bering Strait from northeastern Asia, entering this new world about fifteen thousand years before the present time, although possibly even earlier.[4]

Acorns were among the most important foods for the Paleo-Indians, as they are known to have been for many cultures around the world.[5] Along with several species of oak, the Midwest is home to multiple other nut-producing trees and shrubs such as hickory, walnut, beech, chestnut, and hazelnut.[6] Nuts have a particularly high concentration of fats and oils, precious commodities for surviving anywhere, but especially in cold climates. These first human residents also collected and consumed numerous fleshy fruits, such as blueberries, elderberries, grapes, raspberries, blackberries, cranberries, serviceberries, and wild plums. They also ate an assortment of plant leaves or roots, including violets, wild leeks, arrowhead, sunflowers, and the smartweeds.[7] Over time they came to use plants for building and binding purposes, basketry, medicine, and art. A rich knowledge base of ethnobotany grew over time through trial and error, but also reportedly informed by dreams, visions, and spiritual practices.[8] People were learning how to live in this land, and each successive generation gained knowledge and passed it on.

As time advanced the people occupying West Michigan also became less migratory and began staying in certain places for longer periods. Agriculture appears to have first been practiced around 100 BC as a means for supplementing foods obtained through hunting and gathering.[9] Interestingly, the three earliest staple crops—corn, beans, and squash—were all nonnative species to Michigan, having originated in Central America and the Southwest. Crop development, as well as the presence of artifacts made from raw materials that had no local sources, shows that trade and movement over long distances was occurring.[10] As people interacted with each other, cultural exchanges and advancements were taking place. Some of the most impressive evidence of cultural sophistication comes from the Hopewell.

The Mound-Building Hopewell People

The Hopewell were part of a vast network of early midwestern North Americans who were known for building mounds, a practice that appears to have its origin among the Mayans in Central America. The Hopewell and their kin in northwest Indiana and central lower Michigan were one of the most northerly manifestations of this broad cultural practice. The Grand Rapids area was a population center for the Hopewell, as evidenced by two extensive sets of mounds, the Converse and the Norton.

The Converse Mounds were located on the west side of the Grand River in contrast to the Norton Mounds, which were constructed approximately two miles downstream after the river turns to the west, on its south side. The Converse Mounds occupied an area that later became known as missionary land between present-day Bridge Street and Wealthy Street in Grand Rapids. This was the largest Hopewell ceremonial center in the Upper Great Lakes area and included forty to fifty individual mounds, the largest of which was thirty feet high and two hundred feet in circumference.[11] The Converse Mounds were named (with tragic irony) after one of the most important early colonists of the region, James W. "Deacon" Converse. The area was plotted and leveled for development of the young expanding city of Grand Rapids between the late 1850s and the mid-1880s. As the mounds were literally erased from the West Michigan landscape, workers and local observers were quick to collect and sell unearthed artifacts.[12] Michigan State Archaeologist John Halsey writes, "The Converse Mounds became a sad archeological footnote. Our best Hopewellian site was reduced to a handful of artifacts scattered among museums. Other artifacts had vanished into private collections or even the jeweler's crucible."[13]

One of the Norton Mounds that is seventeen feet high and one hundred feet around at the base is estimated to have required over a half million basket loads of dirt. This construction was almost always done in a way that the surrounding terrain did not appear to have been excavated. The lack of any obvious borrow pits speaks to the desire of having the mounds rise up surprisingly yet gracefully from their flat surroundings. It seems the Hopewell were striving not only for sites to bury their important leaders, but for sites that would convey a visual effect as well. This was art worked out on the canvas of the land. Additionally, many of the burial artifacts exhibit exquisite craftsmanship, often making use of materials that had been transported from places as far away as the Rocky Mountains, indicating extensive trade networks.[14] Much of Hopewellian artistic work (both small scale and large scale) indicates a supernatural awareness.

Because there are no written records or oral histories passed down from the Hopewell, it is difficult to decipher how they understood themselves within the context of the midwestern landscape. The Hopewell appear to have been more sedentary than the earlier Paleo-Indians. Current understanding is that they formed small family groups that temporarily occupied certain areas, usually along rivers, and that they shifted seasonally to take advantage of animal movements and weather patterns.[15] However, the mound building indicates that the Hopewell were adept at coordinating groups to undertake large and incredibly challenging tasks. Furthermore, while the Norton and Converse Mounds are most commonly referenced, early histories of Grand Rapids mention numerous smaller collections of mounds. In the nineteenth century an early settler, archaeologist Wright L. Coffinberry, reportedly examined over sixty such groupings, one of which he describes as being located in the lower portion of the Plaster Creek watershed.[16] He reported that almost every time a road was put in or a building foundation excavated, Hopewellian bones and artifacts would turn up. The Hopewell people clearly had developed a sophisticated society that flourished in the Grand Rapids region, indicating that this is good land for supporting people who have a rich culture and sophisticated beliefs.[17] The Hopewell lived in and influenced the landscape for centuries without ruining it.

The Anishinaabeg

By about 400–600 AD the Hopewell people had mysteriously disappeared from West Michigan, and over time new groups of native people moved to this area from the east. Most of these newcomers belonged to a large, diverse, and rather loosely organized collection of tribes and clans known as the Anishinaabeg who spoke an Algonquian language. Oral histories and pictorial accounts in birchbark scrolls tell the story of how their original homeland was along the Atlantic Ocean. However, inspired by visions given to spiritual leaders, they moved westward to preserve their culture from a wave of strangers predicted to come in the future.

During their migration along the route of what today is the St. Lawrence Seaway, various Anishinaabeg families separated from the larger group and established villages. One group moved north up the Ottawa River, which today serves as a provincial boundary between much of Quebec and Ontario. After the main group paused for a time around present-day Detroit, known as the Third Stopping Point, additional movement culminated with a significant meeting at Michilimackinac (the area that today includes Mackinac Island, Mackinaw City, and St. Ignace). Here, possibly as early as 800 AD, the Anishinaabeg split into three groups: the Ojibwe (later called Chippewa by Europeans) who moved north and westward into Michigan's Upper Peninsula, the Potawatomi who ventured to the west and south to eventually settle in southern Michigan and northern Indiana, and the Ottawa who initially occupied Manitoulin Island (situated near the north shore of Lake Huron) and later expanded into Michigan's Lower Peninsula.[18]

Because the Anishinaabeg had been a distinct group for centuries, over time they accumulated their own cultural practices, languages, and teachings that were passed along from one generation to another. A common thread was the presence and influence of spiritual leaders. These were people who had been chosen to enter a multigenerational society that required instruction and initiation.[19] Two of these groups, the Waabanowin (also known as the Dawn Society) and the Jaasikiid (Shaking Tent Seers), were visionaries who helped guide their respective communities with messages from the spirit world. A third group, the Midewiwin, also known as the Curing Society or Grand Medicine Society, spanned across Indigenous tribes from New England to the Great Plains. To become a Mide or practitioner, these botanical experts had to pass through four different stages of knowledge requiring years of concerted learning.[20] The Mide were healers who used spiritual forces, physical herbs, and other practices (songs, chants, sweat lodges, and prayers) to promote health and wholeness among members of the group.

Although the Anishinaabeg had no formal written language, they safeguarded and transferred their accumulated wisdom through stories, trainings, and regular practices. Recognizing the sophisticated knowledge and cultural practices of the

Ottawa helps to correct the erroneous narrative that European settlement was simply an example of a superior group of people replacing an inferior one.

The most formidable and lasting adversaries of the Anishinaabeg were the Haudenosaunee, a group who lived south of Lake Erie and Lake Ontario. Conflicts between the Anishinaabeg and the Haudenosaunee had been happening for centuries. However, these conflicts intensified in the 1500s when six tribes of Haudenosaunee people came together to form the Six Nations Confederacy.[21] This alliance quickly gained strength and became a significant threat to the Anishinaabe communities in the areas we know today as Quebec and Ontario. With losses they incurred from intensified conflicts and from introduced diseases, Anishinaabe life in this region was significantly disrupted. Many groups sought refuge in the west, away from major areas of conflict, and many ended up in Michigan. Therefore, by the time the first French explorers and missionaries arrived in the area, it was populated by a combination of long-term Anishinaabe residents along with more recently arrived war-torn refugee communities.[22]

Social Organization of the Ottawa

The actual designation of "Ottawa" was first used by the French (from "Outaouais"); it means "traders," a name given to this group because of their active engagement in bartering and exchanging goods throughout the upper Midwest. At least four major subgroups of Ottawa were recognized (Kiskakon, Sinago, Sable, and Nassauaketon), all of whom were friendly with each other.[23] Below these four major divisions were multiple local bands each identified by its own totem (bear, otter, grey squirrel, black squirrel, etc.). And within local bands there were extended family and nuclear family groupings. The various organizational levels each had a leader or chief, and people lived together in small or large villages, depending on the season and landscape. Movement, realignments, and the comings and goings of individuals and groups happened constantly, undermining the Euro-American notion of Indian tribes with distinct territories and a single defined chief. The upshot of this social organization is that a single Ottawa individual had nested layers of identity. Ottawa people were woven into a dynamic social fabric of relationships through which they were supported and blessed, and to which they made contributions. The Ottawa had a strong sense of belonging, which fostered a dedicated and intense allegiance to one another.[24]

The tribal designations later applied by colonizers were not recognized by the Indigenous people themselves. In fact, an Ottawa would likely have identified him- or herself first by their family, second by their clan, and quite likely beyond that as simply Anishinaabeg.[25] Marriage was one way that many Native people, including the Ottawa, maintained close ties with other groups. Marriage enlarged a family's circle of allies who could provide help during difficult times and offer support when conflicts arose. Marriages across tribal lines (at least those involving different tribes who were in good standing) were not only allowed but encouraged, a practice that today is recognized as having benefits for promoting genetic diversity as well.[26]

Connected through trade, marriage, and geography, the various Anishinaabe groups refreshed and re-formed their relationships at major gathering locations such as the rapids of the Grand River. For generations this site had been an important social hub, primarily for the Ottawa, but for other groups as well, yet it was never a permanent settlement of a defined collection of individuals. Some Indigenous people were likely always present at the rapids, but it would not necessarily have been the same group of people month by month or even week by week. The fluidity of this way of life geographically, socially, and culturally was difficult for European immigrants to understand. Even though the people who consistently used West Michigan were labeled as "Ottawa," the composition and character of any one group of Ottawa was constantly influenced by social interactions and mergers with other groups.

Living Well in the West Michigan Landscape

Knowing how to live in a land without destroying it required a great deal of intelligence by the Anishinaabeg, intelligence that emerged out of a deep respect for the earth. Over time they had accumulated knowledge regarding how to capture animals for food and fur, when and where certain plants could be collected for food and medicine, and what materials were useful for making pots, baskets, and shelters. The Ottawa of West Michigan practiced agriculture in particular locations that favored reliable harvests. They also used fire to promote beneficial vegetation and to clear out forest undergrowth for easier movement.

The Ottawa were especially known for their skilled craftsmanship. For example, up to one year was invested in building a single birchbark canoe—a distinctly

Indigenous American vessel that prior to colonization was completely unknown to Europeans. Some of these canoes were forty feet long, required ten to twelve paddlers, and could carry up to six thousand pounds of cargo.[27] The Ottawa were also known for their world-class basketry. In 1922 Charles Belknap wrote,

> In my young days I watched the Indian chop the riverbank elm and roll it into the water to soak; then after days, split it into sections about six feet long and with a wooden mallet pound the sections until the growth could be split into splints. Then on a shaving horse with wooden vice jaws they shaved it to even thickness and width and it was ready for the weaver.

He also praised the artistry involved:

> I have watched the basket weaver . . . as with dreamy eyes and patient hands she wove in and out different colored feathers, sweet grasses, and fern stems, staining them with the juices of wild berries. Each design possessed a meaning and gave the basket its own individuality.[28]

An important aspect of living well in the land was not to impact any area too much. Like many Indigenous groups, the Ottawa moved regularly in concert with seasonal availability of resources that sustained their sophisticated culture and complex spirituality. As a specific example, sometime in the late 1600s or early 1700s, an Ottawa subgroup from the northwest portion of Michigan's Lower Peninsula began using West Michigan repeatedly during the winter months. For many years this group spent their summers at a place called Waganakising, which the French later named L'Arbre Croche, near current-day Harbor Springs on the north side of little Traverse Bay.[29] At this site they would plant crops (maize, beans, and squash), and then after harvest time they shifted south along the west coast of Michigan in their canoes and spread out into interior regions such as the Grand River basin for the winter.

During the winter months people were sustained both by harvested produce and also by the fall berry crop and abundant game in southwest Michigan. In late winter and early spring when the maple sap started flowing, they tapped the trees for sugar, after which they gathered again when the waterways thawed near the mouth of the Muskegon River for their annual trek back up to Waganakising.

Timing of these movements was influenced by the annual runs of a variety of fish that moved from Lake Michigan up into inland rivers and streams to spawn. This was a patterned nomadic existence that alternated between semipermanent family or clan villages during the winter and a much larger presence at Waganakising during the summer. The Ottawa were hunters, gatherers, and agriculturalists, supporting themselves with a diversity of foods and other culturally important materials collected from the landscapes in which they lived and through which they moved.

Ottawa movements were not a tightly choreographed, regularly repeated production. At times some family or clan groups lingered or stayed at certain locations longer than others, and some places would host multiple groups for longer times. These were fluid populations, coming together into larger groups for a while, breaking off into subgroups at other times, moving and gathering and remaining and shifting as seasons, group affinities, and weather conditions changed.[30] Outside threats from enemy tribes would at times motivate larger groupings and could bring about fresh alliances. The Ottawa were also known to take in wandering individuals from other groups, particularly Potawatomi or Ojibwe but at times even individuals from more distant tribes. Newly included members from outside groups represented additional opportunities for fresh insights, teachings, practices, and the building of relationships. In this way, cultural identity, similar to geographic location, was mobile and fluid.[31] Historian Charles Cleland wrote, "people who organized their lives around small, kin-based groups where reciprocal exchanges and an egalitarian ethic prevailed needed to develop impressive social skills." In addition, they needed "encyclopedic knowledge" of their environment. "Each person needed the know-how of hundreds of skills to turn wood, bone, skin, and bark into the necessities of survival. The Anishinaabeg were a knowledgeable, skillful, and resourceful people."[32]

The Indigenous people who lived in the Plaster Creek watershed had minimal impact on the creek. They lived in the watershed without feeling the need to control it or alter it in unsustainable ways to serve their own personal desires, accumulate goods, or promote their own economic gain.[33] A conservation ethic of care, both explicitly and implicitly, governed most of their practices.[34] As current residents of the Plaster Creek watershed, we are challenged to unlearn ways of living that are harmful or unsustainable and find ways to honor the legacy of the Ottawa who have lived here for generations.

Honoring Chief Blackbird's Legacy in the Plaster Creek Watershed

One September morning in the early years of Plaster Creek Stewards (PCS), our program coordinator, Nate, excitedly approached Dave with an idea. "We really should go visit the power line right-of-way that runs through the Black Hills—I think there are some prairie plants in there." This moment is memorable for me (Dave) because, while I knew that Nate was an excellent field botanist, I also knew that it was unlikely any native prairie plants would be growing in the highly urbanized Black Hills neighborhood near downtown Grand Rapids. However, Nate had noticed what looked to be a stand of tallgrass prairie on the south-facing slope of these hills. As we chatted, he pulled up some aerial views on his laptop and pointed out to me the powerline that bisects the hill like an electric shears that has run through a thick head of hair. We made plans to visit.

The Black Hills neighborhood occupies a raised area that was essentially an island that rose out of the original Grand River floodplain. Today this section of the river has been straightened, constrained with cement walls, and relegated to the northwest portion of its floodplain. The rest of the former broad flat floodplain is now filled with industrial activity, roadways, parking lots, and warehouses. This sea of industrialization includes the Grand Rapids Sewage Treatment Plant and Waste to Energy Facility. The possibility of a remnant natural area still supporting native prairie plants in this landscape was highly unlikely.

After parking along the north side of Hall Street by Kensington Park, and walking across the baseball field toward the power line, I could see why Nate was excited. Swaying in the morning breeze was an unmistakable stand of tallgrass prairie—dominated by classic prairie indicators that included Indian grass, big bluestem, and switchgrass. Further up the slope were patches of little bluestem, broom sedge, and a variety of other prairie grasses and dryland sedges. Mixed in was an abundance of wildflowers that are typically found in high-quality savannahs and prairies: showy goldenrod, hairy and violet bush clovers, lance-leaved loosestrife, showy tick trefoil, Culver's root, pinweed, wood sage, and many others.

As we made our way through this fascinating habitat, it occurred to me that many of the more abundant native plants in this spot are plants that had culinary or medicinal uses for the Ottawa, including wild coffee and a native sunflower that we later identified as *Helianthus hirsutus* (hairy sunflower). We began wondering if this was less a pristine prairie remnant and more of a cultivated natural garden.

Quite surprisingly, we later learned that hairy sunflower is a special concern species in Michigan because of its rarity. We were the first to document it officially in Kent County. What an unlikely oasis for native plants here in the middle of industrial Grand Rapids.

With subsequent research, we discovered that the Black Hills (basically one large hill named after the black oak trees that still grow there) is a village site where Chief Blackbird once lived. From this perch, the chief could see up and down the Grand River. He could also look to the south and view the sacred waterfall of Ken-O-Sha as it tumbled over a gypsum outcrop down into the floodplain.[35] Historical records detailed how the Ottawa frequently burned this specific site, which contributed to the open aspect of the woods and the success of prairie species who thrive in fire-prone areas.[36] The power company's practice of clearing woody growth from the right-of-way has acted as a surrogate for controlled burning, perpetuating this patch of prairie. Today when PCS staff collect seeds of native plants from here, we label them "Chief Blackbird genotype," honoring the legacy of the Ottawa people who cared for this land. These native species almost certainly represent lineages that date back to the early 1800s, before Europeans began to arrive.

PART 2

THE HISTORY OF PLASTER CREEK

ACKNOWLEDGING OUR COMPLICITY

CHAPTER 3

Interactions between the Ottawa and European Immigrants

It was a hot, humid day on August 29, 2021, when I (Gail) got out of my car and began walking to the Grand River in the center of Grand Rapids. The Grand River Bands of Ottawa Indians were hosting a ceremony to commemorate the two hundredth anniversary of the treaty signing held in Chicago on August 29, 1821. This treaty had been brokered between the Anishinaabe people and representatives of the U.S. government. I could hear the steady beat of a drum and several voices rising in song to greet people as we gathered. A local Ottawa tribal leader eventually welcomed the crowd and explained the historical significance of this day. He described the plaque recently installed along Fulton Street on the west side of the Grand River. The plaque has a map from 1836 that depicts natural landscape features including local creeks while also showing the land divided into square-mile plats for settlement.[1] In the upper left corner of the map there is a notation that reads "Indian Country," a small section of land on the west side of the river. With this Chicago Treaty of 1821 Europeans secured all the land east and south of the Grand River (including the Plaster Creek watershed) while Native Americans retained land to the west and north, although subsequently this territory was also transferred to the United States in the Washington Treaty of 1836.[2]

Music filled the air—the drumbeats and the singing surrounded the assembled people and caused a quietness to settle over the ceremony. Listening to the music, I experienced a deep sense of lament for the pain and suffering we, as European settlers, have caused the Indigenous peoples of North America, in particular the

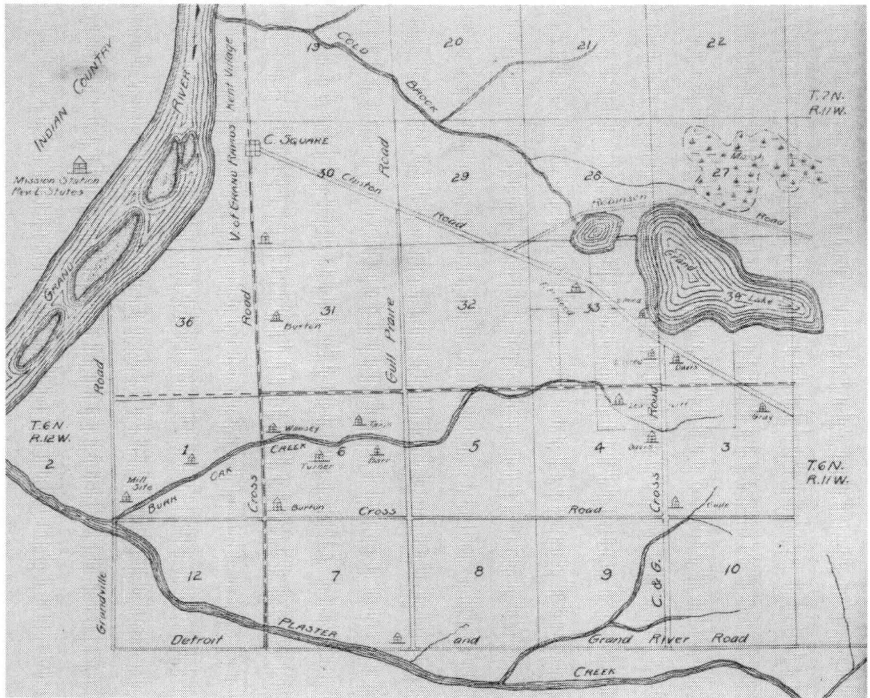

FIGURE 6. A 1920 rendering of an 1836 map of Grand Rapids, Michigan, showing "Indian Country" to the northwest.

PHOTOGRAPH COURTESY OF GRAND RAPIDS HISTORY CENTER, GRAND RAPIDS PUBLIC LIBRARY, GRAND RAPIDS, MI.

Anishinaabe alliance of the Ojibwe (Chippewa), Odawa (Ottawa), and Potawatomi of Michigan. When the music concluded, the president of the Northern Michigan Ottawa Association rose to speak:

> We do not share a collective memory of the 1821 Treaty event. The Ottawa opened up their homelands on a humanitarian basis. The United States operated with discovery, expansion, and exploitation. The Ottawa maintain that the Doctrine of Discovery does not apply to our lands. The Ottawa People have made many land cessions, sometimes under duress, to the State of Michigan and the United States of America. It is exciting to see the original Indigenous caretakers of this land honored and commemorated in this way. *We continue to participate and work toward*

FIGURE 7. Women from the Grand River Bands of Ottawa Indians enacted a water blessing at the two hundredth anniversary of the 1821 Treaty.

PHOTOGRAPH COURTESY OF DOWNTOWN GRAND RAPIDS INC.

> *forming a more perfect union* [emphasis added]. We hope this treaty commemoration and plaque will advance that goal.[3]

This tribal leader's words were moving. Two things stood out as I listened to his comments. First, the Ottawa chose to share their land with European settlers out of humanitarian compassion. The Ottawa recognized that the Europeans needed land to grow food for their own families and responded with generosity. They did not anticipate, at first, the suffering and ethnic cleansing that would happen. It is important that European Americans recognize the unselfish humanitarianism that led Indigenous people to share knowledge, insights, and gifts with them. Second, despite the broken trust, damaged relationships, and environmental destruction the Ottawa have endured at the hands of European settlers and their descendants, this leader spoke of still desiring to participate in "forming a more perfect union" with the United States. The generosity of spirit displayed in the midst of such historical and current suffering was humbling for me to witness.

The ceremony concluded with a Blessing of the Waters by a group of Ottawa women of all ages, who according to Indigenous tradition are the water protectors. It was a simple and beautiful blessing held at the river's edge. The musicians played again as the women enacted the water blessing. This commemorative event is one that I will long remember because it demonstrates that interactions between the Ottawa and European Americans are continuing and have opportunities to grow, despite a violent and painful history.

Settler Colonization

European immigrants inserted themselves into the cultural and ecological landscapes they encountered in North America in what is best described as settler colonization. To *colonize* is to impose one's presence into a new place with little regard for the well-being of current inhabitants. When European immigrants came to North America, they did not seek to fit into this land and the human flourishing that was happening here.[4] Europeans paid little attention to the history of this place and the wisdom and insight Indigenous people had accumulated while living here for centuries. Such disregard is especially notable given the numerous accounts of how Indigenous people helped early immigrants. But the white settler colonists were intent on taking control with their own rules of engagement and gave little consideration to their impact on Indigenous peoples' cultures, languages, or lives. This self-serving approach was also manifest in the lack of regard for the ecological well-being of the land. As a result, the earth and many of its inhabitants suffered. As Native American scholar Daniel Wildcat writes, "Nature and culture cannot be divorced—biological diversity and cultural diversity are inextricably connected."[5]

Indigenous Encounters with Europeans in the 1600s

Prior to European settlement, Michigan was largely a peaceful region, well populated by both long-standing Anishinaabe communities and those who had recently relocated here because of conflicts with the Haudenosaunee (Iroquois) in the east. The first personal encounters between Anishinaabeg and colonists began during the early 1600s. Sometime around 1621 French explorer Etienne Brulé traveled up the St. Mary's River and continued into Lake Superior, accompanied by a group of Wyandots (whom the French dubbed Hurons) serving as his guides. Another French explorer, Jean Nicolet, is known to have navigated the Straits of Mackinac into Lake Michigan in a large canoe, accompanied by seven Wyandot men in 1634. Like many of these early explorers, both Brulé and Nicolet learned multiple Native American languages and by all accounts were treated well not only by their guides, but also by the various tribes they met on their journeys.[6]

About fifty years later, a Jesuit mission was set up at the rapids Brulé had navigated by Father Jacques Marquette in 1668. This place, an important gathering spot for Indigenous people known as Bow-e-ting, was called Sault Ste. Marie by the French. Shortly after that, in 1671, Father Marquette helped to build a chapel at another long-standing Anishinaabeg gathering place called Michilimackinac, sixty miles to the south. Thus began an era of establishing missions, trading posts, and forts, a pattern that continued well into the nineteenth century. These stations, set up by both the French and the British, would later serve as entry points for waves of westward-bound immigrants. The gathering sites stood at important intersections of waterways, along portages, or at important locations where food was seasonally available. Historian Richard White points out that Indians were not attracted to trading posts and missions; trading posts and missions were attracted to the Indians.[7] Therefore, to say that Father Marquette founded Sault Ste. Marie in 1668, or that Louis Campau founded Grand Rapids in 1826, neglects the reality that Marquette and Campau were welcomed and cared for by native people who for centuries had been occupying these places.[8]

The Possibility of Coexistence

From the mid-1500s to the mid-1700s, Indigenous Americans and white explorers and settlers coexisted relatively well in the Great Lakes region. For much of this time France was the dominant European presence in this area. The French government anticipated a future in which the Indians acknowledged the ultimate governance of the king of France. However, the envisioned future was not one of forced removal or cultural erasure.[9] Portraying their nation as a benevolent presence to the Indians, the French claimed to mediate among Indigenous groups and provide for them. While clearly paternalistic, the French envisioned a future of coexistence, not one of replacement, and history would have transpired much differently for Indigenous Americans if this approach had persisted.[10]

Owing in part to the long-term presence of French explorers and traders, France developed a deeper understanding of Anishinaabeg culture than any other nation involved in colonizing North America. In fact, one criticism of the early French explorers was that in terms of clothing, behavior, and appearance, they came to resemble the Indians quite closely.[11] Alliances were also strengthened by marriages between French explorers and Anishinaabe women, resulting in a group of people known as Métis. The Métis were generally well respected and often served as important connectors between the two cultural groups.[12] Establishing relationships (usually mutually beneficial relationships) with different bands and tribes was the primary way that France asserted its presence and exerted some measure of control in the Great Lakes area. The French also cultivated alliances so that Indians would be less likely to trade their goods with the British, who had a presence both south and north of the Great Lakes region.

Trading Posts, Missions, Intermarriage, and Disease

Although white settlements began to appear in northern Michigan in the early 1600s, it wasn't until two hundred years later that West Michigan saw its first mission and trading post. During these two centuries the interactions between

Anishinaabeg and colonists resulted in changes to each group.[13] When deemed strategic and beneficial, colonists appropriated certain aspects of Indigenous ways of life and the Anishinaabeg appropriated certain tools and materials from the colonists. Through these interactions, both groups changed, and a somewhat balanced relationship emerged. However, as white settlers became more numerous, that relationship became increasingly one-sided.

The first trading post in West Michigan was established by Madeline (sometimes referred to as "Magdalene") Marcot LaFramboise and her husband Joseph at the confluence of the Thornapple and Grand Rivers near present day Ada, Michigan. Madeline and her six siblings were Métis. Her mother was Ottawa and her father was French, an early explorer who later served as an agent for the Northwest Fur Company in St. Joseph, where Madeline was born. After her husband died in 1806, LaFramboise set up several trading posts in the Grand River basin, including one near the convergence of the Flat River and the Grand, a site known today as Fallasburg. By 1820 LaFramboise decided to retire to Mackinac Island, transferring her trading post at the Thornapple River to a recent arrival from New York named Rix Robinson. She was a remarkably successful businesswoman at a time when men dominated the fur-trading enterprise and nearly all aspects of white society.

Rix Robinson was the third of thirteen children, born in 1789 to parents who farmed and kept a blacksmith shop in Massachusetts. He avoided being drafted for the War of 1812, but he did work as a sutler, one who distributed goods to wartime troops. This work led him to Michilimackinac where he became acquainted with John Jacob Astor, a leader in the American Fur Company, a relationship that later brought Robinson to West Michigan, where he met Madeline LaFramboise.[14]

In some ways, Robinson was an anomaly among the early settlers. He took over LaFramboise's business in 1821, the same year he married an Ottawa woman named Pee-miss-a-quot-a-quay (Flying Cloud Woman). The couple had one child, John, who later became a well-known Methodist pastor in the Grand Rapids area. After the marriage broke up, Robinson married another Ottawa woman, Se-be-quay (River Woman), who had been educated at Michilimackinac. Se-be-quay was the daughter of Chief Ma-ob-bin-na-kiz-hick (Chief Hazy Cloud) and was the sister of another Ottawa chief, Noah-quag-e-shik (Chief Noonday). Se-be-quay and Robinson never had children but were known for their generous hospitality and fair treatment of customers. They ran the trading post in Ada for many years and established additional stations along the Grand and Kalamazoo

Rivers.[15] Robinson was fluently bilingual in Ottawa and English, accomplished in hunting and fishing, and an avid reader. He held several political offices as West Michigan became more heavily settled, including supervisor for the Township of Kent in 1834, supervisor of Ada Township in 1840, associate judge of Circuit Courts for Kent County in 1844, state senator in 1845, and a member of the State Constitutional Convention in 1850.[16] Robinson was described by other colonists as one who "took up the wrongs of the Indians always, and had them redressed."[17]

About the time Rix Robinson took over the Thornapple River trading post, a Baptist missionary named Isaac McCoy was tasked by Governor Lewis Cass to set up a mission and school in West Michigan.[18] McCoy visited the rapids on the Grand River in 1823 but encountered Indians unhappy with recent treaty outcomes and thought it safest to return to the friendly confines of the Carey Mission that he had earlier established along the St. Joseph River in 1822. In November of 1824 McCoy made a return trip with several companions (one of whom was another missionary named Rev. Leonard Slater) and met Rix Robinson's brother-in-law, Chief Noonday, a notably generous and reliable friend of the early settlers, near Gun Lake. The Ottawa leader accompanied McCoy's entourage back to the site of the rapids. They arrived on December 1, 1824, at which time McCoy, with the assistance of Chief Noonday, selected the precise location for what would become known as the Thomas Mission.[19]

This mission was established on the west bank of the Grand River, immediately south of the current-day intersection of Bridge Street and Front Avenue in Grand Rapids, approximately one mile north of where Plaster Creek joins the Grand River. Further upstream a short stretch of the river fell nearly twenty feet in elevation, creating a series of rapids. This area had been a major gathering spot for Indigenous people back to the time of the Hopewell. During the 1824 visit Chief Noonday also showed McCoy a salt spring and some gypsum rock south of the mission along the river, near the mouth of Plaster Creek.[20] Charles Belknap writes that the water from the salt springs was "very agreeable to man and seemed much liked by the birds [passenger pigeons]. They [the birds] fed also on the grass and on the oak ridges to the west. I have seen a hundred acres densely covered with flocks going and coming about these marshes."[21] The Ottawa considered the gypsum outcrops and the nearby salt meadows sacred. It was their belief that "the spirits fed there."[22]

Construction for the mission began the next year, and by the end of autumn 1825 the Thomas Mission opened.[23] Native people had kept much of the terrain along the rapids clear for a variety of cultural activities, and they had planted a peculiar circular array of wild plum trees here, possibly for ceremonial activities.[24] Downstream where the river swung westward, much of the north bank, where sunlight was optimal, had been improved by the Ottawa for agricultural purposes.[25] By all accounts, once the mission had been set up a time of mutual coexistence occurred. McCoy only served for two years, succeeded by Rev. Slater who took over the mission and remained there until 1832, about the time the mission closed.[26] Rev. Slater was subsequently appointed postmaster of the emerging town of Grand Rapids.

In 1826, one year after the Thomas Mission had been established, Louis Campau moved to West Michigan to build a trading post and blacksmith shop on the opposite side of the river from the mission.[27] Campau had formerly initiated the first trading post at Saginaw back in 1815 and had been encouraged to begin this trading post on the Grand River by William Brewster of Detroit, a businessman in the fur trade. After becoming established in Grand Rapids, Campau subsequently set up trading posts at locations known today as Muskegon, Manistee, Kalamazoo, Lowell, Hastings, and Eaton Rapids. The fur trade was accelerating at this time, and Grand Rapids became a significant hub where Indians would bring furs and exchange them for dried goods, ammunition, beads, blankets, and whiskey. Later on, maple sugar, blueberries, cranberries, moccasins, and handcrafted baskets were also traded.[28]

Described as a shrewd and successful businessman, Campau was known to actively seek out animal pelts by traveling among villages in West Michigan. He often wore Indian clothing such as a buckskin coat and moccasins. He was an energetic storyteller, typically mixing Ottawa or French words into his English, and with his fluency in these three languages as well as his cultural adeptness, Campau was an important interpreter in later treaty negotiations. In 1831 he was the first individual to officially purchase land in Grand Rapids, which included the land around his trading post, blacksmith shop, and cabin.[29]

Another powerful dynamic at this time was the devastating effect that European-borne diseases were having on Indigenous people. White immigrants brought diseases to which Indigenous people had little immunity.[30] Since Indigenous people did not keep domesticated animals as Europeans did, they had never been exposed to pathogens that passed from these animals to humans, and they were highly susceptible to diseases such as smallpox, chicken pox, and the flu.[31] Many colonists, including the authors of *The History of Kent County*, interpreted the pandemics to be divine will: "Storm and flood and disease have created sad havoc in the ranks of the aborigines since the occupation of the country by the white man . . . the great dispensations of the Unseen Ruler are demonstrated."[32]

Great Lakes Indians had suspicions that the diseases were being spread by the colonists. Some Europeans also recognized this possibility and on at least one occasion reportedly gave their Native hosts contaminated blankets, one of the earliest examples of biological warfare.[33] It is not clear how successful this attempt was, but there is no doubt that European diseases devastated Indigenous communities. Within a relatively short span of several decades, at least 60–70 percent of all native North American people died from disease, and in some areas the mortality rate was over 90 percent.[34] The rapid decline of Indian populations was accompanied by an erosion in the confidence of religious rituals and medicinal practices, which had little impact on this new wave of pathogens. Combined with reduced availability of game due to the fur trade and widespread deforestation, the pandemics that ravaged Native American communities resulted in cultural disarray, profound confusion, and deep sadness.

Land Improvement and Ownership

A prevailing mindset among settler colonists was that the new landscape they were moving into needed "improvement." By improving the land, its value increased, and rightful ownership could be procured. Such thinking justified taking land from Indigenous people since settlers thought they were only moving through the land without significantly changing it.[35] With religious conviction, Lewis Cass, governor of Michigan and President Jackson's secretary of war, wrote that the Ottawa were not worthy inhabitants of the land:

> There can be no doubt . . . that the Creator intended the earth should be reclaimed from a state of nature and cultivated; that the human race should spread over it, procuring from it the means of comfortable subsistence and of increase and improvement. A tribe of wandering hunters, depending upon the chase for support, and deriving it from the forests, and rivers, and lakes, of an immense continent, have a very imperfect possession of the country over

> which they roam. . . . The forests which shelter them are doomed to perpetual unproductiveness. . . . Our forefathers, when they landed upon the shores of this continent, found it in a state of nature, traversed, but not occupied, by wandering hordes of barbarians.[36]

Early accounts are replete with descriptions that illustrate an unapologetic ideology of white supremacy by the U.S. government. In his Fifth Annual Message delivered in 1833 to the general public, U.S. president Andrew Jackson declared,

> That those tribes cannot exist surrounded by our settlements and in continual contact with our citizens is certain. They have neither the intelligence, the industry, the moral habits, nor the desire of improvement which are essential to any favorable change in their condition. Established in the midst of another and a superior race, and without appreciating the causes of their inferiority or seeking to control them, they must necessarily yield to the force of circumstances and ere long disappear.[37]

This belief was paramount as European colonists expanded into the Great Lakes region. The rising new nation of the United States of America prioritized the accumulation of financial wealth at the expense of the land and its people.

And yet, this justification was inadequate even on its own terms, because the Ottawa did transform the land through their farming, and colonists ironically called those areas "Indian improvements."[38] Indians also taught the settlers how to grow crops in this new land, and within mere decades, one of them—corn—had become a critical component of every homesteader's farm. Yet because the Ottawa did not practice agriculture with the type of expansive land conversion that settlers considered appropriate, they were deemed unworthy occupants of the land. Many nineteenth-century West Michigan writings echo the arrogance of Cass and Jackson:

> The savages found here, even within memory of the pioneers, could never be brought within the fold of civilization. Their occupation of the entire peninsula at a time when the American cultivators of the soil required it for development, was an outrage on the advancement of that day. . . . The United States, acting on the strict principles of just government, determined that he who would cultivate the land should possess it.[39]

Because colonists considered Indigenous people inferior, their ways of living in the land were devalued. Many of the key elements of Indigenous worldviews—respect for nonhuman creatures, living in ways that fit into the landscape, an emphasis on giving back to the creation that gifted them with provisions—were considered naïve and uneducated. Settler colonists referred to Indigenous people with the same words that they used to describe the land in which they lived: "wild," "untamed," and in need of "improving."[40] In 1903 historian Francis Parkman wrote that the Indian "will not learn the arts of civilization and he and his forest must perish together."[41]

Perceptions of Inferiority and Superiority

Because European immigrants generally believed Indigenous Americans were biologically, culturally, and intellectually inferior, coexistence became increasingly difficult and eventually was perceived by colonists as an impossibility.[42] Vestiges of these notions remain and still misinform today. The fallaciousness of such thinking is quickly exposed after an honest appraisal that the Anishinaabeg knew how to live in the land without destroying it. In more specific terms, the Anishinaabeg never had to deal with a stream like Plaster Creek, so badly mistreated that it threatened their own well-being. While life is never perfect anywhere, the quality of life for Indigenous North Americans prior to colonization may have been as high as any group of people on earth at that time.[43]

The assumption of European superiority was often perplexing and offensive to Native Americans.[44] Indigenous people were typically not opposed to developing relationships with colonists, but they were expecting balanced relationships where mutual responsibilities were met and where promises made were promises kept. The mixing of these two cultural groups actually led some Indigenous groups to consider the European immigrants as inferior. Historian Charles Mann reports that some Great Lakes Indians thought the French had "little intelligence in comparison to themselves" and that in general Europeans were considered weak, untrustworthy, and dirty. Common European practices such as blowing one's nose into a handkerchief and saving the soiled rag in a pocket disgusted the Indians.[45] Indigenous women were alarmed at how white men treated their wives, recognizing that gender roles in most Indigenous cultures were much more balanced than displayed by these newcomers.[46] The Ottawa of West Michigan did not want to live near Dutch immigrants because they found them to be dirty and smelly.[47] Many groups, including the Ottawa, interpreted dishonesty by the colonists and failure to own up to treaty obligations as disgraceful behavior.[48]

Land Cession Treaties

The flow of immigrants from the east coast into the basins of Lake Ontario and Lake Erie caused a reactionary westward movement of many Ottawa, Potawatomi, and Huron into the Kalamazoo, Grand, and Thornapple River valleys where for a time they could avoid conflicts with settlers. But colonists, as well as treaties, tended to follow the Indians westward. The treaties strongly influenced the dynamics between whites and Indigenous Americans, and therefore the way human existence impacted the landscape. In 1819, Governor Cass was instructed to secure treaties that would take large sections of the Michigan Territory from the Indians. His mandate was to gain this land as cheaply as possible and convince the Indians to move westward, somewhere beyond Lake Michigan.[49] The first of these treaties to have influence in West Michigan was the 1819 Treaty of Saginaw. It targeted approximately one-third of the lower peninsula, and negotiations took place near the present-day city of Saginaw. Louis Campau was hired to assist in these proceedings along with many other agents, traders, soldiers, and interpreters. In addition, supplies for this meeting (including large volumes of alcohol), as well as the U.S. Third Infantry were sent to Saginaw on the U.S. cutter *Porcupine* out of Detroit.[50]

Lewis Cass opened the meeting with a speech in which he laid out the U.S. government's intention to peaceably buy the Indians' land and help them settle into small reservations. He cautioned them that their hunting way of life would become increasingly untenable and that they would have to transition to permanent settlements and learn how to farm. This directive surprised most of the Indian leaders at least in part because they had been farming for centuries. Furthermore, they had been led to believe that this meeting was designed to negotiate a peace accord in the aftermath of the War of 1812. In an initial public reply to Cass, an Anishinaabe leader named Ogamawkeketo (Chief Speaker) responded,

> You do not know our wishes. Our people wonder what has brought you so far from your homes. Your young men have invited us to come and light the council

> fire. We are here to smoke the pipe of peace, but not to sell our land. . . . Your people trespass upon our hunting grounds. You flock to our shores. . . . The warm wave of this white man rolls in upon us and melts us away. . . . Our children want homes: shall we sell from under them the spot where they spread their blankets?[51]

Given the volumes of alcohol that were consumed and other underhanded attempts at coercion, violent outbreaks and raucous behavior typified these meetings.[52] In the end, an agreement emerged that confined the Indians to small reservations and guaranteed them the right to hunt and fish on the land they ceded, which became increasingly difficult to do over time with the increased presence of white homesteaders. Louis Campau earned over $1,000 for his services at these negotiations, an amount equivalent to five years of wages at that time.[53]

A second major treaty relevant to West Michigan Indians was the 1821 Treaty of Chicago. Lewis Cass also orchestrated this treaty with a similar approach. Eventually bribery, alcohol, and disingenuous promises prevailed over the strong resistance of some Ottawa leaders.[54] This agreement resulted in the cession of much of southwest Michigan from the Grand River southward to the Indiana line, including the Plaster Creek watershed. In this treaty the U.S. government pledged to the Ottawa an annual sum of $1,000 in perpetuity, and $1,500 annually for ten years to support a teacher, a blacksmith, and someone to train them in European-style agriculture. One square mile of land was to be set aside on the north side of the Grand River in support of these development efforts. In addition, the Ottawa were assigned certain small reservations in which to live and a larger, albeit small portion of the total acreage of the treaty, in which they could hunt and gather food.[55] Few of these government commitments were ever met.

Evidence that a third major treaty was being planned emerged in 1834, when a visitor named Silas W. Titus made his way to West Michigan. Titus was an agent of President Jackson, assigned to lay the groundwork for the Washington Treaty of 1836. He met with Rix Robinson, Louis Campau, Rev. Leonard Slater, as well as others, and he convinced a group of these early settlers to travel to Washington the following year to assist with negotiations.[56] Several Ottawa leaders, including Mack-a-de-pe-nessy (Chief Blackbird) and Noah-quag-e-shik (Chief Noonday), joined them on the journey. In Washington, Robinson was one of several bilingual whites who assisted in the negotiations. This treaty resulted in the cession of all the Indian lands north of the Grand River up to Michilimackinac. As compensation for his services, Robinson secured private lands for his extended family and was paid $23,000, approximately two decades of salary for a government agent.[57] The Ottawa complained afterward that non-Native people had done much of the negotiating. Augustin Hamlin, who was an educated and respected Métis, declared,

> The words the Commissioners had just heard from the chiefs were not their words, not the feelings of their hearts but the words of white men who wanted reservations and have dictated to them what to say. These men care not for the Indian, but they wish to benefit themselves.[58]

It is difficult to know the role that Rix Robinson played in the shaping of this treaty. Given his direct family ties through marriage to important leaders of the Ottawa, one would expect that he acted as an advocate for the Indians. Yet he helped the government secure an agreement about which the Ottawa were less than supportive.[59]

Even though the results of the 1836 treaty were "not the feelings of their hearts," upon leaving Washington the Ottawa delegation believed they had avoided their greatest fear, which was forced removal from Michigan to territories west of the Mississippi. The Ottawa would now move to fourteen reservations scattered throughout the ceded territory where they would be allowed to live in perpetuity. They could continue their cultural ways while learning new practices associated with European-based agriculture and civilization. The Ottawa were also granted the right to hunt and fish within the ceded territory until American settlers wanted these lands.[60] To the Indians, treaties represented a means for retaining at least some of their way of life amid the chaos of colonization.[61] For people whose identity was woven into the land in which they lived, forced expulsion to western territories was the worst possible outcome. How could they build birchbark canoes in a land with little water and no birch trees? How could they gather their nutritious nuts and sustaining medicines in places where those plants did not grow? How could they leave their buried relatives and the place-based stories that taught them how to live as honorable people? And what about the Native people who already lived in those distant places who spoke a completely different language and were not inviting them to come? While regrettably and admittedly defeating, treaties came to be seen as the only option.

To make matters worse, when the official treaty of 1836 ratified by Congress was publicly posted in Michigan, the Ottawa were shocked and frustrated. Without seeking approval from the Indians, the U.S. Senate had amended the document to limit the use of the reservations to only five years instead of in perpetuity, stating that if the Ottawa wished to remove themselves to the west, they would be given free land there.[62] Furthermore, some of the monetary concessions were altered as well, but even the terms that hadn't changed were not fulfilled, which greatly angered the Ottawa.[63] One can only wonder how differently history would have played out in West Michigan if even the original unjust agreements had been upheld as agreed upon.

These three treaties—Saginaw (1819), Chicago (1821), and Washington (1836)—resulted in nearly all of the Indigenous lands of Michigan's Lower Peninsula and the eastern half of the Upper Peninsula being transferred into U.S. jurisdiction.[64] In the aftermath of these accords, land became officially available for homesteaders from the east, and Michigan's white population rose quickly—from 8,765 in 1820 to 31,640 in 1830 and 174,543 in 1836.[65] With this burgeoning European presence intent on clearing and farming land, broken treaties with formidable U.S. military backing, and ravaging pandemics, the future was increasingly bleak for Michigan's Anishinaabeg.

Removal and Assimilation Strategies

The Indian Removal Act of 1830 had authorized President Jackson to grant lands west of the Mississippi River in exchange for Indian lands within existing state borders. In 1833 a group of Michigan Ottawa were forcibly moved west. This was not a move the Ottawa chose nor one they could refuse. Relocation plans were met with bewilderment, deep sadness, and resistance. One of the Ottawa leaders in West Michigan declared,

> Here we have buried our dead, and here we should remain to protect their graves. This is our home. . . . Here we were reared on the banks of the beloved O-wash-ten-ong (the Grand River), whose beauty has become our pride and boast. Here we have held our councils, prosecuted our trade, and preserved peace and friendship with all nations. Why go to a strange land to mingle with strange people? What evil have we committed? Why thus sacrifice that which is most dear to the heart of every chief and warrior?[66]

The group was first settled in present day Kansas and later relocated to Oklahoma. More than half of the original group that left Michigan died en route, leaving only about two hundred individuals when they eventually settled in Oklahoma where there was no wild rice, no black ash for making baskets, nor any birch trees for making canoes.[67]

Other groups of Michigan Ottawa were more successful at avoiding governmental efforts of removal. Some remained on a limited number of reservations. Others moved east into present-day Ontario, fleeing from the oppressive U.S. influence. Despite all the government efforts at cultural erasure, there are still three federally recognized Ottawa tribes that exist in Michigan: the Grand Traverse Band of Ottawa and Chippewa Indians, the Little River Band of Ottawa Indians, and the Little Traverse Bay Bands of Odawa Indians.[68] The Grand River Bands of Ottawa Indians have been seeking federal recognition for nearly thirty years, and as of this writing, they have not yet been granted that designation, which would unlock federal benefits for the tribe.[69] The continued presence and contribution of the Ottawa in the twenty-first century, despite concerted efforts at cultural erasure, speaks to their indelible resilience.

A second way of eliminating Native Americans was to convert them into "civilized" people, extracting Indians from their culture and assimilating them into European ways of living. All aspects of Indigenous life were deemed in need of change—their language, clothing, diet, behavior, and religion. In the Civilizing Fund Act of 1819, the U.S. government assigned much of the civilizing efforts of Native Americans to missionaries. Through their evangelistic efforts and the education that occurred in mission schools, missionaries were tasked with transforming Indigenous people into "respectable" citizens.[70] According to Indian Commissioner Luke Lea, it was "indispensably necessary that they [Indians] be placed in positions where they can be controlled."[71]

Often Indigenous children were forced to leave their families and communities and relocate to mission-based, government-funded boarding schools where they were instructed in the ways of civilized living. Students were forced to abandon their traditional cultures, and at times were subjected to physical, emotional, and sexual abuse.[72] These schools persisted as an approved government policy until after the passing of the Indian Child Welfare Act of 1978, which finally gave Native American parents the option of not having their children attend the government schools.[73] Three of these boarding schools in

Michigan continued late into the twentieth century, the last of which was not closed until 1983.[74]

The many efforts to assimilate Indigenous people into a European American way of life failed to produce the results the settler colonists hoped for. Indians were committed to their ways of life and resisted the assimilation efforts. In *History of the City of Grand Rapids*, Albert Baxter expressed surprise at this hesitancy to assimilate:

> It is a source of wonder . . . that the Indians, by contact with a superior civilization and the continued efforts of teachers and missionaries, did not renounce their savage ways and habits and learn to live like their white neighbors.[75]

These two focused approaches of removal and assimilation were also reflected in the way colonists interacted with the land. Combined with a Doctrine of Discovery–infused assumption that whites have the right to dominate Indigenous people came a religiously bolstered justification to exert dominion over the land by imposing European land practices. This approach involved removing trees from the land and, once cleared, forcing the ecology of the land into European-style farming systems. Homesteads with farms replaced the flourishing biodiverse forests that had been present. Asserting control over the people and the land were foundationally conjoined. To promote reconciliation ecology, we need to acknowledge and lament this history and then work to create healthy, respectful relationships with both the people who have been wronged and the land that has been harmed.

Truth-Telling about the Past

An important part of telling the truth about West Michigan history is to rewrite the narrative of hostile, ignorant Indians and upright, intelligent pioneers. Even though the historical records were written by whites, they report time and again the friendly and helpful initial interactions with Indigenous people in West Michigan.[76] In the 1881 *History of Kent County* the Ottawa were described as "a noble people, rich in natural wealth, free from impurity, honorable and sincere. . . . Their services cannot be overestimated."[77] Violent encounters between Indians and whites occasionally occurred, but among the Michigan Anishinaabeg, most of these hostilities were fallout from coerced treaties, unfulfilled promises, dishonest dealings, and racist disrespect. Another part of truth telling is to acknowledge that a people whose way of life respectfully fit into the land were replaced by a people who took whatever they wanted from the land. Vestiges of that settler colonist mindset are still with us today. The current condition of Plaster Creek is but one example of the careless way we continue to live in the land. What is needed is a humble acknowledgement that Indigenous ways of life hold important teachings that can guide us to live more sustainably on the earth.

CHAPTER 4

European Settlement in West Michigan and the Impact on Plaster Creek

In June 2009 Plaster Creek Stewards (PCS) held its first workshop for residents interested in learning about the watershed, and we were joined by then mayor George Heartwell who offered his congratulations and encouragement for what we were beginning. Mayor Heartwell had recently traveled to New Zealand and learned how the government structure there had reorganized itself from eight hundred governing units to only eighty, and these eighty governing units were organized according to watersheds. Such a novel idea to American ears! Mayor Heartwell talked about the Grand River as one of the major assets for Grand Rapids and about how stormwater runoff posed threats to the health of our local water. Heartwell also described how the problem of combined sewage overflow in the Grand River had been a challenge for more than fifty years and that this long-standing problem was corrected with a massive sewer separation project. Heartwell emphasized a triple bottom line approach—that Grand Rapids needs to move forward in ways that promote the economic, social, and environmental sustainability of our region. While Heartwell's insight and leadership enabled Grand Rapids to make great strides in addressing environmental and equity concerns in the city, there is still a long way to go because the history of Grand Rapids creeks and rivers has not always been positive. Having the mayor of our city provide his blessing as we were starting to do this work was inspiring.

Mayor Heartwell retired in 2015 and was replaced by Mayor Rosalynn Bliss, who has been similarly affirming of PCS. Historically, not all the leaders of Grand Rapids have had the vision to care for local waterways as we will see in the coming pages.

Contemporary Grand Rapids covers an area of more than forty-four square miles and is the second largest city in Michigan. Current population hovers around two hundred thousand. Population growth in West Michigan began in earnest in the 1800s as European colonists settled in the area. First appearing on the 1800 federal census as Michigan Territory, Michigan became the twenty-sixth state admitted to the union in 1837.[1] By 1870 Grand Rapids had a population of more than 16,000, doubling to 32,000 in 1880. Population growth continued, and by 1900 there were 87,000 people living in Grand Rapids. By the time of the Great Depression the population had grown to more than 168,000. Growth has been steady and consistent except during decades when there was economic disruption. In 2021 Grand Rapids was ranked 125th for size among cities in the United States.[2]

In the early days of European settlement, gypsum mining produced great wealth for the region, but after several decades furniture making emerged as the major industry. Grand Rapids was positioned close to where forest clear-cutting was happening, and the felled timber could be floated down the Grand River to Grand Rapids where many furniture companies set up business. Since the late 1800s the furniture industry has remained a mainstay of the Grand Rapids economy. Today the metropolitan area is home to five of the world's leading office furniture companies. Other industries in West Michigan include automotive parts, industrial machinery, printing, graphic arts, plastics and chemicals, and grocery wholesalers. International businesses play an increasingly important role, with more than fifty foreign-owned firms in the metropolitan area. Tourism is an emerging industry as West Michigan increasingly becomes a popular vacation and convention destination.[3] Agriculture is also a significant part of the West Michigan economy. Statewide, Michigan produces more than three hundred agricultural products, ranking second only to California in diversity.[4] West Michigan is known for the variety of fruits grown in the region, particularly apples, cherries, and blueberries. Having abundant fresh water contributes to agricultural productivity and demonstrates why it is imperative that we take care of local rivers and creeks.

If We Don't Confront History, We're Bound to Repeat It

Learning the history of how the land and water were tended and protected for centuries by the Indigenous peoples living in West Michigan, we are confronted with the reality that it is only within the last two centuries that we see dramatic degradation taking place. In other words, Plaster Creek was a healthy, thriving, life-supporting landscape feature for over 99 percent of the time since it emerged from receding glaciers, and a contaminated life-threatening stream for less than 1 percent of its life span.

As European arrivals settled in West Michigan, their changing perspectives on water impacted the development of the city of Grand Rapids and its supporting watersheds as urban drainage systems were planned, designed, built, and retrofitted in ways that reflected the prevailing view of water. We explore unique perspectives on the history of water in Grand Rapids by listening to stories collected as part of the Plaster Creek Oral History Project (PCOHP). Hearing the stories of current and past residents, as well as current and past employees of the city and county whose work has focused on water issues, offers important insights into how the condition of Plaster Creek has deteriorated during the lifetime of the interviewees, particularly in the last one hundred years. Hearing these voices offers distinctive vantage points in understanding the history of the Plaster Creek watershed.

Most of our conversation partners in the PCOHP are of European American descent. Some of the interviewees are Black, Indigenous, People of Color (BIPOC). Despite a focused effort to interview Indigenous people with lived experience in the Plaster Creek watershed, it was difficult to find residents who have Indigenous roots and particular knowledge or experience living in this watershed. One local member of the Grand River Bands of Ottawa Indians described how few Indigenous people living in this region can trace their lineage to pre-European arrival. When asked if his family has always lived in this area, he replied:

> My mother is full-blooded Grand River. . . . I can track myself to Grand Rapids before any non-Natives were here. So, right now in Grand Rapids there are probably about three thousand natives, but there is probably three hundred of us that are actually *from* here. . . . The other people, I always call them DIs, Displaced

> Indians. You know, they are not really from here. But because Grand Rapids was a draw for—oh, education and work and employment and stuff, it drew a lot of people here. But there is still only about three hundred of us that can track before any non-Natives were here.[5]

This interviewee talked about how Indigenous people perceive the importance of water (water is life), but because he did not grow up in the Plaster Creek watershed, he has had limited experience interacting with Plaster Creek itself. Unfortunately, this constrains what we can learn about Plaster Creek from Indigenous perspectives in West Michigan—and this is all too common and regretful for many European Americans who have little opportunity to interact with and learn from Indigenous people.

Some of the oral history stories we heard reveal how Plaster Creek was a source of delight and enjoyment. Other stories reveal how Plaster Creek was neglected or abused. Industries used it as a dumping ground to get rid of unwanted substances. Farmers used Plaster Creek to drain excess water off their land or alternatively to pump water out to irrigate their crops. Listening to the memories shared by our oral history conversation partners reveals how much the issue of water quantity intersects with the issue of water quality. One example of this connection between water quantity and quality is exemplified in a conversation where the interviewee described his first job at age fifteen in the 1960s working at a farm along Plaster Creek.

> I remember that part of Plaster Creek where I'd work on the farm was used for irrigation and for draining excess water. The farmer took his excess water and let that drain into there. I know he also had a big sprinkler system that he'd set up. . . . And he did have a pump. . . . I think those pipes were probably three to four inches in diameter and I seem to recall (remember this was a long time ago—more than fifty years ago) that he'd pump water out. I recall one time working on something and you'd have these twelve-foot sections of water hose line that you'd clamp together. . . . One of the times it was not properly clamped, and he turned on the water. Of course, it came apart and this huge amount of water came spurting out, just destroying everything, eroding everything near it. I remember him saying, "Quick! Hit the water shut off." And one of us ran to shut off the water. So, that was a whole pumping system. Now that I think about this, we were pumping a polluted creek and you are throwing this onto squash plants and corn plants and everything

> else. Who knows if we were eating heavy metals or other pollutants? I am not too worried about sewage per se, because, you know, it is good fertilizer. But if factories and stuff were putting in, let's say, heavy metals, that's no good. So, who knows? I'm still alive and I ate some of that squash, and beans, and corn.[6]

This story demonstrates how some farmers utilized excess Plaster Creek water to benefit their farms. Yet as the memories came back to our conversation partner, he realized that water quality was not really being considered when the farmer irrigated the farm with water from Plaster Creek. These issues of water quantity and quality were expressed repeatedly in multiple ways by different participants in the PCOHP. Some participants highlighted how water was used and managed by European Americans during the building of Grand Rapids. Others described corrective actions that were taken after degradation had begun. Unfortunately, there is no evidence that European Americans tried to learn from Native Americans how to care for water during the days of European settlement.

Building the City of Grand Rapids by Draining the Landscape

European settlers in West Michigan and their descendants have constantly wrestled with issues of water quantity, and attempts to control water volume led, sometimes inadvertently, to decreased water quality. The dominant European American assumption was that to settle in this place first the trees and then the excess water had to be removed, after which land could be converted into farms, factories, streets, roads, houses, and industrial developments. Once built, roadways couldn't be covered by water because it would impede the movement of goods and people. It is important to note that forest clearing actually contributed to the problem of excess water because, once removed, trees could no longer soak up water when it rained.

One of our conversation partners had a deep sense of Michigan history and geography from within a European American perspective but seemed unaware that his insights, while spoken with a certain sense of neutrality, also revealed a subtle unconscious assumption of European superiority.

> Michigan has some of the wettest ground in terms of soil composition, in terms of topography, in terms of soil types, in terms of the rainfall. Michigan

> was, depending on whose numbers you look at, somewhere between 60 and 70 percent wetland back in presettlement times. . . . The biggest impediment to settling Michigan was not the Indians, was not the French or anything else, it was malaria. The mosquito population in Michigan was so intense, and it was a vector for disease. . . . Michigan was so wet that in order for it to be habitable that water had to be controlled. . . . So as Michigan became developed, [they built] drainage channels and pipes to draw the water table down so that you could use it for farmland, you could use it for . . . building cities and so on.[7]

Note that while this conversation partner is focusing on excess water, he also subtly reveals a common perspective among European Americans—that Native Americans were often seen as an impediment to so-called development. An alternative perspective could have led the new arrivals to learn from Indigenous people how to live in harmony with a land that was so wet with rivers, creeks, lakes, and ponds. How did Indian travel routes and village locations avoid problems of water quantity while preserving water quality? European settlers had a short-sighted utilitarian view of water and did not carefully think through long-term consequences of their actions. In other words, cities and towns in West Michigan (and across the United States) were built without giving adequate thought to safeguarding water. The assumption that to develop the land something had to be done with excess water led to specific actions that then created new problems. Plaster Creek is one of the receiving waterways for the county drains that exist to usher water off the land for the benefit of human activities. Many of these "drains" are straightened, channelized tributaries or sections of streams. It is striking that even calling a stream a drain is such a diminishing act—its myriad benefits are reduced down to one. We now recognize that the dominant nineteenth-century European American way of thinking about water was damaging to local streams, creeks, and rivers. As we will see, perspectives on how to manage water have continually shifted throughout the past 150 years as problems keep arising. We cannot completely undo what has happened in the past, but behaviors can change as we learn better ways to care for water. For example, we now know that wetlands are important for absorbing and cleaning water, and can help to address climate change, so draining wetlands is generally not a good option.[8] We need to develop eyes to see the root(s) of the problems that led to contaminated waterways so that solutions we develop are helpful and lasting.

About the time Michigan became a state in 1837, the office of county drain commissioner was established as a way to address excess surface water. Still in existence today, a drain commissioner is an elected official in county government who maintains the network of channels and ditches, pumps and dikes that keep water levels under control in both upstream and downstream regions. A former staff member of the County Drain Commission described it like this:

> Water is extremely powerful. If you get enough of it flowing in one direction, it can do a tremendous amount of damage. We have basically the obligation of protecting public health, public safety, passable roads, public welfare, and maintenance of an economy. And it relies on this network of pipes and ditches and drains to carry the water away.[9]

In order to fund the system of drains and pipes that made the landscape usable for farming, residential development, and industry, the county drain commissioner was given authority to tax local residents. A staff member of the Lower Grand River Organization of Watersheds described the value of a drain commissioner in this way:

> Michigan is one of [only a few] states that have drain commissioners . . . and they had to figure out how to fund all of this work of managing the streams and working in the streams, so they were able to create a drainage district (which is basically a watershed). . . . They can assess those people. So, it's basically they can tax the people for the work because the people receive the benefit of this drainage system.[10]

This quote further illustrates the presumption that water is a problem that needs to be controlled, and draining wetlands was seen as generating benefits for development. While these notions have *some* merit, short-sighted thinking created new sets of problems, many of which are still with us today. Plaster Creek is a victim of a malady known as "urban stream syndrome," the consistently observed ecological degradation of streams draining urban landscapes.[11]

One conversation partner grew up observing and playing in a suburban, midstream section of Plaster Creek in the 1970s and 1980s, and he describes significant differences between the creek of his childhood and the creek he sees now. His experience illuminates how both water quantity and water quality are elements of the urban stream syndrome.

> I remember very big fluctuations in the depth of the water. . . . One of the biggest impact things that I saw over my years watching the creek is how the creek banks have changed. . . . I didn't realize it necessarily when I was growing up, but when you grow older and learn how things work and you come back and see what it was you were witnessing as a child. . . . And I now realize what I didn't know then is that it's all the runoff from the urban environment where there is all this pavement. . . . Where it would have been a much slower process and there wouldn't have been as much water coming into the creek at any one time with a particular storm, now tons more water is coming in. Now it's turning into a turbulent mess and washing the dirt away from the banks and the trees are falling in.[12]

Building the City of Grand Rapids by Channelizing and Burying Waterways

As the landscape changed from forested land to farms or cities, waterways were often straightened or channelized, and floodplains were developed such that they could no longer provide their overflow services. Channelized streams carry more energy and transport more water, increasing erosion and flooding downstream. Stream channelization is an example of how decisions made in the past have created new problems. A Grand Rapids city stormwater engineer described it this way: "Basically, for years and years, you built a pipe, you put it to the river; the river, the creek or whatever it is, takes it away. Out of sight, out of mind. So, that's what you did with stormwater, you put in a pipe. . . . People just didn't know any better."[13]

As urban development progressed, concerns about excess stormwater and increasing pollution in public drinking water led to burying thousands of miles of creeks and rivers in underground pipes.[14] As some authors have described, this made possible "cost-effective flood protection services through the efficient conveyance of stormwater to a benign waterway environment to facilitate the rapid urban expansion of cities."[15] Burying creeks and streams underground also provided space for development of the city. Businesses and residential neighborhoods could be safely built on top of the sunken and largely forgotten waterways.

Silver Creek is the second largest tributary to Plaster Creek, and it was buried underground in the 1930s, as part of the American New Deal program, which

FIGURE 8. The Silver Creek tributary disappearing into a concrete storm sewer in an urban neighborhood.

PHOTOGRAPH BY DAVID P. WARNERS.

employed millions of mostly unskilled men to carry out public works projects. One conversation partner remembers as a child watching men do this work:

> Silver Creek was turned into a covered conduit by the Works Progress Administration in 1934–35–36 . . . that Franklin Roosevelt developed. And we had a lot of fun watching those guys toting wheelbarrows. No bulldozers, everything was shovel and wheelbarrow. And then they built this concrete square container for the creek. . . . Then after they built it, we got flashlights and walked in it.[16]

Another conversation partner also recalled vividly when Silver Creek was buried underground so the city of Grand Rapids could be expanded. Today Silver Creek runs for four miles underground until it merges aboveground again with the main channel of Plaster Creek.

> In the 1930s they put Silver Creek underground. It starts underground right by the Episcopal Church at Hall and Plymouth, right in their backyard. You can look in there and see the creek . . . and it gets wider and wider as it runs down to that valley and comes out at Standard Lumber. But now it's all underground. I was down there a lot when they were building it. They had a lot of—well not bulldozers, but diggers and they dug the big trench and later put in foundations and built the walls. And it's a covered area, the whole thing is cement. . . . High enough you can walk it. Well, I was smaller, then! . . . I tried it. We went down to about Calvin Avenue. And then it got too scary . . . We had a lot of fun in that creek. We'd dam it up, get shovels and throw stuff in there and make it as big as we could. . . . The whole area changed when they developed it. You know they took away the big hills and kind of flattened them out. Water's always attractive, particularly to kids. They love to horse around near water. And so, we had a good time going into Silver Creek.[17]

Creating Sewer Systems to Manage Stormwater and Human Waste

As Grand Rapids grew, managing water became increasingly challenging. Sewers were needed to capture and control stormwater, and sewers were also needed to carry wastes away from buildings and human habitation. Public perspectives of water included both seeing water as a problem that needed to be controlled, as well as recognizing water as a means for removing sewage away from human settlements. The first sewers were built in Grand Rapids in the 1850s when the city charter was adopted and acknowledged by the State of Michigan.

> In the early days, sewers were no more than pipe boxes, that is, long boxes made of wood planks connected to drainpipes. Many of the area hotels laid their own pipes to direct sewage to exterior ditch drains. These sewers were sometimes made of wood, but a survey that was conducted in 1904 found sewers also made of brick, vitrified pipe, cement pipe, wrought iron pipe, cast iron pipe, and concrete-brick.[18]

By the 1860s cities across the United States began to construct sewage systems, and they always combined sanitary water and stormwater into a single, combined sewer system. At times of significant rainfall, sewage flowed directly into the nearest creek, stream, or river. Proponents of combined sewers argued it was more cost effective to dispose of sewage into local waterways and let stormwater runoff carry it away, eventually into receiving lakes or other water bodies.[19] The dominant belief at the time was that running water purifies itself. So there was an assumption that removing human waste, industrial effluents, and stormwater in one combined sewer system was both efficient and environmentally neutral.

The assumption that sending human sewage to surface waters was benign continued for decades with little thought given to what would happen downstream as the waste accumulated. This type of degradation increased to a point where citizens began to raise their voices in protest. In Cincinnati, Ohio, for example, a naturalist wrote a report in 1902 describing Mill Creek, one of their main urban waterways flowing to the Ohio River: "In 1878, the 'Mill Creek was clean, with sandy banks and pebbly bottom. Now it has become a vile open sewer, the sand is saturated with sewage, which decays and gives off deadly gases, destroying all fish and insect life.'"[20] Natural waterways in Grand Rapids were also used as waste-transport conduits.

> All the brooks and creeks in and around Grand Rapids ran to the Grand (river). The little streams, most of which became underground drains with the growth of the city, flowed out of or through the neighboring townships. . . . The streams came to be contaminated on their way to the river, and the question arose as to which governmental unit was to blame for the pollution which inevitably had to reach the river.[21]

In the 1890s, Plaster Creek (as well as Coldbrook Creek) was used as one of these urban conduits to carry sewage to the Grand River.[22] Note the stark contrast between European American and Native perspectives. European American settlers used water to transport raw human sewage compared to the Ottawa who believed that "water is life" and lived in ways that protected surface waters.

About the time combined sewers were gaining widespread acceptance in West Michigan new scientific evidence challenged their safety. Research began to show that some communicable diseases were waterborne, and discharging sewage into streams raised public health risks for downstream communities. Water quality became an increasingly important issue throughout the United States in the early twentieth century, coinciding with a growing concern about bacteria in water. As awareness of waterborne illnesses increased, wastewater treatment facilities became a partial solution to contaminated water. In 1931 Grand Rapids introduced its first wastewater treatment facility, located where Plaster Creek enters the Grand River on Market Street, about one mile downstream from the center of the city of Grand Rapids.

The national debate over wastewater treatment at this time centered on whether it was more economical to treat wastewater prior to discharge into rivers and streams or to treat the receiving surface water before it is distributed as drinking water. The commonly accepted view was that "it is often more equitable to all concerned for an upper riparian city to discharge its sewage into a stream and a lower riparian city to filter the water of the same stream for a domestic supply, than for the former city to be forced to put in wastewater treatment works."[23] This premise justifies an upstream city passing along the costs of cleaning water that it contaminated to its downstream neighbors. This mentality, no doubt, contributed to the public's lack of attention to water or awareness of what happens to water when it leaves their vicinity.

Placing creeks underground in storm sewers appeared to solve a wide range of problems believed to be caused by natural water in urban environments.[24] Stormwater seemed to magically disappear, and because people didn't see what happened to water after it moved into a storm drain, they were blinded to the problems this practice caused in local waterways. For many years human waste was added to stormwater runoff because the economic savings were considered more important than the costs to environmental health. "Since large cities already had combined [sewer] systems, and the costs of replacement were extremely high, cities continued well into the twentieth century to build combined sewers and to discharge their untreated waters into adjacent waterways."[25] Grand Rapids eventually stopped building combined sewers and, in fact, began a major sewer separation project in the late 1990s.

One interesting historical tidbit is that in the 1930s the City of Grand Rapids operated a piggery within one hundred yards of where Plaster Creek joins the Grand River on the campus of the sewage treatment plant. At the time raising live-stock so close to a sewage treatment plant and a creek was considered acceptable. By the 1950s the piggery was abandoned when new laws made it cost-prohibitive. In the 1970 "Annual Report for the Grand Rapids Wastewater Treatment Plant," then superintendent Otto Green provided this history:

> In the 1930s the garbage disposal problem in the City of Grand Rapids was becoming quite acute due to population growth and the type of disposal used at that time. . . . The operation became too costly and the value too great, so an alternate method had to be chosen; hence, the Piggery came into being. The most logical site for this operation was the Sewage Treatment Plant grounds because of the wastes that would have to be treated. . . . Every morning at 7:00 AM 60 tons of garbage was trucked in for feeding some 1,000 hogs. . . . During a year's time, approximately 3,000 hogs were cycled through the process. . . . The operation continued into the 1950s. At that time, the State handed down an edict that all garbage being consumed by animals in this manner must be brought to a boiling point. It was decided at that time by both parties concerned that this was not practical; so, the plan and the building were abandoned. . . . It was just as well because of the many years of ineffective treatment of the wastes.[26]

Today we would recognize a piggery close to a water source and a water treatment plant as a risk to public health—another example of shifting perspectives affecting what we consider appropriate and tolerable.

Twentieth-Century Industrialization and Its Impact on Plaster Creek

While using Plaster Creek to remove sewage had an early negative impact on the creek, during the twentieth century new industries degraded water quality even further. In European and American cities prior to the mid-1800s, small neighborhoods typically managed water with a localized supply and treatment approach that included collecting rainwater in cisterns and designing useful channels in narrow roads and alleys. However, when the industrial revolution came in full force, it was no longer possible to manage city water flow using preindustrial methods. Much greater quantities of water were needed for industrialization, and as urban development took place, the issue of water *quantity* intersected more and more with water *quality*.

In Grand Rapids, as in many cities throughout the United States, the drive for industrial development that began in the late 1800s and early 1900s led to the degradation of its many creeks and streams as well as the Grand River. People viewed local streams and rivers in a utilitarian way—how can this stream be used as a means to increase economic profit and advance industrialization? One of our conversation partners described the impact this way:

> As the city grew in the 1850s, 1860s, 1870s, industrial development happened here, and they basically channelized [Plaster Creek] because they wanted to control where it would go. They didn't want it flowing outside of its banks. It was both flood control and space saving. The other thing is that back in those days they were pretty naïve about what the environmental consequences were of taking something like that and channelizing it. I mean, space was valuable. They wanted as much space for a factory or a development as they could, so they basically straightened it, filled in the meanders and the wetlands.[27]

As city developers were directing excess water into pipes and drains, new problems emerged. First, the *natural hydrology was lost* as impervious surfaces increased and more stormwater was directed to creeks through engineered drainage systems. By the mid-twentieth century more impermeable surfaces were being built—rooftops, streets, sidewalks, factories, parking lots, highways—which prevented stormwater from soaking into the ground. Between the time of the Great Depression in the 1930s and the year 2000, five state or national highways were constructed that cut through the Plaster Creek watershed, along with countless other roads. Stormwater runoff became an increasingly serious challenge as streams like Plaster Creek were receiving much greater volumes of water than they ever would have received under presettlement conditions. Second, the large volume of stormwater collected from city streets and emptying into storm drains *picked up contaminants*, including road grit, pet waste, lawn clippings, and automobile effluents. As one conversation partner rightfully identified, "whether it's oil from cars or fertilizer from lawns or salt from roads, it all enters into this drain and ends up going into Plaster Creek."[28] During these years water quality in Plaster Creek declined significantly.

The common assumption that moving water purifies itself led people to be careless for many decades in their use and treatment of water. Industries dumped unwanted substances into local creeks, lakes, and rivers, assuming that these substances would just float away and disappear. Several conversation partners in the Plaster Creek Oral History Project described memories of their childhood from the 1930s, 1940s, and 1950s when they saw toxic substances being discarded into Plaster Creek. This first memory was shared by a man in his late eighties, and these memories are quite vivid.

> Sad to say, there were factories that were in operation when we were kids, like Kelvinator and the finishing company there, and the gas station had a garage underneath and . . . I mean, everything went out a pipe down into the crick. And there were different times when we could tell what color the paint company was making because that's what the color of the crick was. . . . And Kelvinator, in those days, they made what would be [called] iceboxes. . . . The inside was metal and it was shaped something like the plastic sleds today, only probably a little bigger. And the ones that were damaged or they couldn't use . . . ended up in the crick also. The crick was quite a dumping ground, unfortunately.[29]

Another male conversation partner in his late fifties also described what his neighborhood smelled like when he was a child.

> So my first memories were—it was a pretty swampy area in the corner there, behind the Kelvinator plant. . . . So we would go down there quite a bit. . . . The real memory was that you could *smell* the lacquer, paint, and you could see a lot of rainbow colors. That is my most *visual* memory.[30]

We also heard from female conversation partners who described extensive dumping into Plaster Creek. This interviewee who grew up in the 1950s near Plaster Creek describes the careless attitude the public seemed to have toward Plaster Creek then and she claims still exists.

> When I was a kid, dumping wasn't against the law like it is now. Because people didn't know as much about it then as they do now . . . people figured [whatever was dumped] would just go in the creek and go away. . . . I think there was a lot of stuff that got dumped in there. And people viewed nature differently then. I think it was [viewed as] something there that was to be *used* and *not to be taken care of*. Or maybe people didn't realize they could do permanent damage. . . . To me, it seems as though Grand Rapids has just kind of given up on Plaster Creek. It's kind of an urban wasteway. It's pretty heavily polluted. I don't think we pay attention to it . . . and it would take a lot of work to get it back.[31]

Some of our interviewees didn't just point fingers at other polluters but remembered and acknowledged their own complicity. One of our eighty-year-old conversation partners remembers his own negligence as a boy.

> Well, in those days people didn't think too much about pollution, it wasn't really a factor. I don't know what people thought when they dumped sewage here—the Grand River went to Lake Michigan. I don't know what people thought—maybe they thought it would magically disappear! But people had no qualms whatsoever about throwing things in the crick or in the river. It didn't bother anybody. I say "they," but me also. I never gave a thought to that.[32]

As we've seen, it wasn't only actions and decisions made by industry, business, and government that led to the degradation of Plaster Creek. Many ordinary citizens were also contributing to the problem.

The expansion of residential neighborhoods in Grand Rapids that began in the late 1880s and has continued to the present time has also impacted water quality.[33] At first, little thought was given to how residential areas might affect water quality. What mattered was creating enough space for the homes that were needed for people who worked in the factories and industries. As the residential communities expanded in both the urban and suburban sections of the Plaster Creek watershed, planners overlooked how this newly emerging land use would impact local waterways.

Some of the damage was caused by ignorance or unconscious assumptions that led to destructive behavior. For example, people are attracted to water, and some residents in Grand Rapids purposefully purchased their homes to be near water, including Plaster Creek. One of our conversation partners described how it is very common for people to buy a house because of its location on a stream, and then homeowners decide they want to be able to see the stream, so they remove trees and add a lawn.

> So they mow right up to the stream, maybe they even build a deck over the stream, not realizing that, you know, that activity in the riparian area can cause that stream bank to become unstable. And so, you know, it's not intentional, they enjoy it, they're wanting to enjoy it, but they are impacting it.[34]

When the deep roots of streamside vegetation are removed, streambanks become vulnerable, and parts of the land break off into the stream. As urbanization has

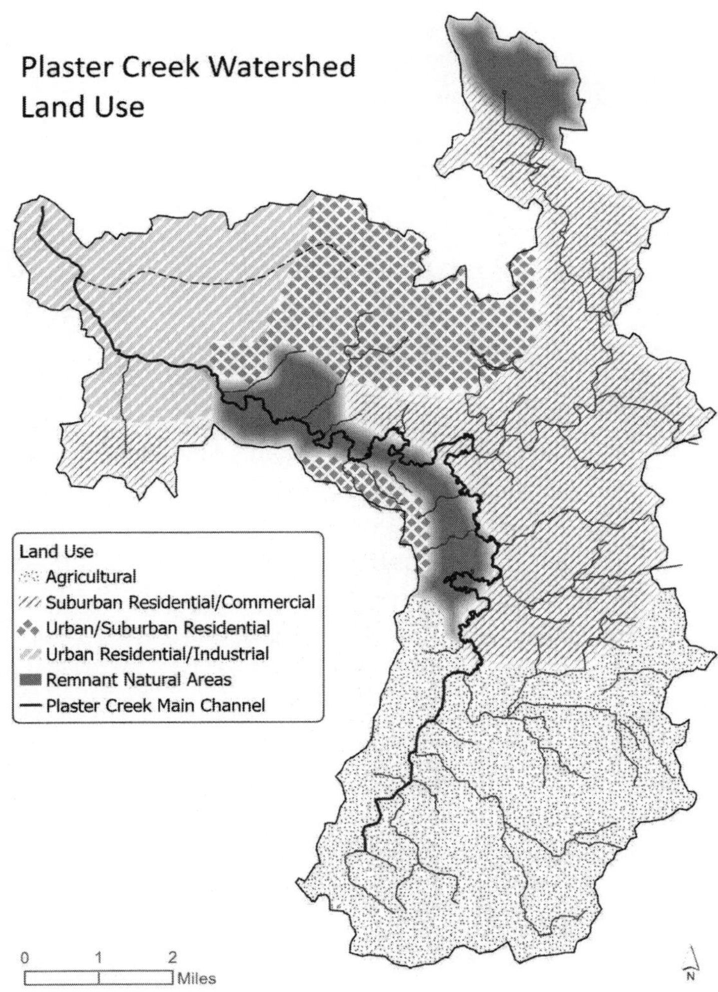

MAP 2. Major land uses in the Plaster Creek watershed.

CREATED BY NELLIE ANDERSON-WRIGHT.

increased in the Plaster Creek watershed, the combination of more runoff and less vegetation has made the streambanks more susceptible to erosion, which increases sediment in the creek, harming fish and aquatic organisms.

Taking Corrective Action to Improve Water Quality through Ongoing Monitoring

The story of Plaster Creek is not simply one of continual destruction over the past 150 years. As problems have been recognized, solutions have been attempted, sometimes leading to improvements, sometimes not. It is noteworthy to observe the change of perspectives in recent decades. Today there is a growing movement to intercept stormwater where it falls, allow it to soak into the ground, find more natural ways to stabilize streams, and provide flood control—all with the hope of improving water quality.

As we have seen, water quality had degraded throughout the United States by the early twentieth century. The federal government created a structure for regulating discharges of pollutants into the waters of the United States in 1948 under the Federal Water Pollution Control Act. Yet water quality remained an issue of serious concern and took on national significance when the Cuyahoga River in Cleveland dramatically caught fire in 1969.[35] The U.S. Environmental Protection Agency (EPA) was established in 1970, and water quality became a focus as a result of a global social and environmental movement in the 1960s and 1970s. Growing public awareness of water pollution led to the passage of the Clean Water Act in 1972 that significantly reorganized and expanded earlier efforts.[36] Under the Clean Water Act, the EPA established and implemented pollution-control programs such as setting wastewater standards for industry as well as national water-quality recommendations for pollutants in surface waters. The Clean Water Act made distinctions between point source pollution and nonpoint source pollution. Point source pollution is any substance that is directly deposited in water that could damage a person, animal, or ecosystem. Factories and sewage treatment plants are two common contributors to point source pollution.[37] As we have seen, Plaster Creek has been the recipient of much point source pollution during the last one hundred years.

Nonpoint source pollution is harder to measure and control. It happens when rainfall or snowmelt flows over the landscape, picking up pollutants and moving them into wetlands, lakes, rivers, and groundwater. Nonpoint source pollution includes excess fertilizers, insecticides, and herbicides from farms and residential areas; oil and toxic chemicals from runoff and energy production; sediment caused by erosion; salt from irrigation practices and roads; bacterial contamination from livestock, pets, and faulty septic systems, among others. Today many states report that nonpoint source pollution is the leading cause of water-quality problems. In the Plaster Creek watershed nonpoint source pollution contributes harmful effects to fisheries, aquatic insects, and wildlife.[38]

To improve water quality, the effects of both point source and nonpoint source pollution need to be monitored and addressed. Grand Rapids began annual water-quality monitoring of the Grand River and its tributaries in the 1960s, and Plaster Creek has been closely monitored since the late 1980s and has consistently been below the threshold indicating good water quality.

Improving Water Quality through Combined Sewer Separation

Since the 1972 passage of the Clean Water Act, water quality in the United States has generally improved. One mechanism for improving water quality has been the separation of sanitary and storm sewers. In West Michigan the wastewater collection system covers a geographical area of approximately 125 square miles. Grand Rapids struggled with combined sewer overflows for at least five decades, resulting in environmental consequences, as well as financial and social impacts. During the 1960s, there were fifty-nine points in the city of Grand Rapids where raw or partially treated sewage could flow into the Grand River during significant rain events. In 1969, Grand Rapids dumped an estimated 12.6 billion gallons of raw sewage directly into the Grand River.[39] Eventually there was enough public outcry and political will to catalyze state and local leadership to implement a sewer separation project. One of our conversation partners who is a retired waste management professional described the relationship between water quality and wastewater treatment and how perspectives on managing human waste keep changing.

> I live here, in this community, and I say that you wouldn't want to live here if it wasn't for our wastewater treatment plant. . . . [If you go] back to the 1920s, this plant started because there was no wastewater treatment. Waste was just dumped

> in the river, and it went downstream and the people living in Grandville were at that point upset. There's a bend in the river and they were taking the brunt of that waste. So, that led to the construction of this treatment plant in the mid-1930s . . . [Water is] reclaimed, restored for use again. We use water to clean things up, and everything that gets cleaned up comes here. Then we separate the water from what we are actually trying to throw away or dispose of, and the water gets recycled back into the environment. What we remove are what we now call "bio-solids" and there is a national/international effort to find better ways to reclaim value from that also. . . . So that is the future of wastewater treatment, finding more ways to reclaim value from things that have been disposed of.[40]

The Sewer Improvement Project in Grand Rapids that launched in the 1990s to successfully separate sanitary sewers from stormwater sewers cost $400 million. Today there are no combined sewer overflows and there is no untreated sewage entering the Grand River. Grand Rapids' state-of-the-art wastewater treatment system processes forty million gallons of wastewater every day. This combined sewer separation project has helped to improve Plaster Creek, particularly at its confluence with Silver Creek.

> The whole issue of separation of sewage from storm water has basically been solved at least in the Grand Rapids area. . . . And that was one of the problems with Silver Creek—there was a cross contamination that was still going on between the [sanitary] sewer system and the stormwater system. . . . I think that the city is probably ahead of most in the country in terms of the speed with which we've addressed it.[41]

However, some residents in Grand Rapids still do not understand there are separate sewers for sanitary waste and for stormwater, and that anything placed into a storm drain (e.g., pet waste or used motor oil) will flow directly into a local creek and eventually into the Grand River with the next rain event. One of our conversation partners described the public's reaction when she explained this.

> People don't even know that stormwater doesn't go to the treatment plant. . . . People would sit there and go, "Really? Really, this doesn't get treated? This just goes straight . . . ?" And part of that's because we've done a poor job of advertising how well Grand Rapids has done separating the sewers. So people knew that when

> it rains, the plant dumped everything, you know. The sewage [went] into the river, which is not true anymore. . . . But because of that misconception, that it *used* to be treated that way, "Well, the city put it in, it must get treated." People just don't pay attention. So education is crucial.[42]

One conversation partner who worked for twenty-five years addressing pollution in Plaster Creek and other tributaries of the Grand River suggests that Plaster Creek is healthier now than it was fifty years ago, but it depends on how you look at it.

> If you go back to the 1970s, you were dealing with really nasty chemicals getting into the creek. . . . I truly believe Plaster Creek is better. If you look at it from a resource that people can enjoy, and it builds them emotionally and they feel ties to the land, then I don't think it's better.[43]

While Plaster Creek is no longer receiving as much point source contamination as in years past, it still is being degraded by nonpoint pollution through stormwater runoff, which increases dramatically after a major rain event and remains a serious threat to public health. Yet another significant challenge for Plaster Creek is lack of public understanding. One of our conversation partners who used to work for the Drain Commission spoke eloquently about the water-quality challenges he tried to address.

> Nonpoint source pollution is harder to fix than the pollution we have fixed in the last fifty years. . . . We fixed the pipes coming out of factories and the overflows from the city. Those things are much easier to fix because it's basically an engineering solution. . . . But nonpoint source pollution comes from 2 million people living in a watershed and it's really, really hard to change the behavior of every person. . . . I guess the biggest impairment is human ignorance or inertia. . . . So the biggest challenge we have, and biggest impairment, is public education and inertia.[44]

Another conversation partner who also advocated for more public education about stormwater suggested that people need to know what happens to stormwater on their own property.

> Just knowing—even in your own little space, where does the water go . . . anything that people do on their property, in the rain, it ends up somewhere. In the streets,

> you can see those catch basins. . . . It goes down that drain, and it goes through the pipe, and empties into a stream or the river. So there's no treatment. And just having people become aware of that, you know. Once they understand where their water goes, then they'll start looking around and understanding the system more.[45]

To promote reconciliation ecology, we begin by increasing public understanding, to recognize and acknowledge what has happened, and then provide concrete options for changing behaviors. This enhanced awareness is critically important if there is any hope for restoring our degraded watershed. The dramatic changes to Plaster Creek over the last several centuries that began when settler colonists arrived are primarily the result of not carefully counting the full cost of urban development on local waterways.

Protecting Urban Waterways through Regulatory Action

Eighty years ago, the prevailing assumption in urban planning was that water needed to be moved away from human structures as fast as possible. Today we know that vision was short-sighted. It is now recognized that widening, deepening, or channelizing streams may be the quickest and easiest way to drain stormwater off the land, but these actions severely damage aquatic ecosystems. Over the past fifty to sixty years there have been continuing shifts in thinking about managing stormwater with new tools for controlling water quantity. One of our conversation partners described the change in perspective this way:

> By the 1970s and 80s . . . we'd learned a lot more about leaving things in natural floodplains. It used to be when they dug a ditch, they dug it straight and they dug it deep because they wanted to get the water out of there. Now we understand the benefits of having the wetlands and the meanders to help to manage it. . . . I think today we realize that simply digging it straight and deep doesn't really solve the problem; it moves the problem downstream.[46]

Today developers who propose new projects in the city of Grand Rapids have to meet the federal and state requirements demonstrating how they will capture stormwater on-site if they increase impervious surfaces. New developments need permits to show that the project will not increase the volume of water reaching local streams and rivers. The City of Grand Rapids employs stormwater engineers who are

> responsible for both making sure the city lives up to their obligations as a National Pollution Discharge Elimination System Permittee, which is basically our permit from EPA to discharge stormwater through our system to the waters of the state. And as subparts of that, it means I regulate both soil erosion control and stormwater management for people coming who want to do construction projects in the city.[47]

One of our most knowledgeable conversation partners, a female staff person who worked for the State of Michigan in the Water Resources Division, summarized the importance of capturing stormwater where it falls as a means to help protect and restore waterways.

> It's the cheapest and most effective if we can keep the water that flows on your property there. That's when the big promotion of rain gardens [began]. . . . Rain gardens in a lot of ways are filter strips that can keep water more on-site or at least cause the water to flow through, so it takes out a lot of the sediments. If you can keep the sediments out, you can keep a lot of the pollutants out, because a lot of them attach themselves to the soils then you get a double whammy when it ends up in the stream.[48]

The Plaster Creek watershed exists in several townships that don't have the same regulations as the city, which can create tension between economic development in the rural areas and water-quality protection in downstream, urban sections of the watershed. This geographic disparity has water quality implications for the whole region.

Protecting Urban Waterways by Increasing Storage Capacity

One way to handle large volumes of stormwater is to put in reservoirs or relief basins so the stormwater has some place to spread out and reduce its damaging impacts. This is what naturally happens in a healthy floodplain. Detention ponds and retention ponds help to control flooding *and* maintain the health of local waterways. One of our older conversation partners (born in the 1930s) described how Plaster Creek has been a lifeline for the city. As the conversation unfolded it was clear that he had an astute understanding of the paradigm shifts that have occurred in managing and caring for excess water.

> Plaster Creek—all creeks are lifelines for different reasons. They have to handle the stormwater runoff. Not the sewage water, but the stormwater . . . and because of the development and culture today we are putting more and more water directly into it. So the creek has to handle a lot of water in a short, given time. The creek has this capacity, but we cannot overtax it. I think the measures taken by the city to build holding ponds that absorb water are good measures. . . . I do think in the 1950s there was a culture to straighten out the river or the creeks and let the water get through as fast as you can. I think that is being rethought today. They want to keep creeks the way they are, and they want to limit the amount of water that goes into them. Water will get there eventually, but not all at once. I have built detention ponds myself. I was a contractor, and a lot of parking lots were turned into detention ponds. And there would be a big manhole in the center of the parking lot so that when the water got deep enough it would just [overflow] to the nearest creek, instead of everything washing out in one big rush of water. Then the detention pond would just slow everything down. Maybe it would take a day to get rid of all the water so that the creek would handle it.[49]

Grand Rapids has also historically struggled with how to handle flooding in the residential sections of the city. One conversation partner in the midstream section of the Plaster Creek watershed described the flooding that occurred on the streets in her neighborhood in the 1980s until the city added a retention pond.

> [There] was a field that was connected to the intersection, a field our children would play in. . . . But when there would be a severe storm, or maybe even not so severe, the manhole covers in front of our house would pop off and geysers would come out of them. The water entered the field right there from the storm sewer. . . . Then the actual area of the ditch, which was dry most of the time, would become a raging river, and would then proceed to flood the intersection. The city was very concerned about it. But our children just enjoyed it very much. They would get out in their raincoats and bare feet and play in the (flooded) street and have a good time. Then the city, in trying to remedy its situation, decided to put

> huge cement conduits under the field. Then we heard that the city had reclaimed the property . . . to make a retention pond so that, as we know is now ideal, that the water stays as close to where it lands as possible.[50]

While the fenced-off retention pond provided a solution that helps to control flooding, children in that neighborhood now have less opportunity to play and enjoy water, which impacts their long-term relationship with nature. While this is regrettable, often trade-offs like this have had to be made.

Protecting Urban Waters through Low-Impact Development and Green Infrastructure

New technologies and practices often referred to as "low-impact development" have been introduced in the twenty-first century to help protect local waterways. Low-impact development (LID) is an approach to land development or redevelopment that uses nature as a model to manage stormwater at the source.[51] In the past decade LID has become a widely accepted design approach in many areas of the United States. The goal is to keep stormwater soaking into the ground where it falls, rather than running off—by conserving or restoring natural areas whenever possible, by maintaining the runoff rate and duration from a site thereby minimizing the impact on hydrology, by using green infrastructure strategies that infiltrate and evaporate runoff, and by implementing proper maintenance.[52] Green infrastructure refers to practices that harvest or reuse stormwater in landscaping, which helps to reduce flows to sewer systems or surface waters. Green infrastructure is cost-effective, offers environmental, social, and economic benefits, and can strengthen community engagement.[53]

By encouraging LID and green infrastructure, the hope is that the relationship between water and the surrounding landscape would more closely mirror conditions before European settlement. One of our conversation partners articulately described the shift in thinking that has occurred in the last two decades.

> So, the whole idea of managing stormwater has now been—you do as much as you can up at the upper end of the watershed, wherever that happens to be, or around the periphery of the watershed so that you can keep the water on the ground as much as possible. It's still directed into places where it doesn't do

> damage, but we have now realized that floodplains and wetlands have benefits, not only for environmental reasons but for stormwater management. When you get a big rainstorm that generates huge flooding, if you can keep that water in the floodplains, it slows the volume down in the channel and it doesn't do nearly as much damage to the channel. The city of Grand Rapids, where Plaster Creek flows through the city of Grand Rapids—there's not a whole lot of room anywhere to reconstruct those floodplains, and the kind of stormwater storage that you have to do is extremely expensive. It is a lot more expensive to put detention ponds underneath a parking lot than it is to keep the water in its natural places upstream. So it used to be that it was just economic considerations. People looked at swamps and said they are not good for anything, let's just fill them in. We now know better, but it's taken us forty years to kind of learn that lesson. . . . There are things that we can do upstream that . . . keep a lot more water on site. . . . You've got to solve the problem upstream so that the concentration of flow doesn't get down to the bottom where it does all the damage.[54]

Working to solve the problem of stormwater runoff in upstream areas is less expensive than mitigating the problems downstream in crowded urban centers. The goal of LID is not to return to some idyllic past before the degradation became so severe. The goal is to develop strategies that allow for development without causing harm to the land and water. The most striking part of this new way of thinking about stormwater is the idea of infiltration and, as one of our conversation partners explained, enabling stormwater to be "recycled and reused."[55] With the introduction of green infrastructure in recent years, cities are able to be developed (or redeveloped) without increasing pollution and contamination to urban waterways. For cities to remain viable and thriving they need a mix of new development and careful upgrading and maintenance of the infrastructure that is already in place.

> A city can't run if we don't have money from development. . . . Once you get too restrictive [with regulations], you could hear, "Well, we're not going to build in the inner city." And [Grand Rapids is] still more restrictive than any of the outliers. . . . Dealing with the Michigan Department of Environment, Great Lakes, and Energy and the EPA, they've been very pleased with what the city has been able to do. . . . Our goal is to take [stormwater] out of the system. . . . We need more green infrastructure to . . . take that water out, getting those native plantings

> everywhere we can, getting the banks stabilized. And public education is still number one, because none of this is going to happen without it.[56]

Changing the mentality of directing stormwater into storm drains as quickly as possible and stressing the value of retaining stormwater on site to decrease stormwater runoff are important for educating the community. This transition will lead to downstream improvements in urban waterways. So we see again the intersection of water quantity and water quality.

Despite years of working to address problems in the Plaster Creek watershed, serious problems remain. One conversation partner who has been working professionally to address problems with urban waterways for the past twenty years mentioned her surprise at the ongoing and dramatic fluctuation in water levels in Plaster Creek, despite all the efforts to address the problems. She claims that "flashiness" remains one of Plaster Creek's most significant problems.

> Maybe one of the most memorable spots of Plaster Creek for me is right towards the mouth of the stream. I wasn't aware of how flashy, meaning the level can rise and fall very quickly. It was probably early spring. We selected our sampling sites and we put in stakes of where we wanted the sampling site to be and then we put in measuring rods. We had poles with measurements so we could measure the flow. We *thought* we had them in a logical place. But during and after a rainstorm, it's six feet under water. We just had no idea that it was *that* flashy. I mean, we couldn't even begin to reach our sites, the banks were so overflowing. So that was a warning—[we were] not realizing how much water comes through there.[57]

As these problems with water quantity and water quality have been revealed throughout the decades, possible solutions have been posed and tried, sometimes leading to good results, sometimes leading to new problems. The key takeaway we glean from these continually changing perspectives is how European Americans have fundamentally altered the relationship humans have with water. Developing the ability to recognize our implicit assumptions is important for initiating lasting restoration.

The phrase commonly used now to describe how developers and builders design in order to manage stormwater, best management practices, also reveals the influence of a European American worldview, where controlling or managing water is the goal. This is a stark contrast with how Indigenous people have viewed themselves in relation to water—as a reciprocal relationship, where people and the earth thrive together. European Americans have much to learn from Indigenous peoples. As one Indigenous conversation partner reminds us, "Water is the source of life. Everybody's drawn to water; . . . it is sacred."[58] Some of the recent shifts in perspective on watershed care that advocate for mimicking natural processes honor Indigenous ways of living albeit unknowingly. Acknowledging that there is much to be learned from Indigenous people is an important step in the reconciliation process. Motivating the average citizen to pay attention, reappreciate water as a source of life, and take steps to care for the water over which they have agency will lead to improvements for the whole community—both the human community and the nonhuman community. It is not an either/or choice.

Wendell Berry succinctly summarizes what is needed if we hope to correct our abuses:

> The mentality that destroys a watershed and then panics at the threat of flood is the same mentality that gives institutionalized insult to black people and then panics at the prospect of race riots. . . . We would be fools to believe that we could solve any one of these problems without solving the others. . . . The changes that are required are fundamental changes in the way we are living. . . . All meaningful contact between ourselves and the earth is broken. . . . If we are to hope to correct our abuses of each other and of other races and of our land, and if our effort to correct these abuses is to be more than a political fad that will in the long run be only another form of abuse, then we are going to have to go far beyond public protest and political action. . . . What I am saying is that if we apply our minds directly and competently to the needs of the earth, then we will have begun to make fundamental and necessary changes in our minds. . . . The principle of ecology, if we will take it to heart, should keep us aware that our lives depend upon other lives and upon processes and energies in an interlocking system that, though we can destroy it, we can neither fully understand nor fully control. And our great dangerousness is that, locked in our selfish and myopic economics, we have been willing to change or destroy far beyond our power to understand. We are not humble enough or reverent enough.[59]

There are ways to interact with water so that it benefits humans and enables thriving human settlements while also benefiting other creatures and sustaining the complexity of the natural world. Our worldviews shape our actions, and we must acknowledge how we have often interacted with the natural world carelessly. At the heart of acknowledging our complicity is recognizing that worldview differences have led to different outcomes for the natural world. This acknowledgement sets the stage for taking meaningful restorative action.

CHAPTER 5

Worldview Contrasts and Ecological Fallout

It has been fascinating to compare what was taught to me (Dave) about the history of West Michigan while growing up in this place with what I have learned by reading historical documents while doing research for this book. One of the contrasts that has emerged so clearly is how differently the Ottawa and the European immigrants understood themselves, the land, and each other. In short, these two groups of people had dramatically contrasting worldviews.

A particularly compelling example of this worldview-level contrast is illustrated by two quotes recorded just one year apart. They show how two groups of people were witnessing the same dynamics, but their interpretations could hardly have been more different. In 1887 Andrew Blackbird, a well-educated Ottawa and son of Chief Blackbird, authored *The History of the Ottawa and Chippewa Indians of Michigan.* In this fascinating account he writes,

> the land the Great Spirit has given us in which to live, to roam, to hunt, and build our council fires, is no more to behold. Where once so many brave Algonquin and the daughters of the forest danced with joy, danced with gratitude to the Great Spirit for their homes, they are no more seen. Our forests are gone, and our game is destroyed. Hills, groves, and dales once clad in a rich mantle of verdure are stripped. Where is this promised land which the Great Spirit had given to his red children as the perpetual inheritance of their posterity from generation to generation? Ah, the pale-faces who have left their fathers' land, far beyond the ocean, have now come and dispossessed us of our heritage with cruel deceit

> and force of arms. . . . Our happiest days are o'er, and never again shall we enjoy our forest home.[1]

One year later, in 1888 the Grand Rapids Board of Trade, intending to attract additional immigrants to West Michigan, published a book titled *Grand Rapids as It Is* in which the authors wrote,

> It is known of all men that for many years this state has been the chief producer of pine lumber in the union; no other commonwealth has placed nearly so much nor so good pine lumber on the markets of the entire country for many years past. The gross product for 1887 was well toward five thousand million feet, valued at $65,000,000 and this annual total will not be very largely decreased for the next decade to come. . . . The hardwood wealth of the state, yet undeveloped, is greater than the pine wealth ever was. This hardwood wealth, consisting chiefly of beech, maple, oak, elm, ash, hickory, butternut, birch, basswood, and sycamore . . . is almost innumerable in quantity, and unsurpassed in quality. There is also a vast amount of hemlock, cedar, and other evergreen timber wealth in Western Michigan. Grand Rapids is admirably located to secure the very choicest of this forest wealth.[2]

These accounts show how both cultural groups valued the forests. Indigenous Americans valued forests because these ecosystems sustained life—their own and the many other species needed for survival. European immigrants valued forests because they contained resources that could be harvested. To Indigenous people a forest was full of gifts, and harvesting these gifts was done in a context of mutual responsibility and ecosystem flourishing. To the Europeans, a forest that was left standing was being wasted. By clearing the land, human progress was advanced, wealth was accumulated. Yet in the process, the forest ecosystem was destroyed.

Worldviews Reflected in Landscapes

While outcomes like deforestation, stream channelization, floodplain loss, point source pollution, and stormwater runoff help to call attention to the fact that there are, indeed, problems with Plaster Creek, these are not the *causes* of the creek's problems. Instead, they are symptoms that have resulted from behavioral patterns of people who are living out a particular worldview in this particular watershed. To truly recognize the heart of the problem of environmental degradation, we need to identify deeply seated worldview assumptions that tolerate and even encourage these kinds of dangerous outcomes. This chapter offers a summary of worldview differences between the Indigenous people of North America and the European settler colonists who began arriving in North America in the seventeenth and eighteenth centuries.

A worldview is a set of presuppositions that we hold consciously or subconsciously about the basic makeup of the world.[3] Every worldview addresses four basic questions: Who am I? Where am I? What is wrong? What is the solution? In other words, a worldview reveals a person's basic assumptions about how the world works, how it ought to work, and the role humans play within it. A worldview includes attitudes, values, stories, and expectations about the places we inhabit, which inform and influence behaviors and actions. Worldviews are informed by ethics, religion, philosophy, science, and cultural values. Although there is no single homogeneous Native American or European worldview, there are common themes that were part of the way these two distinct lineages of people understood themselves and the world in which they lived.

Because worldviews are lived out in places, the character of a place in many ways will reflect the dominant worldview held by the people who occupy that place. The Ottawa lived in ways that reflected their basic worldview principles. When the prevailing Anishinaabe worldview was displaced by a European-dominant worldview, the West Michigan landscape changed dramatically. While the worldview differences between European immigrants and Indigenous Anishinaabeg were myriad, we will highlight four themes where sharp contrasts come into focus: understanding of relationships, religion, economy, and land.

Understanding of Relationships

The Anishinaabeg lived in a world they understood to be full of beings, and they understood themselves as living in relationship with these coinhabitants. Being *in relationship with* streams and trees, squirrels and deer will likely seem strange to those of us who come from European ancestry. The Enlightenment worldview with its emphasis on human exceptionalism reduced the concept of relationship to merely interactions between people. But in general, a relationship is present whenever two things are interacting with each other and influencing one another. The word "relationship" is used in broader contexts today to describe the interplay between different nations, cultural groups, businesses, or communities of faith. An even more expansive definition of relationship is seen in the discipline of ecology, the study of relationships that occur among living organisms and between living and nonliving elements in an ecosystem. When we notice the breadth of ways the term "relationship" is actually used today, it is curious how seldom most Americans consider our own species' relationships with nonhuman creatures that share the places where we live.

And yet we are certainly influenced by the many living and nonliving elements that exist within the environments that surround us. Our actions also influence those elements in ongoing back-and-forth relationships. For example, a large tree in the backyard of a house signals that there is a relationship between that tree and the people who live in the house. The tree shades the home and yard, moistens the air that the residents breathe, absorbs carbon, dissipates wind, and provides nest sites for birds that fill the yard with activity and song. The tree also provides visual textures of rough gray bark, verdant green vegetation, and a palette of changing colors each fall. In turn, the residents influence the tree whenever soil is dug and roots are encountered, when branches are pruned, leaves are raked, and fertilizer is spread, not to mention the children who may climb the tree, hide behind it, or swing from its branches. The people and the tree are in an ongoing relationship, influencing each other back and forth as time moves forward. If the tree was suddenly snapped off in a storm, it is likely the family would miss its presence and the memories its absence evoked. Wendell Berry writes, "We do not understand the earth in terms either of what it offers us or of what it requires of us, and I think it is the rule that people inevitably destroy what they do not understand."[4]

For millennia, Native Americans have lived on the land in ways that recognized and celebrated their relationship with the nonhuman creation. They understood that humanity was a part of the natural world and their worldview focused on how humans could fit into this broader world of beings. Indigenous people believed and still believe that human survival is dependent on the well-being of other creatures that provide them with food, medicine, clothing, and shelter, creatures who contribute to their physical and spiritual health.[5] Indigenous scholars Raymond Pierotti and Daniel Wildcat write,

> Perhaps the best way to think of this is that Native people lived their lives as though the lives of other beings mattered, i.e., that all other living organisms should be taken seriously. . . . They also realized their own lives were intimately intertwined with those of these other organisms. Most importantly, they recognized that the human being is not the measure of all things. Rather, humans exist as but one small part of a very complex ecosystem. This contrasts to the Western view of nature that sees human beings as above the rest of nature.[6]

Recognizing that human beings are intertwined in relationships with creation led to a more humble and less domineering understanding of humanity. Daniel Wildcat emphasizes that "it makes a critical difference whether humankind thinks of the natural world as consisting of resources or relatives."[7] Relatives are those with whom we have relationships, forming a community of interacting creatures whose well-being is collectively dependent on the well-being of the whole.[8]

Understanding of Religion and Spirituality

The Ottawa have had a sophisticated understanding of religion and spirituality, which is impossible to encapsulate within an entire book, let alone a few pages. Many stories and teachings were lost due to the intense assimilation efforts that Indigenous people have endured over time. Furthermore, some of the religious teachings of the Ottawa are considered culturally sensitive and inappropriate to discuss outside the Ottawa community. Yet main themes and observations are recognizable and offer some similarities and some marked contrasts to the European version of Christianity that was brought to this continent and cultivated here.

The Anishinaabeg recognized and worshipped a Great Spirit, named Kitche Manitou, who was the Creator and the ruler over all things. Out of nothing Kitche Manitou made rock, water, fire, and wind, and from these elements the physical world was created.[9] After everything was made, Kitche Manitou set in place the Great Laws of Nature for the well-being and harmony of all things. These laws governed the placement, movement, rhythms, and continuity of life, birth, growth, and decay. All things lived and worked by these laws.[10]

The Anishinaabe belief in a Supreme Ruler and Creator was a consistent starting point with Christian (and Jewish) monotheism, yet early records by Jesuit missionaries voiced surprise and concern over the myriad spirits that Great Lakes Indians recognized. Awareness of a spiritual reality was certainly part of Christian faith, but the spiritually enlivened landscape that the Anishinaabeg perceived was far beyond the spiritual reality for Europeans and was considered unacceptable.

The most notable of these spirits was Nanabozho, a great helper of people when they summoned him, but also known as a fun-loving trickster.[11] He was credited with teaching people which plants to use for medicine and how to catch fish from the lakes. His exploits formed a major part of Anishinaabe mythology. Not all spirits were good-natured like Nanabozho. For example, Windigo stalked the winter woods, and if a family was overtaken and died in a winter blizzard, it was understood that Windigo had paid them a visit.[12] More benign spirits, or "manitous," were present in certain landscapes, and others were connected to certain species, helping to direct animal behaviors and movements. Part of the reason for paying respect to a slain animal after a hunt was so that its individual spirit would report back to that species' manitou that the people were respectful and should continue to be blessed with available game.

Religious beliefs influence daily behaviors and practices. Respect for all living things is a foundational belief for the Anishinaabeg. This attitude was a critical part of "Bimaadiziwin," which translates as "the Proper Conduct of Life" or "the Good Life."[13] Bimaadiziwin included small acts of gratitude like leaving a humble token of thanks when harvesting food, but it also included broader cultural norms such as showing kindness to strangers, even to one's own personal detriment. Bimaadiziwin was enacted by the generally friendly way early explorers and voyageurs were welcomed by the Anishinaabe. In the *History of the City of Grand Rapids* (1891) a European traveler told of becoming lost and sick while exploring in Michigan:

> Lost my compass . . . lost my trail, and when night came on, I was lost. I tied my horse to a tree, took saddle for a pillow, wrapped my blanket around me, laid down, hungry, sick, lost and discouraged; tried to sleep, but the unmusical voices of wolves kept me wakeful. While thinking I had made a fool of myself in leaving old Connecticut for this useless tramp through the wilds of Michigan, I was startled by the sound of a footstep, and a minute later an Indian was at my side. I arose and followed him to a . . . camp. He conducted me to the chief. . . . I was kindly received, given something to eat, and furnished a bed of skins, with

> my feet to the fire, where I slept. I was given a decoction of herbs which relieved me from my sickness. . . . After remaining two or three days and recovering from my fatigue and sickness, having seen none but Indians, I was furnished by the chief with a young Indian for a guide, who with his pony conducted me to a white settlement.[14]

The Anishinaabeg also believed that the Great Spirit sees all things and that it is impossible to hide one's actions, either good or bad. Andrew Blackbird explains that this awareness motivated the Ottawa to be honest and upright in their dealings with others, owing to their trusted role as regional traders. The teachings that collectively informed Bimaadiziwin were not considered to be hard rules that must be followed. Instead, individuals were expected to be attentive to these teachings and, in response, shape their life accordingly within the context of accountability provided by their family and clan.[15]

Cultivating Bimaadiziwin fostered certain character traits that the Anishinaabeg valued, which included careful listening, patience, humility, perceptive insights, and clear and convincing oratory. Such skills were needed in community deliberations where important decisions were made through consensus of the entire group. Therefore, when choosing a leader, the Anishinaabeg were drawn to individuals who were valued members of the group because of their generosity and humility. One critical characteristic that was sought when considering who should be a leader was the lack of desire to be the leader.[16] In group deliberations it was important that the leader made sure everyone had a chance to speak their mind and that everyone was convinced their perspective was taken seriously. Through careful commentary and negotiations, the leader needed to unify the wisdom of the group, no matter how diversely opinionated the group might be.

Into this rich cultural and spiritual landscape European immigrants arrived with a decidedly different understanding of religion. The most notable and damaging was the belief that the religious understanding of Europeans was superior to all others. This worldview premise was justified and framed by the Doctrine of Discovery that Pope Alexander VI laid out in his official 1493 declaration, *Inter caetera*. Pope Alexander wrote that Christians who "discovered" lands occupied by non-Christians have the right and duty to take control of those lands to advance the Christian religion "and that barbarous nations be overthrown and brought to the faith itself."[17] Pope Alexander elevated Christian believers above all others and justified cultural genocide of non-Christian groups throughout the world. The Doctrine of Discovery was at the heart of colonization, and its racist and ethnocentric views infiltrated North America as European immigrants settled in the United States. In the 1823 case of *Johnson v. McIntosh* the U.S. Supreme Court unanimously affirmed this document, with Chief Justice John Marshall writing, "the principle of discovery gave European nations an absolute right to New World lands."[18] European settlers worked to conquer and dominate the land and its occupants because their identity of superiority over both had a religious basis. Jazmin Murphy has written, "Christianity has deep, painful, historical associations with the obsession of dominance."[19] The mindset of conquering this new land and taking control of it with religious zeal is a concrete manifestation of the Doctrine of Discovery.

Another contrast between the religions of these two groups was in the way religion was practiced. The formal manifestation of Christianity involves a temporal rhythm, generally weekly, when faith communities come together in collective worship. There was no such weekly meeting time for the Anishinaabeg, but instead spirituality was more integrated throughout the nuances of daily living. Religious festivals and celebrations were integral to Anishinaabe spirituality, but the rhythmic practice of worshipping inside a structure (house of worship) was a foreign concept to the Ottawa, as was the search for religious knowledge by reading from an ancient book.[20]

Understanding of Economy

Another significant worldview contrast is in the exchange of goods and services. European economies were market based, using some form of currency that was earned and then later spent for the purchase of property, supplies, or goods. Personal security was advanced by building up currency or by building up goods that could be readily exchanged for currency. For those of us who have been raised in a monetary-based economy like this, it is challenging to grasp how economics within Anishinaabe culture worked. Wealth was measured in Anishinaabe economics in the strength of relationships and the lived experiences that knit people together into communities. The Anishinaabeg existed within close-knit family units, but also within larger extended family groupings, and beyond that as part of a particular clan.[21] Social connections were essential not only for promoting a sense of belonging, which contributed to emotional and psychological well-being, but these connections were also pragmatically essential for survival. During times of disease, injury, drought, conflict, or famine, people needed to take care of each other, especially those with whom they shared a close relationship. In addition, the accumulation of material goods, which was a sign of wealth to colonists, would have made life more difficult for the Anishinaabeg who were frequently on the move.[22]

A gift-based economy functioned in the Anishinaabe communities. In a gift economy when an individual obtained something of value (by killing a large game animal, discovering a useful group of plants, collecting a robust harvest of crops, etc.) that blessing was dispersed and shared throughout the community.[23] In this way strong relationships were fostered, and one's esteem in the community grew in accordance with one's generosity. The practice of readily giving things away and the expectation that others would freely share their items of value was a point of consternation for the colonists. Early French explorer Antoine Cadillac was perplexed by this behavior and critically commented,

> the good hunters profit the least from their hunting. They often make feasts for their friends or their relatives or distribute the animals they have killed among the cabins or the families of the village. . . . Their only idea is to feed the people, and as the whole tribe gets the benefit.[24]

Gift giving was also a kind of insurance policy because a gift given was understood to be a gift received. Other families or villages would reciprocate such behavior when they had items of value, and in this way over time people cared for each other and strong relational networks emerged. Gift giving reminded both the giver and receiver that they needed one another. This practice was initially extended to early European immigrants as well. Anishinaabe gifts to settlers were also deliberate political gestures; they sought to integrate the settlers into Anishinaabe networks of reciprocity. In 1891 an early settler of Grand Rapids wrote,

> The Indians who lived here when the white men first entered are represented to have been peacefully and amicably inclined, often aiding and succoring the pioneers in time of need, providing game or fish. . . . In most seasons the Indians not only supplied their own families with meat, but often when a deer was slain presented their white neighbors with choice pieces of venison.[25]

The Anishinaabeg not only gave gifts to humans, but also extended gifts to the nonhuman creation in gratitude for the way it sustained them. Similarly to the exchange of gifts between people, when the land gave a gift, reciprocity was inspired.[26] James Schlender, writing about the Ojibwe, comments:

> Plants were to be treated in a respectful way with ceremony, prayer, and an offering. While gathering only a few and praying, an offering of tobacco was often made as thanks and in recognition of the sacrifice that the plant was being asked to make. In this dignified manner, the plant was honored, the medicine obtained, the Creator thanked, and the cycle of life ensured. After all, isn't it true that everything is related and that human beings are dependent on the rest of creation?[27]

Potawatomi scholar and author Robin Wall Kimmerer explains how she leaves a gift of tobacco when harvesting wild leeks, and also plants some of the leeks into forests where they have disappeared as offerings of thanks.[28] These small reciprocal gifts were regular practices of daily life for the Anishinaabeg and consistently reinforced their dependency on the earth, fostering a sense of reverence and humility. In a world animated with countless beings, it made sense to thank a bay for providing fish that alleviated your hunger, and to thank a tree for providing medicine that made your headache go away. Living in a world that supplied gifts came with the realization that long-term thriving required the ability of the land to continue providing those gifts. For that thriving to happen, life had to be lived carefully, in ways that gifts could continue to be offered, received, and reciprocated.

Understanding of Land

The Anishinaabeg inhabited land they believed was alive with countless beings—animals, plants, rivers, lakes, and a dynamic spirit world. Therefore, the language they spoke, Anishinaabemowin, was a much more lively and animated language than any of the dialects that were spoken by waves of arriving European immigrants. For example, in English, 30 percent of all words are verbs, but in Anishinaabemowin verbs make up 70 percent of the total word count. This notable contrast reflects how differently the Anishinaabeg perceived the land compared to the colonists.[29] Kimmerer explains that to English speakers a bay is a noun, but to the Anishinaabeg, a bay is a verb. It is being a bay and it expresses its bay-ness with a specific collection of water and creatures, light and wind in a certain way at a certain time on a particular day. The following day the bay will be expressing its bay-ness with different water and creatures, light and wind, similarly to how people's moods will shift from day to day. The same understanding was applied to hills and mountains, streams, and trees.[30] To the Anishinaabeg, the land was alive with being-ness. Additionally, creatures that in English are recognized as being alive, such as a squirrel, a bird, or a tree, would never have been referred to as "it" in Anishinaabemowin. These are individual beings who are as much a she or he as one's sister or brother. Kimmerer writes,

> This is the grammar of animacy. Imagine seeing your grandmother standing at the stove in her apron and then saying of her, "Look, it is making soup. It has gray hair." We might snicker at such a mistake, but we also recoil from it. In English, we never refer to a member of our family, or indeed to any person, as *it*. That would be a profound act of disrespect. *It* robs a person of selfhood and kinship, reducing a person to a mere thing. So it is that in Potawatomi and most other Indigenous languages, we use the same words to address the living world as we use for our family. Because they are our family.[31]

The language spoken by the Anishinaabeg shows how they understood themselves as living in a world that was enlivened by creatures with whom they shared the land.

European worldviews considered humans as the preeminent species and understood their association with nonhuman nature to be largely proprietary, one of mastery and subjugation. Human beings were considered to be separate from and superior to the rest of the world in which they lived. A dogmatic belief in the possibility of continual human progress fed into a vision that a utopian future led by economic growth and technological innovation is possible. The land was seen as containing resources to be used for economic gain, often for short-term, utilitarian purposes. "Growth in prosperity and scientifically founded technological progress are the two indispensable allies on the way to a better future."[32] Since humanity was understood to be superior, it was assumed that human advancement would occur at the expense of other species and the land itself.

By living for multiple generations in the same animated landscape, the Anishinaabeg developed intimate knowledge of the various creatures and places that supported their existence. But beyond simply knowing particular hills and creeks, shorelines and swamps, the land held memories of events, many of which were portrayed in stories, songs, and dances. Births and deaths happened within the land, ancestors were buried, battles were fought, animals were hunted, injuries incurred, blizzards survived, all within particular locations in the landscape. Life in all of its challenge, joy, and meaning played out in the land causing the land itself to be alive with experiences, lessons learned, insights gained. The Anishinaabeg could not conceive of their own existence as somehow separated from or outside of the land; they were embedded participants. Historian Charles Cleland writes, "The land and the Anishinaabeg were one complete thing, neither to be understood apart. This relationship was one of kindred expressed by them as the relationship between dependent children and the provider, *Nokomis*, grandmother earth."[33]

The deep connection that the Anishinaabeg had for the land included a recognition that pressing it too much was detrimental both for the land and for themselves.[34] In the Great Lakes region, Indigenous agriculture was done in relatively small, temporary patches. These agricultural activities supported relatively large gatherings of people, and in fact, the practice of raising crops benefited from a sufficient workforce. But during the winter months, most food came from hunting, which could not sustain concentrated crowds of sedentary people. Therefore, groups were more spread out on the landscape during winters when they were not growing crops.[35] Seasonal environmental rhythms also dictated times of social gatherings such as maple sugar harvesting, fish runs, and waterfowl migrations. When and where food was plentiful, larger groups (often of mixed tribes) would congregate, but when and where food was scarce, human population densities were scattered more lightly across the land. The Anishinaabeg were people in motion, never pressing places beyond the land's capacity to continue supporting the lives of its creatures, many of whom they depended on for their own health and well-being.

Because the Anishinaabeg viewed themselves as belonging to the land, the idea that they could own land never developed.[36] There were territories within which certain groups were recognized as having the right to harvest food and medicine to sustain their lives. But people never *owned* these lands that produced the goods, and in fact they often shared areas with other groups, particularly when resources were abundant. By contrast, many European immigrants were driven westward by the very opportunity to own land because in Europe they had been too poor to do so. Once land was owned, it was understood that the purpose of a particular parcel was to benefit the one who owned it. A great deal of confusion arose because the European understanding of land and landownership simply did not make sense to the Anishinaabeg.[37] Theologian Willie Jennings writes about an Indian named Massasoit who stated to an American colonist,

> What is this you call property? . . . It cannot be the earth, for the land is our mother, nourishing all her children, beasts, birds, fish, and all men. The woods, the streams, everything on it belongs to everybody and is for the use of all. How can one man say it belongs only to him?[38]

Kimmerer describes this worldview contrast by writing:

> In the settler mind, land was property, real estate, capital, or natural resources. But to our people, it was everything: identity, the connection to our ancestors, the home of our nonhuman kinfolk, our pharmacy, our library, the source of all that sustained us. Our lands were where our responsibility to the world was enacted, sacred ground. It belongs to itself; it was a gift, not a commodity, so it could never be bought or sold.[39]

Somewhat curiously, early colonists recognized that even though Indigenous people did not "own" land, they certainly did manage the land with regular burning. Setting intentional fires conveyed multiple benefits. The flames could be used to drive game and the vegetation that grew back after fires was highly palatable and would draw game in. Clearing the undergrowth in a forest also made it much easier to move about and also helped control insect pests. This service was appreciated by the early immigrants, and they noticed that when the Indian fires stopped, the forests became much thicker and were more difficult to traverse. In 1881, the authors of *The History of Kent County* reflected,

> The woods then resembled an immense park; there was scarcely any underbrush, few grubs, and no small trees. The annual burning of the grass by Indians had left the forests clear of all such obstructions, and the eye dwelt with delight upon the vista that extended before it under the leafy archway of the immense roof that expanded above in every direction. . . . All the very early settlers agree in their recollections of those beautiful forests. . . . A coach and four could have been driven anywhere with safety in those grand old woods.[40]

This idea of using fire to enhance the land's ability to support life was a notion that was not familiar to European immigrants. Learning why and how Native Americans used fire is proving to be extremely helpful as this important conservation tool continues to be rediscovered.[41]

Given that the land occupied by the Ottawa is framed by the Great Lakes, water held particular importance and respect.[42] The Ottawa had always been involved in trading, moving corn and tobacco from southern lands northward to Lake Superior and beyond, returning with meat, hides, and other goods from northern tribes. This movement of goods, often involving exchanges between the Potawatomi and Ojibwa, was done on water, and the Ottawa were masters at navigating the Great Lakes and their tributaries. The Ottawa were also master craftsmen, creating canoes constructed from cedar frames with birchbark coverings that were sewn together with spruce roots and sealed with pine pitch. These incredibly lightweight and highly maneuverable canoes took many months to build and could carry up to three tons of goods.[43] Water also supplied the Ottawa with fish, their most important and consistent source of protein. But fish were not the only food that came from water. The Anishinaabeg had originally moved westward with vision-based instructions to keep traveling until they came upon the food that grew on the water. They knew their destination had been reached when they found wild rice (an aquatic species that grows in standing water) in the Great Lakes region. For these reasons and more, to the Anishinaabeg water is life, a sacred gift that was given to ensure the ongoing flourishing of the world in which they lived.

The newly arriving European Americans certainly recognized that water was critical for growing food, satisfying human thirst, navigation, and more. But in the same way they viewed trees and animals as resources to be harvested, they also came to see water as a resource that could be brought under control to generate financial gain. Permanent high-density settlements were set up near water because of its many benefits, which also led colonists to think about water as a problem given its temperamental surges caused by storm events and spring meltwater. During the 1800s as small towns emerged and began growing into larger cities, the prevailing European American worldview recognized that to live permanently near water provided both opportunities and challenges. Historian Theodore Steinberg has written:

> As the [nineteenth] century progressed, a consensus emerged on the need to exploit and manipulate water for economic gain. A stunning cultural transformation

> was taking place, a shift in people's very perception of nature. By the latter part of the nineteenth century, it was commonly assumed, even expected, that water should be tapped, controlled, and dominated in the name of progress—a view clearly reflected in the law.[44]

As the human population in West Michigan shifted from people who belonged to the land to people who desired to have the land belong to them, the character of the land itself was transformed. As succinctly stated in *The History of Kent County*, "the face of the wild land was changed."[45] Thus began a dangerous decline in the health of the nonhuman creation.

Broadly speaking, Indigenous worldviews cultivated balanced relationships among humans and between humans and the natural world while Enlightenment-informed European worldviews encouraged personal advancement and a largely one-sided relationship between human beings and the natural world. What the Anishinaabeg appreciated and realized much better than the coming wave of European immigrants was that the health and well-being of humanity is intimately dependent on the health and well-being of the land.[46] While the Ottawa understood themselves to be a small part of the larger natural world with an emphasis on fitting in well, Europeans understood themselves as in control, with a mandate to assert dominion over a natural world they viewed as external to themselves. The lingering effects of this worldview are at the root of our environmental and social problems today. Daniel Wildcat writes, "In short, land, air, water, and life, which depends on the first three elements, are under siege by humans guided by a worldview with roots so deeply embedded in the ideas of Western civilization that it is part of an unconscious, taken-for-granted 'reality' that has become second nature."[47]

Honest Acknowledgement of What Was Lost When the European American Worldview Became Dominant

As the prevailing European American worldview has held sway in the United States over the past few centuries, the human–creation relationship has been severely damaged; people groups have become estranged and environmental health has declined. Degradation of the natural world must be "understood as related to humankind's development of societies and cultures disconnected in fundamental ways from the landscapes and seascapes, the places where they are situated."[48] Writers Fred Bahnson and Norman Wirzba argue that ecological amnesia has set in.

> Ecological amnesia—this condition is a fairly recent development in the history of humanity. It is a form of amnesia that, while having a philosophical expression, takes root because of the ways we live in the world. Its most basic cause is the practical separation of people from the land. This separation takes 2 forms: *physical* (a matter of location) and *existential* (a matter of how we relate to others). . . . People living [in cities] may have no understanding or appreciation for the ecological contexts and responsibilities that make their living possible. . . . This is problematic because what people do not see and understand they will less likely value and protect.[49]

While this quote does not openly acknowledge the role of settler colonization, it does summarize some of what has been lost when the European Enlightenment worldview became dominant. This fundamental change in worldviews has had huge implications for the way people have thought about and interacted with water, including Plaster Creek. Instead of understanding water as life-giving, water became viewed as something that should be controlled for convenience, comfort, safety, and financial profit. The human–creation relationship shifted from respecting and caring for water so that its provisioning services could continue for all creatures, to a view of dominance and utility, forcing water to serve primarily the human species. To manage and constrain waterways, particularly in locations where cities were being established, water needed to be dammed or directed into channels, culverts, and sewers for the purpose of benefiting humans. Wildcat succinctly summarizes what has been lost by saying, "Nowhere are the anthropocentric features of the modern American worldview and modern notions of history more obvious than in our inattentiveness regarding water."[50]

Many North Americans today have lost an appreciation for our relationship with water and how dependent our lives are on the rain that falls from the skies, flows across the landscape, and collects in pools, ponds, and lakes. One of the consequences of this lost relationship is that water has essentially become invisible to us; most Americans do not pay much attention to water. While this lack of awareness of water has become commonplace in the United States, it is not true of people everywhere. Each of us (Gail and Dave) has had the opportunity to teach in New Zealand. When you first meet an Indigenous person from New

Zealand (a Māori), they typically introduce themselves by identifying the mountain nearest to their home and the watershed in which they live. They situate themselves by telling of their place in the natural world, which forms an important part of their identity and shapes their introduction to the conversation. This is quite a contrast to most North Americans, especially urban and suburban residents, who typically give little thought to their place in the natural world. We've observed this with Plaster Creek watershed residents. When we began this work most Plaster Creek watershed residents didn't know of Plaster Creek's existence, let alone its dangerously contaminated condition.

The creek's condition is easy to overlook because of a general lack of appreciation for the human–creation relationship. Practices that damage the creek have become accepted as collateral costs for supporting the good life as defined by a European-based Enlightenment worldview. These same factors have induced a general apathy about environmental issues globally. The strands of awareness that attach our physical, emotional, and spiritual well-being to a healthy earth have been stretched so thin that we are left with an illusion they no longer exist. This is a worldview that has deceptively led us to the dangerous belief that our personal well-being is somehow irrelevant to the condition of the only planet on which we are capable of living.[51]

We need to acknowledge that broken relationships among people and between people and the land are perpetuated through worldview-level beliefs that result in decisions made on a daily basis. Since it is these damaged relationships that have brought about environmental degradation, trying to fix the degradation without addressing the relationships will fail to achieve lasting results. As Kimmerer writes,

> Restoring land without restoring relationships is an empty exercise. It is relationship that will endure and relationship that will sustain the restored land. Therefore, reconnecting people and the landscape is as essential as reestablishing proper hydrology or cleaning up contaminants. It is medicine for the earth.[52]

When we are able to recognize how relationships have been broken and when we are able to acknowledge our complicity in that brokenness, then we are prepared to begin restoration.

PART 3

THE NEW STORY OF PLASTER CREEK

COMMITTING TO RESTORATION AND REPARATIONS

CHAPTER 6

The Emergence of Plaster Creek Stewards

On a wintry morning in December 2008, a group of concerned community partners in West Michigan gathered to discuss the latest information about the Plaster Creek watershed. The Michigan Department of Environmental Quality (MDEQ) had just reviewed and approved a Watershed Management Plan for the Plaster Creek watershed developed and written by staff from a local civil engineering firm, Fishbeck, Thompson, Carr & Huber. Representatives from these groups gathered with staff from the West Michigan Environmental Action Council (WMEAC), Grand Rapids Environmental Services Division, and Calvin College to discuss implementing the new Watershed Management Plan. During this meeting, an MDEQ senior staff member turned to the Calvin faculty, pointing her finger, and gave us a direct invitation. "Calvin College, we could use your help! There are people in the upstream reaches of the Plaster Creek watershed who refuse to listen to us, because we are part of the government. But they are people of faith and maybe they will respond to you because you share a common religion. Will you help us?" This direct request for us, a Christian liberal arts college, to help a government agency caught us by surprise. But we were not completely unprepared to answer this call either. To understand why we were well positioned to respond to this challenge a bit of history about Calvin is required. This chapter will describe how Calvin College became involved in watershed restoration and how over time Plaster Creek Stewards (PCS) became a leader in local initiatives to clean up urban waterways.

Higher Education and Community Engagement

For almost a century higher education has sought to expand their role to serve the common good and to apply knowledge to larger community and societal issues. Since the 1990s there has been a substantial movement within higher education to urge more robust contributions from academia to contemporary problems. The notion of the "scholarship of engagement" was first coined in 1996 by Ernest Boyer, then president of the Carnegie Foundation for the Advancement of Teaching, in which he called for the academy to become a more vigorous partner in the search for answers to our most pressing social, civic, economic, and moral problems.[1] Award-winning professor of urban planning Kenneth M. Reardon argues that universities and colleges are ignoring their moral obligations unless they bring their teaching, scholarship, and research to bear on pressing community needs.

> Public and private colleges and universities have been subjected to a steady stream of criticism throughout the 1990s, both for a lack of research that addresses our major environmental, economic, and social problems and for a failure to prepare graduates fully to meet the challenges of socially responsible citizenship.[2]

These challenges raise questions about how institutions of higher education begin to do the work of genuine community engagement. How do university faculty listen to community members and learn from them about the challenges their communities face and the solutions they are working toward? Can spaces for mutual learning be created? These questions (and others) situate community engagement within the context of what constitutes real participation and highlights the need for more authentic embracing of diverse peoples. "We must recognize that communities are not voids to be organized and filled by the more knowledgeable; they are well-developed, complex and sophisticated organisms that demand to be understood on their own terms."[3] Serious dialogue about what real partnership means for communities and universities has led to important shifts in understanding and practice. Academic partners need to move beyond seeing themselves as the expert, and community partners need to move beyond seeing themselves as in need of outside expertise. Genuine partnership requires face-to-face interaction, deepening trust levels, and a willingness to step outside of traditional comfort zones to be present and listen carefully to one another. This type of engaged scholarship is collaborative in nature and relational, and at its best focuses on emancipatory purposes.[4]

Engaged Teaching and Scholarship at Calvin

Conversations about these national trends in higher education were swirling around within the Calvin College community in the 1990s and early 2000s. Calvin College (now Calvin University) has existed in Grand Rapids for over 140 years and for nearly 60 years has been actively involved with and invested in the local community. Calvin has been recognized as a national leader among faith-based colleges and universities in the service-learning movement, which connects college and community in concrete ways to address real human problems. In *Commitment and Connection: Service-Learning and Christian Higher Education*, the work of Calvin College is described "as a serious attempt among faculty and students to learn *with* the community, *through* the community, and *from* the community, not merely *in* the community."[5]

Between 1995 and 2005, Calvin's Service-Learning Center experienced a significant growth in academically based service-learning, with faculty across many disciplines redesigning courses to include a service-learning component. Faculty in the natural sciences launched the Calvin Environmental Assessment Program (CEAP), a service-learning initiative, to foster a habit of stewardship based on attentiveness to place. CEAP increased our understanding of what it means to be embedded in natural and social systems, enabling us to start paying more attention to that which is closest at hand. For example, because we reside in the Great Lakes region, we recognized the importance of water and the current issues and challenges the region faced. This awareness led to faculty designing course content that connected these contemporary issues to theoretical frameworks being taught in class. Examples of service-learning projects that faculty organized for students through CEAP included collecting data on campus water quality in a chemistry class, creating maps of local West Michigan watersheds in a geography class, and conducting botanical inventories in a plant taxonomy class (which led to the discovery of two species growing in remnant forests along Plaster Creek whose survival is threatened in Michigan). In the early 2000s Calvin faculty began learning that the Plaster Creek watershed, home to the college itself as well as many of its faculty, students, and alumni, had been deemed the most contaminated urban waterway in West Michigan. Wading, swimming, even touching surface water could have detrimental public health consequences.

Early Efforts of the Plaster Creek Working Group

This growing knowledge led us to begin attending meetings with community organizations and agencies actively working on environmental concerns around water. We began learning about efforts to slow down the damage being done to Plaster Creek. We did site visits to Plaster Creek in various locations and started to get to know the creek. We saw eroded stream banks and downed trees caused by excess stormwater runoff. We observed cows wandering through the creek on farmers' land, contributing to the bacterial contamination of Plaster Creek. We learned about some of the problems, but there was a lot more to learn.

These early efforts of the informally named Plaster Creek Working Group led to several half-day brainstorming sessions to talk about possible next steps. By 2007, Calvin had received two grants that focused some attention on the Plaster Creek watershed: one environmental education grant funded by the Environmental Protection Agency (EPA) to develop high school science curriculum, and one from the National Science Foundation to develop a Young Scientists Academy to build research skills among middle schoolers. At a December 2007 brainstorming session with community partners, we focused on four questions: (1) What unique contributions can we make, as a college, to the work already being done? (2) What gaps exist that we could potentially help to fill? (3) What would we like Calvin to be known for ten years from now? (4) What concrete steps do we need to take to get there (staffing, funding, grants, other resources)?

It's valuable to mention at this point how we (Gail and Dave) emerged as collaborative leaders of this watershed restoration project. Gail, as an urban studies scholar-practitioner, was then serving in the Provost Office at Calvin as the director of Community Engagement assisting faculty to envision how their teaching and research could serve a larger community beyond the campus. Dave, as an ecology and botany professor, was intent on engaging students in his classes with real-world environmental problems through service-learning. As we learned more about Calvin's complicity in the creek's condition, we also worked to help

Calvin develop a response to the watershed degradation. Gail served as convenor of the early brainstorming sessions, and Dave helped recruit fellow faculty and staff to participate. Going forward Gail and Dave made decisions together about how to proceed in crafting a response to the needs as they emerged.

Ongoing Meetings with Community Partner Organizations

Six months later, in June 2008, a group of Calvin faculty, administrators, and staff along with representatives from community organizations working on watershed issues gathered in another one-day workshop. We pooled our efforts to think critically and creatively about future possibilities for Calvin to work with the primary stakeholders involved in watershed management and restoration. At this workshop, we learned that the Grand Valley Metro Council had recently established a watershed alliance called the Lower Grand River Organization of Watersheds (LGROW). We learned about LGROW priorities for working with municipalities and how the Plaster Creek watershed, as a subbasin watershed, fits within the structure of LGROW. We learned about early efforts to monitor *E. coli* levels in Plaster Creek. At this workshop we were introduced to the Nonpoint Source program within MDEQ, and we learned that a revised Plaster Creek Watershed Management Plan had just been approved.

Through careful listening, Calvin faculty and staff began to consider the unique contribution Calvin could make to the work already underway to restore Plaster Creek. So we posed several big questions: What additional research or monitoring is needed within the Plaster Creek watershed? Can we identify Calvin faculty who teach specific courses that could include a service-learning monitoring component—macroinvertebrates, channel measurements, stream morphology, land use, oral history with residents in the watershed, computer modeling? How do we foster connections between Calvin faculty and community partners working in the watershed? How can Calvin focus educational efforts on fostering a sense of place and help people connect to water? Can we explore new angles to reach our constituent community, including the idea of sustainability as important to businesses? These early brainstorming sessions in December 2007 and June 2008 were quite beneficial in building relationships of trust with community partners as we pondered and considered the contributions a college could make to an important issue of community concern.

The stage had been set. The broad conversations about community engagement that had been happening at Calvin for more than a decade and the specific conversations about the degraded local watershed that had been taking place during the previous four years prepared us to both hear and respond when the catalyst question came to Calvin on that wintry morning in December 2008 to help MDEQ reach people unwilling to cooperate with government officials.

Turning Point—Summer Workshop in 2009

Several faculty members at Calvin College led by Gail and Dave took up that challenge from MDEQ and sought the endorsement of the college to begin outreach to local congregations. With generous internal support from the Calvin Center for Christian Scholarship, the following summer we organized and conducted a three-day workshop for local congregations held at the Calvin Ecosystem Preserve Interpretive Center. This workshop brought together a wonderfully diverse group of people, all around the topic of creation care in the context of the Plaster Creek watershed. Participants varied in age, race, gender, and denominational background, and all were interested in learning about local environmental issues. Participants in this workshop learned about the state of this damaged watershed, why it matters, and what could be done to begin restoration. For three intense days we heard presentations, went on field trips, shared meals together, worked in large and small groups, and welcomed guest speakers. In the end representatives from five local congregations and the denominational headquarters of the Christian Reformed Church in North America presented action plans to be implemented over the next eighteen months. This was a very exciting time of awakening both to the deplorable condition of Plaster Creek and the call for congregational environmental action.

Mayor George Heartwell participated in this first workshop, and in response to a question about the involvement of faith communities in sustainability efforts, he admitted that although an ordained pastor himself, he feels a love/hate relationship with the church at times. He loves the potential that the church holds but hates the way the church so often falls far short of that potential. Mayor Heartwell argued that the faith community in West Michigan has been very good at showing mercy, but not very good at doing justice. He hasn't seen a passion emerge for environmental justice the way it has for social justice.

Having the mayor spend a morning at our workshop presenting his ideas and perspectives on what is needed in Grand Rapids showed how important the work we were launching is for the city and region. From early on we hoped that PCS could serve as an entry point for members of faith communities to become actively involved in environmental care.

We did not realize at the time how significant these preliminary meetings, summer workshops, and organizing efforts were to establishing a long-term mission for the work of watershed restoration and reconciliation ecology. It is only in retrospect that we realize how these early steps set the stage for significant accomplishments to come. One of the participants in that 2009 summer workshop was later interviewed for the Plaster Creek Oral History Project and was asked how he first began to care about his local watershed.

> The first time I felt interested and attached was when Plaster Creek Stewards had our initial get-together. When you are listening to the stories of people who are passionate about watersheds and environmental justice, then you become passionate about your watershed and environmental justice. That's when Plaster Creek became important to me. And probably for the first time in my life I could identify the watershed I lived in, and I knew how my watershed was doing. [It was] the first time I ever began to consider the consequences of some of my actions in the watershed where I live.[6]

The summer workshop with congregations in June 2009 was a defining moment—a turning point in the work for watershed restoration. The group collectively made a strategic decision to rename ourselves as "Plaster Creek Stewards," dropping the more mundane name, Plaster Creek Working Group. We now had a cadre of Calvin faculty, congregations, community organizations, and others who were committed to implementing action plans to begin restoring Plaster Creek. And then another surprising thing happened. The *Grand Rapids Press* ran a story about our efforts, emphasizing the theme of the workshop, Creation Care on the Homefront. It included photos of participants (including a staff member from then senator Carl Levin's office in a suit) actually working *in* Plaster Creek looking for aquatic insects that are indicators of water quality. A local philanthropist saw the article and made an unsolicited, anonymous donation of $10,000 to encourage this work to continue. This gift provided enough funding to create our first part-time staff position, and PCS was launched.

Key Decisions in the Formation of PCS

Over the course of the next eighteen months from June 2009 to December 2010, the faculty leaders of PCS along with the part-time program coordinator began crafting a vision to shape the work. We carefully identified what Calvin College, as an institution of higher education, could do (and what we could not do, i.e., advocacy and lobbying). We developed a mission statement: "Plaster Creek Stewards is a collaboration of Calvin University faculty, staff, and students working with local schools, congregations, and community partners to restore the health and beauty of the watershed."[7] We identified initial focus areas for our work: education and outreach, research, and on-the-ground restoration. We developed a three-year strategic plan and specific goals for each focus area to set a clear direction.

As we began to think and talk about ways to motivate people from the campus community and the larger Grand Rapids community to get involved in this work of watershed restoration, we knew that a new paradigm would be needed for envisioning the human relationship to the natural world. We resonated with writers who articulated the importance of personal experience with nature as a catalyst for restorative ecological action, and this helped to inform our approach.

> Fundamental, significant, and lasting environmental change will occur only when avenues are created for people to *physically, intellectually, socially, and spiritually connect with the natural world* [emphasis added]. Accordingly, it assumes that the generation of environmental virtues—attentiveness, respect, admiration, care, and love—are rooted primarily in our experiences of nature. Human beings can alter their minds, an intellectual act, but they must also change their hearts, an emotional endeavor, for real change to occur.[8]

We came to recognize that we needed an approach that connected mind with heart, and heart with hand; we needed to connect knowing and doing. We also came to realize that ecological restoration as an applied, scientific practice didn't go far enough. Creation care needs to be more than just reconciliation between people and the land; reconciliation is also needed between different people groups who are living together in the land. For us, reconciliation ecology is about reconciling people to each other while also reconciling people to the earth—rural and urban, wealthy and poor, Indigenous and immigrants. For damaged land to be healed, people living in that damaged landscape need to understand each other and work together to repair the land.

As Calvin faculty continued to learn more about our place, we learned how degradation of the Plaster Creek watershed over the past 150 years has inequitably impacted low-income communities of Black, Indigenous, and People of Color (BIPOC). We must admit that during our early workshops and planning sessions only a few Black people joined us, and no Indigenous or other people of color were present. We understand now how much was missed because of their absence. It's too easy for white people to intellectualize issues of inequity and not feel the impact of the harm that is being done. However, serious conversation has continued about the responsibility we have as a Christian liberal arts college to address an environmental justice problem that previously had been invisible to us. Could we build meaningful reciprocal relationships working together on restoration in concrete ways? Could we use the tools of our disciplines to discern and determine steps that are truly part of a lasting solution rather than continuing to be part of the problem? These questions became topics not only to guide course content and faculty research, but also for building intentional relationships with those most impacted by the degradation. This matter continues to challenge us, and while we have become better at engaging BIPOC individuals in our work and decision making, we keep striving to reach those who are impacted by injustices in this watershed.

As concern for the Plaster Creek watershed continued to grow, we realized we would need funding for some of the projects we envisioned. We applied for numerous grants, and in those early years very few of our proposals were funded. Gratefully we received several small internal grants from Calvin that helped us keep organizing and planning. However, another defining moment came in 2010 after we had completed our first comprehensive strategic plan. Through this planning process, we were able to recognize more clearly what we could accomplish with internal funds and for what specific activities we would need external funding. In the spring of 2011, we applied for a grant from River Network, a national organization working to protect the waters of our country.[9] To our surprise, we were one of five organizations selected from a national pool of more than 120 applicants to receive a capacity-building grant. This first external grant gave us funding for two things: (1) to initiate an oral history social research project to engage local residents in this watershed work; and (2) to hire a full-time program coordinator to focus our educational efforts and expand our capacity to implement restoration projects on the ground. More importantly, this River Network grant included technical assistance and an invitation to join the inaugural group launching the Urban Waters Learning Network (UWLN).[10] The UWLN is a national initiative funded by the EPA that builds collaborative working relationships throughout the United States to conserve, restore, and revitalize America's urban waterways. The UWLN fosters solutions that advance water equity and environmental justice, builds healthy ecosystems and resilient communities, and addresses the disparate impacts of environmental degradation and climate change. As a member of the UWLN, PCS was introduced to national leaders in the watershed restoration movement. This, in turn, positioned us for additional funding, technical assistance, rich learning from peer organizations, and many valuable mutually collaborative relationships.

By the fall of 2011, we were regularly convening a group of community partners interested in collaborating with PCS to submit a major grant proposal to MDEQ to expand educational outreach, study the hydrology of Plaster Creek, and install four large green infrastructure projects within the Plaster Creek watershed. This proposal was funded and became the first of five large grants from MDEQ to PCS between 2012 and 2023. With this funding support, PCS to date has installed seven large bioswales, restored three large floodplains, and created more than 130 curb-cut rain gardens in urban neighborhoods.

As the work of PCS has flourished, we have been strategic as we develop plans for grant projects. Based on research findings, we intentionally design projects in the upstream, midstream, and downstream reaches of the watershed within each grant application, always considering what restoration is needed upstream to create a positive impact downstream. This approach enables us to reach multiple communities and residents in different parts of the watershed and helps to foster an increased understanding of upstream–downstream connections. The U.S. EPA Region 5 has created the System for Urban Stormwater Treatment and Analysis Integration, a model to create low-impact development at strategic locations in urban watersheds. The Plaster Creek watershed was chosen as a pilot site in 2012 to evaluate best management practices for addressing urban runoff.[11] There are now multiple entities working to address water quality and stormwater-related concerns in Plaster Creek including PCS, Michigan Department of Environment, Great Lakes, and Energy (EGLE), City of Grand Rapids, Kent Conservation District, LGROW, WMEAC, Friends of Grand Rapids Parks, River Network, and suburban and rural municipalities.

This collaborative work has expanded to include a regional green infrastructure program called the Grand River Rainscaping Program.[12] In 2016 PCS joined several other watershed organizations to design an outreach program focusing on the larger Lower Grand River watershed in West Michigan. The goal of the Grand River Rainscaping Program has been to increase awareness among residents about the importance of low-impact development and to provide technical assistance in designing and installing green infrastructure at residential properties. This collaboration among organizations working in different subwatersheds of the Lower Grand River watershed provides an example that other regions could emulate to build public awareness about how residents can care for their local waters. The way forward is to take small, focused steps. As one of our conversation partners aptly said,

> Lake Michigan is a huge body of water; the Great Lakes is a huge watershed. You can't tackle that all at once. So what you have to do is look at these small watersheds, and if all the small watersheds are doing [restoration] types of things, cumulative impacts can start making a difference. But it's really the only way to approach improving the water quality and improving the Great Lakes; you have to do it at this micro scale.[13]

Strategies of PCS

The approach PCS has taken to implement reconciliation ecology has included six strategies that have become hallmarks of the work: education, research, on-the-ground restoration, upstream–downstream connections, engaging faith communities, and shaping future environmental leaders. These strategies help to flesh out concretely what has been outlined to enact reconciliation ecology: recognizing a problem, acknowledging and lamenting our complicity, and making a commitment to take restorative, reparative action to heal the broken relationships. Here we give a brief introduction to these six strategies. In following chapters, we will explore each strategy by examining theoretical perspectives, sharing some historical context, and highlighting key findings from the oral history project. These six strategies provide ideas and entry points for readers interested in practicing reconciliation ecology in their own home communities.

Education

Because PCS is an initiative embedded in a university, education is a primary strategy to fulfill our core mission. In addition to involving students and faculty across many disciplines within the university, we have focused on educating people in local schools, congregations, neighborhood associations, and local businesses. One hallmark of our work has been a concerted effort to *combine education and action.* For example, when we offer an educational presentation on the importance of native Michigan plants to help capture stormwater, we then invite people to work in the greenhouse transplanting native plant seedlings for future restoration projects. Knowledge isn't enough to motivate behavior change. People need opportunities to do something to care for the earth. We never teach about watershed ecology without providing an opportunity to do something to improve the watershed; we never organize action events without first providing education about the watershed. We know that education happens both by listening and by doing. We hope a deeper affection for the stream will emerge as people learn about and practice restoration activities. One conversation partner expressed, "you can help 'save the creek,' so to speak, by helping people connect with it. . . . When you allow people to connect with a place, they have more stake in it."[14]

We need occasions to practice connecting our knowing and our doing. PCS has been inspired by former teachers who regularly took their students outside to learn and who worked to create parks and other gathering places in the watershed for people to enjoy the creek. We will explore the literature of the pedagogy of place and the importance of connecting education with action. We'll also hear stories of teachers and schools who have had a deep impact on creating engaged students who later grew up to become environmental leaders.

Research

PCS has taken a multidisciplinary approach to this work, and research has emerged as a second important strategy. Faculty members in various fields have studied multiple aspects of this urban waterway and have involved students in research projects that use the Plaster Creek watershed as a living laboratory in biology, chemistry, literature, geology, urban studies, history, geography, engineering, and art. It is noteworthy that many of the more than ninety student research assistants we've hired in the last decade have expressed the positive impact their research experiences have had on their own lives. One former student research assistant shared,

> Thinking back on my experiences collecting the oral history of Plaster Creek, one of the greatest impacts . . . would be learning to see how others viewed the world through *their* life experiences. Having conversations with people who were over 65, while I was in my early 20s, and what their experience was with Plaster Creek in their youth, compared to today's youth really put things in perspective, especially for how things could change.[15]

Restoration

Capturing stormwater where it falls is an important contributor to the restoration of urban waterways, and this is best accomplished by installing green infrastructure in parks, on streets, at homes, schools, and congregations. So, the third strategy of the work of PCS has been installing and maintaining native Michigan plants in dozens of community-based green infrastructure projects annually. These native plants are grown in campus greenhouses from seeds collected locally around the West Michigan region. The plant propagation process has been developed and refined over the years. In 2010 PCS grew about four thousand plants, and this effort has expanded significantly. Currently PCS grows more than 150,000 native plants per year.

Upstream–Downstream Connections

The fourth strategy of our work has been to create more awareness of upstream–downstream connections. Many Americans seldom think about how their actions impact others downstream from them. Yet it's common sense—what happens upstream impacts those downstream. People's lives are interconnected in a watershed whether they think about it or not. For example, if upstream residents throw pet waste into a storm sewer that is flushed into the nearest creek, children downstream who play in the creek have a greater risk of being exposed to *E. coli* bacteria. None of us wants to be the recipient of contamination. PCS has made

FIGURE 9. Planting trees is an important part of an education/action community event.
PHOTOGRAPH BY GAIL GUNST HEFFNER

a concerted effort to connect people in upstream and downstream communities and raise awareness that everyone in a watershed is related, particularly because these are often issues of environmental justice.

Engaging Faith Communities

Most faith traditions acknowledge the importance of caring for the natural world. Though communities of faith may emphasize different aspects of the human–earth relationship, there is a common recognition of brokenness and the need to work for wholeness and healing. Historically environmental groups have made minimal effort to engage with faith communities, which is one reason why faith communities have been largely inactive in this work. However, the pattern may be changing. In recent years, some communities of faith have begun to acknowledge their role in creating the brokenness that marks our current crises, and to honestly face what is needed to consider a different future. Congregations have the potential to be influencers and leaders in the vision for restoring the earth. The fifth strategy PCS has emphasized is engaging faith communities, and in the years since beginning PCS, people of all ages and from diverse religious and cultural backgrounds have joined the effort. Many congregations are poised to reimagine a new way forward in seeking reconciliation, finding ways to live in mutually fulfilling relationships with others, and working for the flourishing of all.

Shaping Future Environmental Leaders

The sixth strategy of PCS is engaging youth in the work of reconciliation ecology with the hope of shaping future leaders. The oral history project has provided rich opportunities to listen to residents' childhood memories of Plaster Creek, particularly how life experiences have shaped and motivated them to work to heal the damage done to the environment. Reaching youth is one way to influence their parents, families, and communities to take environmental action. In 2012, during an EPA Urban Waters national training held in Washington, D.C., we were introduced to several national programs that are engaging youth in environmental protection and restoration.[16] Interacting with organizations from other parts of the United States was inspiring. And a new idea for PCS was spawned—a summer education and employment program for high school students. In 2013 we launched the Green Team, recruiting a cohort of high school students who live, work, worship, or attend school in the Plaster Creek watershed. The Green Team program provides a paid work experience combining education about watershed ecology and green infrastructure with concrete work experience in watershed restoration. This youth outreach initiative has been very successful and has expanded since 2013.

A Growing Affection and New Questions

The last decade has been a fruitful one. Between 2012 and 2024, PCS has been awarded more than thirty external grants. We have educated several thousand people about watershed ecology and the need to care for their local environment. We have conducted more than twenty research studies and installed dozens of restoration projects. We have built collaborative partnerships locally, regionally, and nationally, and published articles and research reports. We have spoken at conferences throughout the United States, in Canada, and Japan, and received regional, national, and international awards for our work. Yet there is still much work to do.

Affection for Plaster Creek is growing, and this is deeply satisfying to witness. A common love for the creek waxed and waned between the 1930s through the early 2000s as we learned through the Plaster Creek Oral History Project. Occasionally we heard an older conversation partner acknowledge that a shift may be occurring with a younger generation. "You've got a whole generation that has much more sense to this than my generation. We paid no attention to it. I probably would've dumped stuff into Plaster Creek when I was there."[17] It is encouraging to hear people articulate a growing love for Plaster Creek and begin to care about it as Indigenous Americans have. New relationships are forming as people recognize the importance of taking care of their homeplace.

> The creek is loved. That is maybe a big difference from ten years ago; that this creek has some people who love it and are really trying hard to care for it. So, to the extent that creeks can emote and feel things, it is probably nice for Plaster Creek. And that is a meaningful thing, I think.[18]

As this work of reconciliation ecology has unfolded in recent years, priorities have been established and strategies for watershed restoration have been practiced, clarified, and expanded. Yet what is equally striking to us is the change that has happened within ourselves as we have been doing this work. In the beginning we approached the PCS work as scholar-practitioners—recognizing a community problem, analyzing the issues, attempting to bring our expertise to address the issues, and engaging with others to work on solutions. In the process we have come to see how blind we have been to the depth of pain American colonization has caused to both people and the earth. Listening to and learning from people of color locally *and* nationally has changed how we see and approach this work. We have been angered, humbled, challenged, and motivated to understand how decolonization needs to be an important part of reconciliation ecology. It is not enough for us to just study a problem out there without realizing how we have been complicit and, at times, even contributed to the problems we are trying to address. What is needed is more than Western scientific knowledge. We affirm what philosopher Gretel Van Wieren has written: "For ecological restoration practice to contribute to a more fully flourishing societal restoration ethic, it will need to be solidly grounded in ecological science and practical experience."[19]

This begs the question—Whose practical experience? Whose ecological knowledge? We are asking different types of questions now, not just scientific and technical questions but also questions about power. Whose voice is heard and respected and whose voice is overlooked? Who decides what actions to take and who is ignored? These are big and difficult questions. We have made some significant shifts in understanding, but we also acknowledge that we often don't know what we don't know. Building relationships of trust with Black, Latino, Indigenous, and other people of color will take time and deep listening. Yet *this* aspect of reconciliation work cannot be sidestepped if we hope to see lasting, meaningful change for the healing of the watershed, and more broadly for the healing of the earth.

CHAPTER 7

Developing Engaged Citizens through Place-Based Education

It was a crisp fall morning when I (Gail) arrived at the school. The light was low in the sky, but the sun would soon be shining brightly. A group of nervous eighth-grade students was gathered under a pavilion near the school waiting for instructions from their teachers. There was excitement in the air because the students were outside—beyond the walls of their classrooms—and they were going to be exploring the creek that runs near their school. The science lessons today would not be in lectures or lab experiments but in observations and measurements of the actual stream. What made this experience unique was that there were two groups of eighth-grade students in different places at the same time collecting data for comparison: one group from an upstream, more rural school and the other group from a downstream, more urban school.

Plaster Creek Stewards (PCS) began the upstream-downstream work with these schools by developing learning activities and inviting two middle school science teachers from very different communities at opposite ends of the watershed to involve their eighth-grade classes. This effort included a variety of activities with both schools together, including a bus tour of the watershed so the students and teachers could see how the creek is being affected by different land-use patterns. Developing simultaneous research activities in up- and downstream sections of the watershed, and having the students and teachers get to know each other, has provided rich opportunities for comparisons. The upstream mostly rural and suburban students learn about the inputs from urban and industrial regions of the watershed. The downstream urban students learn about how agricultural areas influence water quality in the creek.

Dutton Christian Middle School is in a farming community and Potters House Christian Middle School is in a highly urbanized area of the city. The eighth graders exploring Plaster Creek had probably never thought about how actions upstream impact places that are downstream. On this particular morning at each location, some students examined the stream profile by measuring contours of the stream bed, and calculated the volume of water that the stream was carrying in each location. Other students studied the water chemistry by measuring pH levels, electrical conductivity, and temperature as indicators of water quality. Another group used nets to collect aquatic insects from each location and then sorted and counted the number and type of insects present in the samples. These aquatic insects, or macroinvertebrates, are indicators of the relative health of the water since some exist in poor water and others only survive in higher quality water. Students learned that macroinvertebrates represent an important lower level of the food chain, and larger fish will not be present unless there are ample macroinvertebrates for them to feast on. Helping the students share their data between schools and compare findings emphasized the connections between upstream and downstream areas. This activity introduced the students to what is needed for healthy waters and why it matters for public health. Meeting people who live in other sections of the watershed also helped students realize their actions have consequences that impact real people in other parts of the watershed. This collaboration between two schools demonstrates concretely the relationships that exist in a watershed. One of the middle school science teachers expressed his appreciation in these words:

> I love it when students start to see themselves as part of this neighborhood, a part of the greater watershed, a part of a country that they are living in, and a part of a global community that they are a part of—but more importantly, when they come to see how they have a part in making their neighborhood, watershed, country, and world a better place as part of God's restorative work.[1]

Building Healthy Communities through Place-Based Learning

Helping students pay attention to what is close at hand, such as a creek in the school's backyard, is an example of place-based education. Places have legacies that are historical and cultural, as well as ecological, and all of these aspects are tied together in ways that define our human–nature relationships. Place-based learning can be one important component of a student's educational experience. In recent decades, educational theorists have begun writing about a "pedagogy of place," which begins with what is nearby and extends outward from there. Place is particular and local. Place incorporates the specific features of geography, biology, history, and social context. And it is rooted in the recognition that people are embodied human beings who are embedded in their natural environments,

> environments that have physical, historical, and social particularities that are integral to the physical life and development of any human. Good teachers in the liberal arts have always recognized this and offer their students some sense of the historical and environmental context within which [their education] is created.[2]

A pedagogy of place is an educational approach that encourages immersive learning to improve the social, economic, political, and ecological life of the places in which the education occurs. For education to have lasting impact, it must be "directive and must always be transformative."[3] But for this to happen, schools and teachers cannot remain distant from the communities in which they exist. Entering into partnerships with neighborhoods, community organizations, and local initiatives opens up opportunities for mutual learning about what matters most in that place. The study of place has significance in reeducating people in the art of living well wherever they are.[4]

The educational literature argues persuasively that for meaningful place-based education to happen, intellectual content needs to be combined with concrete experience. Classrooms and lecture halls are spaces where ideas are presented, discussed, and debated. But students also need to be given opportunities to observe, investigate, test, and learn why the ideas matter. Students of all ages benefit by practicing how to apply their knowledge. Another word for this is praxis—to imagine and then implement, to reflect and then take action. Typically, students learn academic content by topics, specialties, or disciplines. While there is value in going deep into one area of knowledge to learn its complexities and nuances, there is also a need to see how various aspects of knowledge are connected. Place-based pedagogy has the potential to demonstrate the interrelatedness of knowledge and can lead to a more integrated understanding. "The classroom and indoor laboratory are ideal environments in which to narrow reality, in order to focus on bits and pieces. The study of place, by contrast, enables us to widen the focus to examine the interrelationships between disciplines and to lengthen our perception of time."[5] By studying what is close at hand, a student has the potential to make these connections.

> Place-based education takes us back to basics, but in a broader and more inclusive fashion . . . the history, folk culture, social problems, economics, and aesthetics of the community and its environment are all on the agenda. In fact, one of the core objectives is to look at how landscape, community infrastructure, watersheds, and cultural traditions all interact and shape each other.[6]

Writers have argued that the importance of *place* in education has been overlooked for multiple reasons. In American society, for example, we have become "de-placed people for whom our immediate places are no longer sources of food, water, livelihood, energy, materials, friends, recreation, or sacred inspiration."[7] The concept of place is contested especially by those who have been conditioned to value the abstract and general over the specific and particular. Furthermore, much of mainstream American educational curriculum has overlooked the history of the Indigenous peoples who have inhabited particular places and the oppressions they have endured in those particular places. So even place-based education as a movement seldom embraces the history of a place stretching back to Indigenous habitation of that place and how the Indigenous people who were native to that place became displaced. If education is to be transformative, then these oversights must be corrected.

Place-based learning builds strong and healthy communities because it helps people learn the skills of paying attention, of noticing strengths and concerns, of asking probing questions, of discovering what makes the place unique, and of working to recognize and correct problems. "Getting to know home is the most human and necessary of occupations. To give that power of observation to students is to give them something of infinite value and importance—something to do with the rest of their lives."[8] Place-based learning can enable inhabitants to invest in actions that transform a space into a place, contributing to so-called placemaking.[9] This approach involves healing the damaged relationships between different people groups, recognizing that our identities are shaped by the landscape and places where we live. Educational theories abound that suggest ways to capture students' imaginations and spark their interest, but learning to care for the people and the place is of foundational importance. As Wendell Berry suggests,

> Education in the true sense, of course, is an enablement to *serve*—both the living human community in its natural household or neighborhood and the precious cultural possession that the living community inherits or should inherit. To educate is, literally, to "bring up," to bring young people to a responsible maturity, to help them to be good caretakers of what they have been given, to help them to be charitable toward fellow creatures. . . . If this education is to be used well, it is obvious that it must be used some *where*; it must be used where one lives, where one intends to continue to live; it must be brought home.[10]

Learning to care about what is important in one place is often transferable knowledge for learning to care about other places, so in that sense place-based education is not parochial. What is most important is helping students learn to notice and pay attention to what is close at hand and then learn how this place is connected to every other place. Place-based education helps students connect knowing and doing, learning with action. If the aim of education is to develop a human being capable of serving the common good and not just his/her own private self-interest, then education must do more than offer classes on disparate topics, hoping that students will become good citizens and good workers afterward. Writers Matthew Bonzo and Michael Stevens argue, "Education for the sake of creating producers and consumers for the global economy is a very different end from producing members for a healthy local community."[11]

Place-based education has been enacted by educators in the Plaster Creek watershed as illustrated by examples shared during oral history interviews with retired and current teachers. PCS has followed these educators' example, using the local watershed as a context for educating students of all ages—in elementary, middle, and high schools, in college classrooms, and in community education efforts. We envision this work as bringing together theory and practice, serving the dual purpose of teaching important content while simultaneously helping people learn what is unique to this place and what specifically can be done to protect and restore it. To build a healthy community, people and other living creatures cannot flourish unless the place where they live is healthy and thriving as has been taught by North American Indigenous people.

The Watershed as a Learning Laboratory for Local Classrooms

From the beginning, education has been a hallmark of the work of PCS. Since 2009, PCS staff have visited dozens of classrooms in local public and private schools to introduce the watershed concept as a meaningful lens through which to teach course content. Creating age-appropriate learning activities for students in preschool through high school along with accompanying restoration activities that match the learning has been an exciting aspect of PCS's work. Setting in motion an investigation of the Plaster Creek watershed—its problems as well as its strengths—has had wide-ranging results. Students and teachers in K–12 settings have learned basic watershed ecology, the relationship between upstream and downstream communities, and how to restore damaged urban waterways by implementing green infrastructure. Combining academic content with restoration action, either on the school property or at another location within the watershed, has provided many rich learning experiences. We have also led teacher workshops to design curriculum using the watershed as the context for teaching. When local schoolteachers move beyond merely inviting PCS staff to teach in their classrooms and instead teach the content they gleaned from a PCS workshop, this becomes a tangible measure of progress. Helping teachers recognize the role their schools can play in serving the community is an important outgrowth of the teacher workshops and helps advance place-based learning.

> We contend that schools occupy places, not spaces, and a worthwhile question to ask is, how can education happen such that the place in which it occurs is enhanced because the learning happens *there*? Another way to think about this is to ask: Are the residents, businesses, farmers, churches, or apartment dwellers grateful that they are located near your school? Is the neighborhood or environment within which the school exists utilized in ways that enhance the education of the students? And is the learning that the school promotes done so in a way that benefits the broader community to which the school belongs?[12]

Teachers can shape learning activities that open their students' imaginations to things previously not noticed and can play an important mentoring role in their students' lives. Several conversation partners in the oral history project mentioned a teacher who impacted their lives when they were students, and only now as adults do they realize the significance of what the teacher taught them.

One respondent talked about coming back to Grand Rapids after years of study and work in another part of the country. When he visited Plaster Creek, he was surprised by how much it had changed. Yet his earlier education helped him understand what he now saw.

> I took an environmental science class when I was a senior [in high school], and I *loved* that class. . . . After being educated and coming back and seeing what was happening, you start to add it together and you're like, "This is not natural, this is something that is human caused." When it rains, we would see the water levels rise . . . very quickly, exponentially. I remember driving across the bridge [over Plaster Creek] and looking down there after it rained and you see it's this chocolate-milk-looking, churning river. It was a creek turned into a river. . . . And when we'd get longer periods of rain it would even rise up and over the banks and flood the whole forest in there. I remember seeing that several different times when I was a kid. . . . And the banks of Plaster Creek have just eroded away at a very high rate.[13]

What this watershed resident had learned as a child in school in the Plaster Creek watershed provided a basic understanding that has helped him interpret what he was seeing now as an adult.

Interesting stories emerged from teachers in local K–12 schools who have used the Plaster Creek watershed as a learning laboratory for their students. Several long-retired former teachers, who were interviewed as part of the oral history project, described rich learning opportunities for their students when they decided to move their classes outside and make the landscape and watershed the setting for their students' investigation. One retired teacher described using a local park through which Plaster Creek flowed as a hub for some of his classroom activities.

> I'd have to go back to the very late sixties—1968, 1969, in there. I looked for a place to bring students from school to do a variety of outdoor activities. The spring wildflower show there is just incredible. And birding is very good in the spring especially. During migration periods, it is excellent. . . . Over time I really began to use that place as an educational venue. I would bring my students there every year for wildflower walks . . . leaf collections, and you know, there were trees there, like the pawpaws and the black maples, that are not so common elsewhere.

> And so, we would use the place, usually in the spring or right at the end of the school year. . . . We just really enjoyed the place.[14]

One of the most inspiring teachers remembered by several of our interviewees taught at a public school near Plaster Creek in the early 1960s. We want to share his story in detail because it has the potential to inspire others to replicate in their place what he developed at his school. He recognized a unique opportunity and immediately went to work to pursue it.

> I went to Ken-O-Sha School in 1964, the 64–65 school year. So [the stories I will tell you] happened between September of 1964 and 1970. . . . When I was a teacher at Ken-O-Sha we were told that there was a limit on how close anyone could build next to the creek in our area—because of the area being [a holding spot] to prevent flooding in the city of Grand Rapids. . . . We were told it would never be built on. Because I had done some travels to national parks all over the West, I had been on hikes with a ranger, and they would identify the flowers and the trees and the animal markings. Kind of a nature walk. . . . I saw that whole large area—it had to be over a hundred acres right next to the school practically and it kind of drops off there down into the Plaster Creek drainage. The school is back away from the creek. So, I thought, here is a perfect place for the children to learn some science. . . . I decided we are going to have a trail here for the children to see all the spring flowers that come up and where the sapsuckers have drilled into the trees to get the sap. We are going to see where the creek has eroded the banks away and where it is building up on the other side and learn about stream erosion.[15]

This teacher developed a creative sixth-grade curriculum by laying out a trail, marking numbered posts to introduce his students to the flora and fauna of the surrounding area, and eventually he trained the sixth graders to be tour guides at the nature trail. Other school groups and community groups were invited to come out to walk on the nature trail, and the sixth graders were the hosts. In this way, students and community members began to learn about Plaster Creek and the changes brought by the seasons. Often in March or April, when snow melts and spring rains come, there were (and still are) huge volumes of water that flow through this section of the Plaster Creek watershed. For many residents, this was invisible to them. By creating a nature trail and involving sixth-grade students in teaching about it, community awareness was heightened. There's more to the story.

> The Park Department started to come out with chainsaws and cut down dead trees. And I would have to call the school district and the Park Department and say "Wait a minute! You're cutting down some of the houses where the woodpeckers are living. You're cutting down our nature trail." And believe it or not, it went on for three years. And finally, I said to the kids, "We are going to do something . . . we are going to petition the City Commission of Grand Rapids to designate this a nature center, that cannot be touched without everybody agreeing to what's going to be done." We drew up the petition. I took a group of our student council students down there, one kindergartener, one first grader, one second grader, right on up to sixth grade. And they all made a little plea in front of the City Commission. The reaction of the first commissioner was, "I could not have said this better than you did. I cannot believe that you have to do this. We should have done it ourselves a long time ago. Why didn't we see it? We are glad that you saw that this would be a wonderful place to keep natural." So, it was declared the Ken-O-Sha Nature Center.[16]

What is impressive about this initiative is not just the increased understanding of science that the sixth-grade students developed, but also what they learned about citizenship and their sense of agency to create change. Their learning was multidimensional and multidisciplinary. As we shall see, it had a lasting influence on some of the sixth graders who came through Ken-O-Sha School between 1964 and 1970. Eventually this teacher became a principal, and the school expanded to include a fifty-thousand-square-foot addition for special needs children. The school had to consider how to make the nature trail accessible for all of its students.

> We had a meeting of the sixth graders and said, "We want students in wheelchairs to be able to enjoy the nature trail. It wouldn't be fair for all of us to be on it and they can't, so let's see if we can pave it." So, we came up with an idea that we would give every elementary school a chance to pave twenty-five feet, and we would paint that school name, "Paved by Burton Elementary" or "Brookside Elementary" on the pavement. One of the kid's parents worked for the newspaper and got wind of this, and then the television people got wind of what we were

> doing. Out comes the newspaper, out comes the TV crew. And the TV people had us take one of my students, who was in a wheelchair and try to push him down the trail. The camera showed the wheels digging into the dirt and it was kind of muddy in spots and I was having a horrible time pushing it. Well, when that hit the 6:00 news that night I got a call from a company that said, "You let us know how much money you did not raise from the elementary schools. We are going to pick up the rest." So, it was a do-it-yourself project. We had the excavation people come out and dump the hot blacktop on our noon hour. We shoveled it into the wheelbarrows, and we spread it along the trail and raked it out. We had a roller to roll it smooth. So, we did that several noon hours until we got the whole quarter mile trail paved . . . the students did it! The kids that later came in wheelchairs could whip right down the trail. So, things just kind of snowballed. And of course, we had the grand opening of the nature center. There was a huge crowd there for that—the superintendent of the schools and the mayor and a lot of speeches. The whole deal and we cut the ribbon![17]

This history of Ken-O-Sha School demonstrates the integration of the curriculum where biology, geography, civics, and even introductory sociology were incorporated into the elementary school curriculum. A courageous teacher who was willing to innovate, follow the interests of his students, and connect them to the larger needs of the community led to some amazing outcomes. Environmental awareness was raised, the valuing and protection of natural areas was advanced, citizenship skills were introduced, and classroom learning and community issues were connected. One of the most rewarding outcomes is to hear from former students who were impacted by their earlier education experiences. This teacher concluded his oral history interview by saying,

> I just got an email from one of those students who went through the Ken-O-Sha Nature Trail. He is a professor at Princeton University now and just did a book for National Geographic on the universe. He is the head of a department there. And he was one of our guides on the nature trail. I mean, you never would figure little Robert would end up at Princeton. . . . Hopefully the nature trail had a little part in grooming him to understand the environment.[18]

It is remarkable that a student would reach out to a teacher forty years later. Obviously, his teacher had a lasting impact on this former student. This extended story about Ken-O-Sha School is a noteworthy example of a pedagogy of place. Place-based education at Ken-O-Sha School became a catalyst for the City of Grand Rapids to value this section of the Plaster Creek watershed and preserve it as a park in perpetuity. Another conversation partner remembered this teacher forty years after he had moved away. She still credits him for making visible this important creek and surrounding landscape, which has served as a magnet for many years now, drawing people of all ages to enjoy and protect it. "Ken-O-Sha Park is a sizable, pretty important piece of urban green space. . . . It has real value for city kids and adults to learn something about nature."[19] Another former teacher suggests that the trail in Ken-O-Sha Park "gives people not only access but also knowledge about it, just by walking in there. So people have, by their awareness, come to quote 'love' the place a bit more than what happened in the past. When I first started going in there, back in the sixties, I would very seldom meet anyone."[20] Now it is a well-used and well-loved park.

> Every time I am down there, I see somebody biking, walking, running, taking their dog for a walk. . . . It has enabled people to connect better with the watershed, to use it as a place to recreate. . . . Sometimes birding groups will go down there and use it for birding purposes. Other places have used it for educational purposes, schools.[21]

Today the forested floodplain along Plaster Creek near Ken-O-Sha School still exists. An exercise path extends for about a mile through the woods from the school to Eastern Avenue, as well as a mountain bike course on the north side of the creek. In 2021 the City of Grand Rapids completed major park improvements at Ken-O-Sha Park including a new natural playscape using recycled fallen trees, an outdoor classroom, new green infrastructure and daylighted stormwater, new accessible pathways, educational and wayfinding signage, and a nature amplifier along Plaster Creek.[22] The trail in Ken-O-Sha Park has been a magnet for years drawing neighbors to come near to the creek and enjoy it. We've seen Wendell Berry's phrase, "It all turns on affection,"[23] brought to life in these woods.

This forest also represents a high-quality natural area in the watershed and as such provides a valuable ecosystem model for guiding restoration efforts in other localities. The woods also provides literal seeds for our work, from which we grow native plants for other projects. And so, in very real ways, the remnant forest at Ken-O-Sha is acting as a mother ecosystem, by serving as both a reference community and a source of seeds for other projects in the watershed.

In addition to the examples set by these earlier teachers in the Plaster Creek watershed, we also have heard about creative learning experiences initiated by teachers in recent years in local elementary, middle, and high schools. One of the upstream middle school science teachers whose eighth-grade class was involved in the collaborative research project described at the beginning of this chapter reflected on what his students gained when the watershed was the context for their learning.

> The Plaster Creek watershed was a great context for project-based learning. Many of the students live in the watershed. Our school even has a small tributary of the watershed, flowing near our school [that] created a real context for our study. We were able to take what we learned in science class and apply it to our study of the creek multiple times through the year. Students showed increased understanding of the skills used as well as practiced realistic science rather than "recipe" style science labs with specific outcomes. Science is messy and the work with Plaster Creek Stewards helped students get in on the mess. Ultimately, students were able to use what they learned and share that information with a real audience. Students shared what they learned with the principal and a couple of board members as the school prepared to add on to the building. [The students could] share thoughts about increasing the building footprint and the parking lot. I think the best part was how real it was. The real context, the real audience we shared our information with, the real data that was not easy to interpret always and forced us to work through errors. All of this taught really valuable lessons about the process of science and the work that is done in science. [Because] the students shared with representatives from the school board and administration, I think it made it very real for students. A number of students showed skepticism of whether they would be heard. . . . A portion of the new parking lot has permeable surface. I do believe the students showing that they cared and bringing it to the [board's] attention played a role in that decision.[24]

The middle school science teacher in the downstream school also articulated the benefits he perceived for his students when place-based learning was enacted.

> I started engaging Plaster Creek as a regular part of my yearly science curriculum during my second year of teaching through an invitation from Plaster Creek

Stewards at Calvin. [I collaborated] with a teacher out at Dutton Christian School which is located upstream whereas the Potter's House School is downstream, close to where the creek flows out to the Grand River. I was intrigued by this connection, and we had students study water chemistry, physical characteristics, and stream biology at both of these locations to compare. What I appreciated was the actual meeting of these students who live in completely different neighborhoods interacting together. The value of having students learn about Plaster Creek is multifaceted. First, Plaster Creek provides a great example of the impact human beings can have on the environment around us. It provides students the opportunities to see how our actions can bring good or hurt—beyond the walls of our buildings. . . . The watershed provides great locations for students to ponder the beauty that was created and to see its value in being preserved and restored. It also provides great locations for students to come face to face with hurtful realities and to lament. [These learning experiences] also foster a sense of connection to a bigger world and even more, a sense of responsibility and duty toward this bigger world.[25]

One of this teacher's students articulated her concern and sense of responsibility in this way: "You may be thinking why somebody would do so much research and so much testing just for a creek that flows right behind our school. It's not just a creek. It's *our* creek."[26] Hearing directly from students is compelling—a growing affection for the creek has led to a growing sense of responsibility to take care of it.

Most of the schools we have partnered with have chosen to connect education with action. Some of the teachers have organized just their individual classes. Other teachers have organized their whole school to plant rain gardens or take other restorative action on school property. Some teachers have turned their focus beyond their schools to encourage restorative practices in local parks or other public spaces. A teacher from one of the schools that has worked closely with PCS for many years described what still keeps her excited about this work—teaching concepts about the watershed but also connecting them to concrete restoration activity in the school rain garden and beyond.

In our Earth & Space class, we spend some time learning about the hydrosphere. We open with the watershed puzzle activity (developed by Plaster Creek Stewards).[27] We discuss how all development is interconnected in a watershed and

> have a good conversation about social justice using Wendell Berry's Golden Rule, "Do unto those downstream as you would have those upstream do unto you." We discuss watershed vocabulary, and we always work on our rain garden at school. . . . I love giving students the chance to BE OUTSIDE in the watershed. I also love opening their eyes to the justice issues at hand. . . . My favorite is when students encourage their parents to get curbside rain gardens installed at their houses![28]

In addition to working directly with teachers and schools in the Plaster Creek watershed, PCS has also partnered with Groundswell, an initiative of Grand Valley State University College of Education. Groundswell supports K–12 educators in West Michigan to create opportunities for student environmental learning beyond the classroom.[29] PCS and Groundswell share a common commitment to promote community-based learning and student-led projects to protect the Grand River and the Great Lakes. PCS staff have been hired by Groundswell to provide teacher-education workshops, upstream–downstream consultation, and expertise on green infrastructure installation. The partnership that has emerged between these two initiatives at two different universities has provided valuable opportunities to nurture active learners and engaged citizens in our shared community.

Watershed Education in University Settings

In addition to working with local schools and teachers to create opportunities for place-based learning, PCS has also worked to introduce watershed topics into university courses in many different disciplines—geology, engineering, art, education, biology, poetry, and history. Numerous Calvin University professors have utilized the Plaster Creek watershed as a context for their teaching and research. We'll highlight three examples.

In an upper-level plant taxonomy course small groups of students generated botanical inventories of remnant sections of natural areas along the creek. They then analyzed these inventories using the Floristic Quality Assessment tool and compared their assessments to determine the relative natural quality of the sites.[30] Most of the sites were highly degraded, but the students did find several exciting discoveries during this work when they were able to identify two plants, threatened in Michigan, that are still present in a few remnants: beak grass (*Diarrhena americana*) and Virginia bluebells (*Mertensia virginica*). These findings have had relevance for establishing local conservation strategies.

In an introductory photography course, the instructor wanted her students to learn how to use light and dark and introduced the concept of a photogram, which is a photographic image made without a camera. It involves placing items on the surface of a light-sensitive material and then exposing them to light. For this project, the students used the root systems of Michigan native plants from the watershed to create their photograms. The native plants were collected and carefully washed clean by PCS staff, then later presented to the art students with a brief lesson on the environmental services provided by these native plants and their amazing roots. In the process of learning photography skills, art students also learned about the importance of the deep roots of native plants for healing a degraded landscape.

During the same semester an English professor teaching a poetry class introduced his students to the local watershed in a unit on nature poetry. Each student then crafted an original poem about Plaster Creek. These poems and photograms were part of an art exhibit, *Dwelling: Our Watershed in Image and Word*, held at the University Center Art Gallery to celebrate the tenth anniversary of PCS. Viewers were asked to consider, "What does it mean to *dwell* in the Plaster Creek Watershed and how can art play a role in helping us connect with our communities and the places we call home?" These creative class assignments help students learn course content while simultaneously learning how to care for their place. In the process of studying and conducting research in the local context, these university students learned about the problems that are plaguing urban watersheds. The knowledge and skills they gained apply not just in West Michigan but in other regions as well. University students come from home places throughout the world, and what is learned in one place is applicable and transferable to wherever they will find themselves in the future.

Interest in place-based education has led to invitations for PCS to speak at colleges, universities, and conferences in the United States, Canada, New Zealand, and Japan. In 2014 PCS received a Regional Centres of Expertise Award for Outstanding Flagship Project at the United Nations University conference in Okayama, Japan. These opportunities for collaborative learning have enriched the work PCS is doing in West Michigan and hopefully influenced higher education in other regions to focus more attention and resources on healing their local places.

Watershed Education and Outreach in Community Settings

When we launched this work to restore the local watershed, we didn't have language yet for how to practice reconciliation ecology in a particular place. But we did know that we wanted to reach beyond the college classroom to influence the local community to help in this work of restoration. Knowing that people take care of what they love, we began to consider what residents need to know that will spark their affection for and motivate them to take care of their place. And we pondered how to educate community members in living well where they are for the benefit of all.

Starting in 2010 PCS began hosting community education events twice a year. These events have served as vital catalysts for community engagement in Plaster Creek restoration. We advertise these community education events through social media and email to residents who have asked to be added to our mailing list. Educational presentations have always been linked with opportunities for residents to take concrete restorative action.[31] At these events residents learn about some aspect of watershed ecology and then are given opportunities to take specific action to help restore the watershed: planting trees, installing rain gardens and bioswales, or stenciling storm drains with the message, "Dump no waste, drains directly to creek." These regular gatherings for education and action have proven to be effective in deepening community engagement among upstream, midstream, and downstream sections of the watershed. Showing maps during our educational presentations has helped residents to position themselves in relationship with others so they could see *where* they are in the watershed and begin to imagine how their behavior impacts others. When residents meet and get to know people who live in other sections of the same watershed, there is greater urgency to heal this damaged watershed because they have met real people whose lives are being affected. We are not just trying to heal the degraded watershed, but we're also trying to change the relationship people have with other watershed residents. A highlight of these community education and action events is that they attract all ages—college students, young families, professionals, retirees, neighborhood leaders. At one recent gathering we hosted participants who ranged in age from eighteen months to eighty-one years old.

A larger vision of upstream–downstream connections was facilitated by a grant from the Fulbright Canada Foundation. A Calvin geography professor, formerly a Fulbright scholar in Canada, applied for and received a small grant for building citizen understanding through upstream restoration activities in the Plaster

FIGURE 10. Diverse watershed residents working together with a common goal of healing the creek. PHOTOGRAPH BY GAIL GUNST HEFFNER.

Creek watershed. Plaster Creek contributes to pollution that impacts downstream ecosystems and human communities in two different countries. Ultimately, actions in the Plaster Creek watershed impact water quality in the Great Lakes and the St. Lawrence Seaway. This grant allowed us to frame our work in the watershed in terms of cross-border impacts and relations. To implement this Fulbright grant PCS hosted a public education event where volunteers planted trees and native plants in two new rain gardens in the Plaster Creek watershed. New signage paid for by the Fulbright grant highlighted the upstream-downstream nature of the cross-border connections. This grant demonstrated again that the basic watershed concept can be a powerful means to enhance place-based awareness and understanding of upstream–downstream relationships at all scales.

Generating Passion to Care for the Earth

Experience has shown us that without education, meaningful lasting restoration is difficult to sustain. External forces can overwhelm and undo progress that has been made because of the lasting legacy of de-placement ideologies that were introduced with colonization. Caring for the earth requires much more than words or ideas. It requires an ongoing commitment to keep learning about and recognizing the problem, acknowledging our role in creating and maintaining the problem, and being willing to take steps to change our ways of life to heal the problem. Author and educator Richard Louv writes,

> While knowledge about nature is vital, passion is the long-distance fuel for the struggle to save what is left of our natural heritage . . . to reconstitute lost land and water. Passion does not arrive on videotape or on a CD; passion is personal. Passion is lifted from the earth itself by the muddy hands of the young; it travels along grass-stained sleeves to the heart.[32]

Working with local teachers and schools has been an important way to influence human interaction with the living world and to build a movement of passion for watershed restoration. Engaging directly with community residents in education and action has been another way. We have learned lessons along the way that have shaped our approach and deepened our commitment to educating the public to care for that which is closest at hand. Authors Bonzo and Stevens argue,

> So our task becomes leading students toward health, a task that must be not only taught but also lived. Education isn't the only source of the problems, nor is it the solution by itself; educators cannot stem the tide of massive political and economic pressures. But it is a place where healing can begin, can be identified rightly and nurtured.[33]

Our work in place-based education with all ages of people essentially is about trying to answer a question posed by David Orr in *Ecological Literacy*: "How long does it take for one to learn enough about a place to become an inhabitant and not merely a resident?"[34] The contribution we, as educators, can make to helping people inhabit their place with intention and care and not merely live as passersby ultimately serves the common good—for both the living human community and the nonhuman community—in that particular place and beyond.

CHAPTER 8

Assessing the Problems with Applied Research

February 18, 2020, was a typical winter day for West Michigan, about twenty degrees Fahrenheit with eight to ten inches of snow on the ground. These aren't typical conditions for wading in a stream, but that's what my (Dave) students were doing to collect data on the health of the water flowing through Plaster Creek. In this biology class students are taught how to conduct scientific research by using the Plaster Creek watershed as a living laboratory. On this particular day, I split my class into two groups: one would do sampling above and below the road overpass at Eastern Avenue, and the other would sample above and below the road overpass just downstream at 28th Street. With this sampling design, the data collected could give indication of some of the winter contaminants that enter the creek from bridge overpasses, such as sodium and chloride from road salt. Although it was a cold day, students dutifully donned hip waders and proceeded to collect stream flow, water chemistry, macroinvertebrate, and *E. coli* data at their appointed sites.

The first indication that something wasn't right occurred when a student in the macroinvertebrate group asked if what they were finding was normal. When I looked at their kick-net (a one-meter-square wire screen attached to a wooden frame designed to capture aquatic insects) I saw bits of carrots and onions that were mixed in with wads of toilet paper and some other scattered debris. Surprised,

I responded, "No, this is not normal," and I wondered to myself if one of the restaurants upstream was illegally dumping food waste into the creek.

Later on that week we processed the samples in the laboratory, and as the class period progressed, a noxious smell emerged from the samples that had been refrigerated for two days, filling the windowless classroom with a putrid odor. The macroinvertebrate group had an extremely difficult time sorting out aquatic insects from the substrate material they had brought back because the smell was overpowering. Then word came back from the microbe group that they were tabulating extremely high numbers of *E. coli* (an intestinal parasite) at both of the 28th Street sites. What was especially interesting was that the groups that had collected samples from the Eastern Avenue sites were generating significantly different results, with much lower levels of *E. coli* and no vegetable fragments, even though these two locations are separated by only a half mile.

It turns out that the 28th Street groups found an average of nearly eight thousand *E. coli* colonies per 100 ml of stream water, over sixty times higher than what is considered safe for full body contact by the state of Michigan. This number also represents eight times the threshold of what is considered safe for even partial human body contact. We had never measured *E. coli* levels this high during the month of February before. Right away I contacted water quality staff in the City of Grand Rapids and the State of Michigan's Department of the Environment, Great Lakes, and Energy (EGLE). I was told they had been made aware, just days earlier, of a main sewer line break along Plaster Creek between the Eastern and 28th Street overpasses. They conveyed to me that efforts had been taken to divert that flow of sewage through a different series of pipes and that plans to repair the pipe were in place. I was also assured that no raw sewage was currently leaking into the creek and that *E. coli* numbers had already been declining and would continue to do so.

Without knowing it, I had assigned half of my students the task of entering this urban stream to collect data immediately below a site where raw sewage had been pouring directly into the creek. How long this contamination source had been active before it was noticed was not known. How many gallons of raw sewage had leaked into the stream was anyone's guess. Fortunately, we had taken appropriate precautions by wearing gloves and waders, and none of my students was adversely affected. But this laboratory activity did provide a valuable real-world learning experience. The students saw for themselves how degraded Plaster Creek has become and how it poses health concerns for aquatic organisms and for the downstream neighborhoods located along the creek—especially the children who are naturally drawn to moving water.

The following day I walked the stretch of Plaster Creek from 28th Street to Eastern Avenue. It wasn't hard to find the sewer line break. Because of the high-volume flow of the creek, excessive erosion had caused a large tree to fall into the creek. This tree slightly altered the course of the stream, directing even more flowing water toward the north creek bank. This alteration made the erosion even worse, and the soil underneath the sewer line (which runs parallel to the creek) had eroded away causing the collapse of this large cement pipe. There was still ample evidence of raw sewage around the site of the break.

Sometimes observations are straightforward: you look at a stream with chunks of vegetables and toilet paper in it and you know its health has been compromised. But often harmful effects are less obvious, and samples need to be collected and processed to help interpret what is going on. We also learn about a place through stories that accumulate over time as in the Plaster Creek Oral History Project. Indigenous people have learned so much about their places over centuries by living in the land, an understanding that is known as traditional ecological knowledge (TEK).

> TEK is deep knowledge of a place that has been painstakingly discovered by those who have adapted to it over thousands of years. . . . This realm has long been studied by disciplines under headings such as ethno-biology, ethno-ornithology, and biocultural diversity. But it has gotten more attention from mainstream scientists lately because of efforts to better understand the world in the face of climate change and the accelerating loss of biodiversity.[1]

TEK is a valuable way of learning how the world works and has much to contribute to Western scientific perspectives.[2] Unfortunately, during colonization TEK was devalued, and much of it was overlooked. More recently there has been a reawakening to its importance, and efforts to blend TEK with Western scientific traditions are growing.[3]

In my class the students had observational information (visual and olfactory) that something was wrong with the creek. We also had scientific data showing high numbers of *E. coli* bacteria, which we could not see or smell. Research done through Plaster Creek Stewards (PCS) has been informed by observing, collecting data, and interviewing long-term residents, but we have had far fewer opportunities to learn from TEK about Plaster Creek. Historical records have taught us some of the ways the local Ottawa interacted with this creek, and while we can tap into general Anishinaabe teachings about how to live carefully in the land, we have not been able to meet Native Americans whose families actually lived in the Plaster Creek watershed. Much of the TEK that accumulated from the long-term presence of people living in this place was lost when the Ottawa were forcibly removed from this landscape. The loss of the Indigenous people and their knowledge for how to live well in this watershed is cause for lament. Yet we hope someday TEK and Western scientific knowledge will become more integrated in this place, contributing to the healing of Plaster Creek.

Scientific Research—Listening to Creation

In her *Braiding Sweetgrass* chapter "The Honorable Harvest," Robin Wall Kimmerer highlights her personal relationship with wild leeks. When she goes out to harvest leeks, she asks the leeks if it is a good time to collect them. By observing how many leeks are present in a population and what their bulbs look like when she examines them, Kimmerer essentially interprets the answer that the leeks are giving. She emphasizes that in the relationship between people and creation, it is important for people to listen to what creation is telling us.[4]

Scientific research is a way of listening to the world around us. By observing carefully, formulating questions, and designing experiments, scientists are taking part in what amounts to a conversation with the natural world. At times our experiments essentially poke the creation here and prod it there to see how it will respond. Researchers document the conversation as it progresses by collecting data. By analyzing the data, we are effectively translating what the natural world is telling us into terms that we understand. To achieve a healthy human–creation relationship, it would be foolish for humans not to pay attention to this conversation.

The restoration activities of PCS are informed by research that has been undertaken by many different faculty and students from multiple disciplines. Some of this research has been done as part of a class laboratory or longer-term project. Other research has been conducted during the summer by faculty members with student research assistants. The oral history research project was a multiple-year study that collected information and stories about the creek and its impact from more than eighty-five different individuals. The findings from these research projects have been important in guiding PCS restoration activities. All of these research experiences, essentially these human–creation conversations, help us learn more about of the particulars of this place.

Research as Part of a Class

The students who were collecting Plaster Creek samples below a sewer line break were part of a Research Methods class. This is the final required class in a four-semester core sequence for biology majors at Calvin University.[5] This class was first introduced in 2011 and was designed in response to an increased emphasis in higher education to involve undergraduate students in problem-based, real-world research. In this class students learn how to conduct research by planning and carrying out, in small groups, a research project focused on the health of Plaster Creek and its watershed residents. At the end of each spring semester, these projects are each summarized into a written scientific paper and presented in a public forum.

Although the research projects conducted by these second-year students occur for only one to two months in early spring, they have provided helpful insight for understanding the condition of the creek. In some cases, these short classroom-based projects have led to grant-funded research projects or responses from local jurisdictions. As one example, in 2015 a group of three students did a water chemistry project where they took multiple samples from small tributaries flowing into Plaster Creek in different areas of the watershed. They compared the water quality of these tributaries to water from the main channel of the creek. What they found was somewhat alarming because one of the tributaries was significantly different than the others and carried high levels of pollutants. At the completion of this project, I emailed the student report to city and state authorities, explaining that we found "peculiarly high levels of fluoride, sulfate, phosphate, and low dissolved oxygen and pH in one of the tributaries. This study was only done in early spring. Although it's not a publishable study, I can attest that the data reported are accurate." This student report elicited a rapid response by the Michigan Department of Environmental Quality (MDEQ), which included maneuvering a small video camera up into a pipe that was draining runoff into this particularly polluted small tributary. With the help of this camera, MDEQ discovered that one of the nearby industries had an unapproved hookup to a pipe that

FIGURE 11. Calvin University students researching macroinvertebrates in Plaster Creek.

PHOTOGRAPH BY DAVID P. WARNERS

was disposing hidden chemicals into the tributary. The practice was immediately halted, thanks to students who completed a classroom-based research project.

Other classes at Calvin have focused on Plaster Creek for a lab, a series of labs, or a project. Chemistry students have measured and compared water quality variables in the creek at different locations. A geomorphology class has dug soil pits to assess soil layers at different places in the watershed. Learning about soil layers has helped us determine specific types of green infrastructure that fit particular areas of the watershed. Geography students have done numerous projects that have contributed to a geographic information system (GIS) database. In a Social and Cultural History class students explored the history of land-use patterns within the Plaster Creek watershed, researching farms, industries, neighborhoods, parks, and schools, and their findings offered a historical portrait of life in the Plaster Creek watershed over the past eighty years. One of the themes emphasized in this course was how social history brings to light stories that traditional historical narratives often overlook. Engineering students have done several class projects that have informed later restoration work: a preliminary hydraulic model for a section of Plaster Creek flowing through a condominium association that resulted in projects to reduce runoff and erosion; a hydrology assessment for a local ice arena parking lot that resulted in solutions to improve infiltration; a design for managing a six-acre church site, highlighting ways to reduce runoff to the rapidly eroding ravines of a local tributary. These class research projects are all examples of engaged teaching and scholarship that make real-world contributions to restoring local land and water.

Summer Research

While these student research projects have yielded interesting and helpful information, classroom-based contributions are limited in terms of duration and time of year. Other research projects have been done by faculty working with a student or a small group of students during the summer. These projects are funded either with external grants or internally through Calvin's summer research program.[6] We'll describe four types of summer research within the Plaster Creek watershed that have been conducted by Calvin faculty and student assistants: hydrology modeling, bacterial contamination, relative success of native plants, and the impact of restoration efforts on waterborne pathogens.

Understanding Runoff through Hydrology Modeling

A stream is an incredibly dynamic system, changing over the span of years in response to local land-use activities but also changing hourly in response to rainfall and snowmelt events. A watershed system also shows variation in its responses across space, with some areas contributing more runoff, nutrients, or pollutants than other areas. One way to understand these dynamics is with computer modeling. The U.S. Army Corps of Engineers Hydrologic Engineering Center, Hydrologic Modeling System (HEC-HMS) is one approach that looks at an entire watershed and predicts how quickly rain that falls in different locations will make it into the main creek channel.[7] Some of the tributaries drain larger areas, while other tributaries drain much smaller subbasins. Some tributaries drain forested land while others primarily drain roads and parking lots. The HEC-HMS model that was done for the Plaster Creek watershed in 2015 and 2016 was put together by two civil engineering professors along with engineering students.[8] These researchers used information provided by a Calvin geography professor who had delineated twenty-four subbasins in the watershed using GIS. Each of these subbasins essentially represents a miniature watershed nested within the Plaster Creek watershed.

The HEC-HMS Plaster Creek model has helped inform PCS staff where runoff hotspots are located, enabling us to focus our restoration efforts and justify proposed projects in grant applications. This approach was used to focus on a smaller section of the watershed in 2017 by modeling a two-block area in an urban residential neighborhood. This study estimated the amount of stormwater runoff from this area that occurred under presettlement conditions and compared that volume to what is entering the creek today from this same area with its current impermeable roadways, sidewalks, driveways, and rooftops. Because we had been installing curb-cut rain gardens (CCRGs) in this neighborhood the researchers also modeled how much our efforts had made a difference. These CCRGs are similar in size, installed between the sidewalk and the street, and collect rainwater from street gutters. Out of these calculations it was estimated that if one in every eight homes in this two-block area were to install a CCRG, the amount of runoff into Plaster Creek would be equivalent to presettlement times. These results helped us visualize the impact CCRGs could have. Based on these findings PCS produced an informative and inspiring educational video to encourage residents to install

CCRGs in their front yards.[9] Many have chosen to be one of the homes on their block that is part of the stormwater runoff solution.

Investigating Sources of Bacterial Contamination

Understanding runoff volumes is extremely useful in planning for restoration projects, but one of the major health hazards of this creek is something you cannot see. From class research projects we learned that even without leaking sewer lines, levels of *E. coli* bacteria are consistently high and always increase after it rains. Depending on the intensity of the rain event and the time of year, *E. coli* levels in the aftermath of a rainfall event are typically much higher than the Michigan standards that have been set for safe full and partial body contact.[10] This pattern tells us that stormwater runoff is carrying *E. coli* into the creek whenever it rains. *E. coli* is a bacterium that resides in the digestive tract of animals, and it doesn't live for very long outside the body of its host animal. In other words, when high levels of *E. coli* are detected, it means that animal waste has recently been washed into the creek. The public health concern is that when there are high levels of *E. coli* in open water systems like Plaster Creek, those who come into contact with that water are more likely to contract an infection themselves—either through small cuts on their skin, or internally by inadvertently ingesting the *E. coli*. Furthermore, high levels of *E. coli* are likely coordinated with high levels of other microbes that can also make people sick.

When high levels of *E. coli* are detected, another question arises: Where is it coming from? One aspect of this question is to determine where geographically in the watershed the bacteria are coming from. Another important question is what creatures in those areas are contributing to the *E. coli*? To begin addressing these questions, a disease ecologist at Calvin undertook a research project with students in 2015, which was partially funded by MDEQ. This project spanned two summers and included five Calvin students, additional staff and faculty from Calvin, and four amazing sewage-sniffing dogs from Environmental Canine Services.[11]

This study initially focused on ten main tributaries that drain into the central channel of Plaster Creek. Weekly samples were collected from each tributary upstream of where they joined the main channel. Researchers found that *E. coli* levels fluctuate widely across sites and especially over time. Across the ten locations, the average lowest concentration of *E. coli* was 220 colony forming units (cfu) per 100 ml. By contrast, the average highest concentration across the ten sites was nearly 13,000 cfu/100 ml. Wet conditions (soon after rain events) always had higher levels of *E. coli* than dry conditions (at least forty-eight hours since a rain event), and most samples had *E. coli* concentrations much higher than the maximum allowed levels for partial (1,000 cfu/100 ml) or full body (130 cfu/100 ml) contact. In fact, the overall average value for each of the ten sites was considerably above these thresholds. These results were conclusive that fecal contamination is an ongoing problem in this creek and that it is coming from multiple sources.

Based on the initial sampling, the six most contaminated tributaries were identified and investigated further with more refined techniques for better understanding the animal sources of the contamination. Using a more sophisticated test called qPCR it was determined that two of these tributaries were positive for human bacteria at multiple sites, and three other tributaries were positive for both human and ruminant sources (meaning cattle or deer). The following year water from four of these tributaries was evaluated by scent-trained dogs who can detect the presence of human waste in surface waters. These sites were also analyzed again with the qPCR testing. Results showed that human waste was a major contributor in all four tributaries, but human sources were joined by ruminants in three of the tributaries, by canines in two, and by Canada geese in one of the tributaries.[12] What has become clear through this work is that there are multiple sources of contamination even within a single tributary and it is difficult to pinpoint all the sources. A major recommendation from this study was to carefully check all sewer lines that parallel the tributaries and main channel. As was illustrated with the opening story of this chapter, sewer lines often follow the lowest contours of the landscape, which is where water is often running. Leaks in these pipes often enter directly into a waterway.

Evaluating Which Native Plants Grow Best in Urban Places

Another research focus has been to study which native plants provide the most benefit in green infrastructure projects. PCS has installed more than 130 urban CCRGs in residential neighborhoods of the watershed. The precise species composition of a CCRG is planned and designed by PCS staff together with homeowners who are ultimately responsible for taking care of the garden. Since the native plants used in these gardens are put into a highly altered and continually disturbed site (grit from roadways, fertilizers from lawns, salt in winter, etc.), it has been hard to anticipate which species will grow best.

We conducted a systematic study of eleven CCRGs installed in 2015. Student researchers visited the gardens and assessed each species patch for survivorship and performance. Survivorship was simply the number of plants that were still living in year two compared to the number that were planted initially. Performance was quantified as a value between 1 and 10 where 1 was barely noticeable and 10 was thriving. Twenty-one different native species were included in this assessment, and when the results were plotted onto a graph, we were able to differentiate four groups.

Those with both high survivorship and performance are species we can count on to do well with little additional care. Those with low survivorship but high performance are species that possibly need to be planted initially at higher densities if we want a full thriving patch. Species that have high survivorship and low performance may need more than one year before they really look good. And those that have low survivorship and low performance are probably not well-suited to these novel habitats or, if truly desired, may need some extra care for them to do well.[13]

As this study was unfolding, we realized that while survivorship and performance are important variables to evaluate, there is more information we need to think about with these plants. The reason rain gardens are constructed is to help process stormwater runoff, so we also wondered which species are best at reducing water volume. The physiological process of plants taking water into roots, moving it up through the stems and passing it out of small little pores (stomata) on the leaves is called transpiration. With a highly sensitive instrument called a porometer, we are able to measure the rate at which water is being passed out through the surface of a leaf. It turns out not all species transpire similarly. These data were collected over three different summers (2017–19) between 10:00 a.m. and 2:00 p.m. on days when there was full sun. Some days the soil was moist because of recent rains, other days things were very dry, but what we found surprised us. The data were clear that there are consistently fast transpirers and consistently slow transpirers, regardless of conditions, and the rate at which they move water from the soil to the air varied tenfold. The species that seems to move water from soil to air the best is butterfly weed, a showy, orange-flowered milkweed that is somewhat challenging to work with (low survivorship), but clearly an important plant to include in these gardens.[14]

The porometer has also been put to use in a research project that was set up with the Kent County Drain Commission in 2020. Thanks to a grant from the Great Lakes Restoration Initiative and the U.S. Forest Service, we were able to plant over two hundred trees along a section of Plaster Creek called Schooley Drain. This tributary is in the far upper reaches of the watershed and has been straightened for much of its length as it passes through farm fields. The section of Schooley Drain we focused on has stream banks that have become covered with an invasive grass called reed canary grass (*Phalaris arundinacea*). This aggressive species grows down into the channel and impedes the flow of water, which results in flooding, necessitating regular dredging. Reed canary grass does not grow well in shade, so together with the Kent County Drain Commission, we wondered which native tree species are best at both transpiring water and at discouraging reed canary grass.

Seven tree species were chosen for this experiment: sugar maple, red maple, tulip poplar, sycamore, hackberry, bur oak, and swamp white oak. Trees were planted in same-species clusters of four. The dataset we have begun to build will take a few years to complete. We will be evaluating the trees for transpiration rates as well as survival and performance, and we will also be measuring the productivity of reed canary grass in the middle of the four-tree clusters. In the meantime, as the trees mature and our dataset grows, this section of the creek will become increasingly shaded and the water will be cooled, a stream corridor will be developing, insects and birds will be returning, more water will be intercepted by tree roots, and less water will be transported downstream. Sometimes the applied benefits of research can be realized even before research findings have been fully analyzed.[15]

Retention Ponds and Waterborne Pathogens

Another research question we've studied is how restoration activities influence waterborne pathogens like *E. coli* or other dangerous bacteria. Two Calvin professors and a colleague from Duke University along with Calvin students explored this question by studying the inflows and outflows of Kreiser Pond, a retention basin in the Plaster Creek watershed that had been the site of an early restoration project by PCS. Retention basins are holding areas for excess stormwater runoff that usually maintain some standing water even during dry times. With this study we were assessing the impact of our own work, specifically the impact of this project on *E. coli* and other potentially hazardous microbes. Yet our question had broad relevance: When water washes into retention ponds do these microbes simply die in these holding areas or can they be retained and passed downstream during times when stormwater runoff is high? Previous reports in the scientific literature have been inconclusive.

The research findings from Kreiser Pond very much supported the earlier findings that bacteria concentrations varied widely between dry and wet periods. Whenever it rains, the density of bacteria increases dramatically in the tributaries feeding the pond and in the pond itself. And, consistent with previous studies, these researchers also found that the levels far exceeded what is considered safe for human contact. A new finding, however, was that during dry periods, fecal contamination as indicated by *E. coli* numbers declined in Kreiser Pond, suggesting that this method of addressing stormwater runoff also helps to control *E. coli*. One rather alarming discovery, however, was that much of the *E. coli* that were cultured from Kreiser Pond were resistant to multiple different antibiotics. So this work reinforced that Plaster Creek contains alarmingly high levels of bacteria that can cause dangerous infections to those who come into contact with the water, and it showed that many of these bacteria are resistant to the antibiotics that would be used to combat such an infection.[16]

Trying to understand *E. coli* and other microbial constituents of the creek has been an important line of research for PCS. Through this work we have learned that there are multiple sources of microbes in Plaster Creek—geographically and biologically. We have also learned that green infrastructure projects like Kreiser Pond are an effective way to not only decrease the volume of water that flows into Plaster Creek, but also decrease the prevalence of *E. coli*.

Student Reflections

The involvement of students in research has been invaluable for helping PCS design and implement restoration strategies. Students have been helping us listen to the creek and learn from the land, which can lead to changes in the way we live our lives. Our students have also told us that in the process of doing research, they have been impacted and changed as well. To more fully understand this dynamic, we asked some current and past student assistants to describe the impact doing this research has had on them. Student response was overwhelming. Beyond just a sentence or two, many students wrote extensive, thoughtful descriptions of how their research experience has informed the way they understand the world. These experiences are happening at a time in the lives of these young people when their understanding of the world and how it works is expanding rapidly. Therefore, their involvement in a community-based effort like PCS becomes a significant event in their life journey as they are learning how to become contributing members of society. The stories that students relayed clustered into four broad areas, which we highlight below.

Interconnections

Nearly all the students indicated some level of appreciation for learning more about how interconnected everything is. Here are excerpts from two different students:

> It has first and foremost demonstrated that every single part of the environment is connected through the watershed—city schools, suburban mansions, and manure-fertilized fields all come in contact through the water in the creek. Seeing hundreds to thousands of *E. coli* growing on plates from the creek has helped me realize that every little part of the world is connected, and that such connections can be deeply harmful.

> Conducting interviews with people from all walks of life gave me a deeper appreciation of how the natural world weaves us all together, even in cityscapes. I also realized that people's perspectives about the natural world are very much shaped by their geographical context. For example, community members who lived in the headwaters generally had more positive things to say about Plaster Creek than those who lived downstream in more polluted and industrialized reaches of the creek. Overall, my experience with Plaster Creek Stewards helped me connect to a basic, but oftentimes neglected truth: we have an obligation to restore damaged ecosystems, not only for the sake of the creatures living

within them, but also for the physical, mental, and spiritual health of human communities.

Environmental Justice

Some of the students developed a deeper understanding of environmental racism and the need for environmental justice because they were able to see it firsthand. Three of the students wrote:

> Working to restore the watershed helped me better understand the upstream-downstream disparities that exist in my own city, and it prompted me to grapple with my own privilege and how it extends even to my relationship with the environment.

> Working for Plaster Creek I was able to see social injustices, ravaged ecosystems, people who cared, and people who didn't. From that I began to understand a worldview that involved creation care as a key part of a Christian's journey and that this was the direction I was being called to.

> The research experience at Plaster Creek Stewards opened my perspectives to the opportunities within environmental justice. . . . Implementing education for the youth, community organizing, research, and ecological restoration could come to fruition under inspiring leaders. . . . [This experience] has inspired and encouraged me to be part of such movements.

Vocational Direction

As hinted in this last excerpt, several students noted directly how the research experience was pivotal in their vocational understanding. Here are four responses:

> My work with PCS opened me to the possibilities of advancing environmental research and was a pivotal factor in my decision to pursue a master's program

> in which I could build more research experience to aspire to a profession in restoration ecology.
>
> Ultimately, working for PCS was one of those "I get it" moments where a lightbulb goes off over your head like a cartoon character, and I now can see more clearly the path I want to go down as I get ready to graduate and begin my career.
>
> Research work with PCS . . . has allowed me to concretely pursue my vocational journey as an educator in science. I was a bit hesitant when I first applied for the mentor position with the Green Team, but it has strengthened my ability to . . . promote educational and restorative practices.
>
> Seeing how daily practices affect both stream and human health, and its implications on environmental justice issues in our communities, guided me in my decision to become an environmental toxicologist one day. I am really grateful for this opportunity as it has left a beautiful mark in my life.

Cross-cultural Interactions

For others, the opportunity to interact with diverse groups of people—both on campus and in the community—was the most impactful. Two of the students responded with these insights:

> Watching a recently planted rain garden fill up with water or hearing the excitement in people's voices as we explained our work to them are experiences I'm not likely to forget soon. I also had the opportunity to connect with so many different people. The summer crew I worked with was fun, persistent, and diverse, which made my work with PCS all the more valuable. I learned so much about not only watershed restoration but other people and worldviews and I'm so grateful for everything that job taught me.
>
> One of the greatest impacts it had on my vocational work was getting me out of my comfort zone, and . . . talking to people of varying ages and of different

> walks of life. Up until then, I mostly interacted with people from Calvin, which is a pretty small circle.

Each of these student comments reveals evidence of a deepening understanding of reconciliation ecology, not just in theory, but also in practice.

Research Can Transform Both People and Place

Science has historically been portrayed as an unbiased enterprise where researchers are purely objective participants in the process. But the research work that has occurred as part of PCS's efforts has drawn students who see the creek less as an interesting focus of intellectual investigation and more as an environmental and human health concern that pulls at their hearts. Furthermore, in the process of paying attention to the creek, listening to what it is telling us through the data that are collected, and translating that information into hands-on restoration efforts, the researchers themselves become changed for the better. When done well, community-based research can help to heal the place where the work happens, and it has the potential to transform the people who do the work.

CHAPTER 9

Reconciling the Human–Nature Relationship through On-the-Ground Restoration

In the midst of working on this book, I (Dave) spent the better part of October 13, 2020, collecting native seeds with my Plaster Creek Stewards (PCS) colleagues. This is a practice we do throughout the growing season, but one that becomes more focused during autumn when most native plants in West Michigan are producing ripe seeds. When collecting native seeds, we make sure to do so judiciously, never collecting more than 10–20 percent of the seeds in any given population. Harvested seeds are overwintered outdoors in small cloth bags for at least three months, which helps to break dormancy. In late February we begin bringing the seeds inside our greenhouse for germination. To find local genotypes of native plants we visit a variety of nearby remnant natural areas: wetlands, woodlands, and open prairies. Given that prairies were an unusual habitat type in this region, relegated to well-drained soils on west- and south-facing slopes, and only in areas that were regularly burned (as the Ottawa did), there aren't many high-quality prairie sites available today for collecting.

Yet, as described in the story about the Black Hills, we have found native prairie plants can persist in areas where utility line right-of-ways cut through woodlands, especially when the soil is sandy. The power companies don't burn these linear openings, but they do occasionally mow them to keep out woody plants, offering something of a substitute for the historical controlled fires. And so it was that we found ourselves in one of these power line right-of-ways on a beautiful sunny October afternoon with the bordering oak and maple forests beginning their colorful autumn transition.

We were excited to happen upon one section of high-quality prairie remnant in this particular right-of-way, covered by little bluestem, broom sedge, and three-awn grass accompanied by butterfly weed and rough blazing star. But as we walked downslope, this remnant prairie patch abruptly gave way to a weedy collection of nonnative plants including sweet clover, knapweed, ragweed, motherwort, and nightshade. Moving into this weedy spot we started to make sense of why this patch was here. There were new telephone poles that had recently been set in place, with mounds of gravel at their bases. The heavy equipment used to position the poles had seriously disrupted and recontoured the ground, conditions that made it difficult for native prairie plants to persist, but a perfect situation for weedy plants to gain a foothold.

At the bottom of the slope, we came upon a curious ditch, apparently caused by drainage during times of heavy rain. Surprisingly, the ditch banks were not completely covered by weeds, but included large patches of lady fern, wood fern, and other native plants. These plants may have emerged from spores and seeds that had been stored in the soil for years and recently exposed by erosion caused by the drainage. We also noticed that the soil here was not sandy like the rest of the area, but looked dark and fertile, likely owing to the low-lying moist conditions. On one of the banks of this ditch I saw a large clump of a sedge, and when I made my way over to it and looked closely, I found long flowering stalks that still retained some ripe seeds. This sedge was not one that I recognized immediately, so I collected a few stalks for a confident identification later. We looked around carefully, up and down the ditch, but did not see any additional plants of this species, just one clump.

The rest of the afternoon the identity of that sedge festered in my mind. There was only one plant, it didn't look at all like the more common sedges I have come to know here in West Michigan, and it was growing in this curious, highly altered spot. What could it be? Later that evening I consulted the sedge key in my *Michigan Flora* text, and with the help of a microscope was able to learn its name: *Carex virescens*, the ribbed sedge. Further investigation revealed that this species is not common in Michigan, having only been documented in nine of the eighty-three counties in our state.[1] In Kent County there has only ever been one official documentation. And when I looked up the details of that record, I learned that this singular collection had been made back in 1897 by Emma Jane Cole.[2]

Following in Emma's Footsteps—A Trailblazer in West Michigan in the Early 1900s

For anyone who is involved in field botany in West Michigan, Emma Cole is a patron saint. She was raised just outside Grand Rapids in the mid-1800s, during a time when very few women were entering science. She excelled in her high school classes and later in her botanical studies at Cornell University.[3] After returning to West Michigan she taught biology at Grand Rapids Central High School. In 1901 Emma Cole published a book, *Grand Rapids Flora*, that describes many areas around the city where she visited with students and made herbarium collections of plants.[4] Emma Cole was the first paid employee of the Kent Scientific Institute, which later became the Grand Rapids Public Museum. Dr. Garrett Crow, botany professor emeritus from the University of New Hampshire, and I (Dave) have been involved in a project with the goal of visiting all the sites that Emma Cole described in her book to provide an update on how these former gems of biodiversity have changed over the past 120 years.[5] Across the state of Michigan, Kent County is known as a very well-documented county botanically speaking, largely because of all the work that was done by Emma and her students.

Much of the emphasis of our PCS restoration work is to create green infrastructure projects like rain gardens, bioswales, and floodplains that will assist in retaining and filtering stormwater runoff. We do this restorative work using native plants that because of their local adaptations, are the best candidates for successful reintroduction to watershed localities where they used to grow. Native species are also the best plants to use for attracting native insects and birds that are supported by their foliage, flowers, fruits, and seeds. These coinhabitants of the Plaster Creek watershed have in the past been pushed aside to make way for people and for urban and agricultural development. Nearly all native plant species in West Michigan have been in decline since Emma Cole's time. In fact, already in 1901, she wrote how discouraged she was by the lack of concern for preserving West Michigan's natural communities.[6] Because native plants have been declining steadily over the decades, as a consequence native insects and birds are also being lost.

By working to restore health and beauty to the Plaster Creek watershed, we offer a counternarrative for the West Michigan landscape—a new approach where humans welcome back, coexist with, and gain multiple benefits from the diverse species for whom these landscapes were home long before we called it ours. To do this we collect seeds from native plants, sometimes quite rare native plants such as *Carex virescens*, and help enhance the chances that their lineages will be perpetuated into the future. It has been exciting to discover connections with trail-blazing, like-minded countercultural voices of the past like Emma Jane Cole.

The Role of Green Infrastructure in Watershed Restoration

Since colonization, environmental services the land had been providing were lost through massive land conversion and biodiversity reduction. By shifting the view of "water is life" to perceiving water as a problem that needs to be managed and controlled, wetlands and floodplains that removed sediments and absorbed stormwater were replaced by gutters, drains, pipes, and dams that contributed to the degradation of streams and rivers. Ecological restoration emerged as a discipline in response to this widespread environmental damage, to assist in the recovery of ecosystems that have been damaged, degraded, or destroyed.[7] Green infrastructure is an important watershed restoration tool to help bring environmental healing especially in areas where gray infrastructure has been causing environmental problems. When done well, green infrastructure is a great example of reconciliation ecology because its goal is to bring back natural habitats that were destroyed during colonization and European settlement. Re-creating wetlands, restoring floodplains, and daylighting streams are hopeful actions demonstrating that humans *can* make room for native biodiversity to return to the places where it previously thrived.

Types of Green Infrastructure Projects Undertaken in the Plaster Creek Watershed

The green infrastructure projects we have introduced in our watershed restoration efforts have focused primarily on reducing stormwater runoff because this is the trigger that causes so many other problems. Therefore, we can achieve multiple benefits for the watershed when we capture stormwater and let it soak into the ground instead of allowing gray infrastructure to convey it rapidly into the creek. Our green infrastructure projects are all different versions of a simple strategy to diminish the amount of water that makes its way into Plaster Creek whenever it rains. One benefit of installing green infrastructure is that volunteers of all ages can assist, from collecting seeds to transplanting seedlings in our greenhouses to planting native plants in community locations. By learning more about their home watershed, and by working on solutions side by side with fellow watershed inhabitants, residents are learning how to better care for their place and each other.

Rain Gardens

Rain gardens are typically small basins located in a place where stormwater runoff can collect. Residential rain gardens are often located at the base of downspouts or where they can collect water from the drip line of a rooftop. A tricky aspect of designing a rain garden is to make it big enough to meaningfully capture water when it rains but not so big that the plants need to be watered in between rain events. We design our rain gardens to handle a heavy rain event that typically happens every two years. An important consideration when doing this planning is to know what type of soil underlies the garden. Water will percolate into sandy soil more quickly than clay soil. We try to prevent water remaining in a garden long enough to create a mosquito breeding ground. To properly design the size of a garden considering soil conditions and the volume of water coming in, there are rain garden calculators that even nonengineers can utilize.[8]

In the early 2000s the nonprofit group Huron Pines incorporated over one hundred rain gardens into residential and commercial areas of Grayling, Michigan, as part of a stormwater project to keep stormwater runoff out of the Au Sable River.[9] These dished-out rain gardens were positioned between the sidewalk and street and collected stormwater runoff from the street gutters by way of a cut that was made in the cement curb. While teaching Restoration Ecology at Au Sable Institute in the summer of 2010, Dave's class was given a tour of the stormwater project in Grayling by Huron Pines staff. Using lessons learned by the efforts of Huron Pines in Grayling, we began our own curb-cut rain garden project in the

FIGURE 12. Promoting the benefits of rain gardens.
PHOTOGRAPH BY GAIL GUNST HEFFNER.

Plaster Creek watershed in 2015. By 2024 our total count of curb-cut rain gardens in southeast Grand Rapids surpassed 130, with more planned for the future.

Our curb-cut rain garden project, funded by EGLE (Department of Environment, Great Lakes, and Energy), has mainly targeted two downstream urban neighborhoods that have sandy soils to maximize the potential for success. Sites are selected through careful criteria, including volume of water that can be captured at a particular site and homeowner interest and willingness to provide ongoing maintenance. Since these curb-cut rain gardens are installed in the tree lawn near the street, we work closely with the City of Grand Rapids for easement permission. Each homeowner who meets the criteria is invited to help select plants for their garden and must agree to maintain the garden after an initial year of assistance from PCS. This project has been a wonderful way to engage the community and bring native plants, insects, and birds back into residential neighborhoods. The curb-cut rain gardens have also provided great opportunities for doing research.

Bioswales

A bioswale is essentially a very large rain garden. Bioswales are often designed to collect stormwater runoff from parking lots, allowing the water to soak into the ground and to be taken up by plants before flowing into a local waterway. Our first large bioswale project was constructed on Calvin's campus in partnership with Calvin's Ecosystem Preserve and Native Gardens. The horseshoe-shaped vegetated basin collects water from a two-acre parking lot and slowly moves it through thick stands of native plants and three small check dams before it has a chance to enter a raised storm drain from which it flows into Whiskey Creek, a tributary to Plaster Creek. Prior to the construction of this bioswale, also funded by the Michigan Department of Environmental Quality (MDEQ), rainwater from the parking lot had eroded a steep gully, introducing high volumes of parking lot runoff and sediment directly into Whiskey Creek. The bioswale now captures that runoff, causing much less rainwater to flow into Whiskey Creek, and the runoff from this parking lot that does eventually reach Plaster Creek is much cleaner. Where there was once a thick stand of invasive buckthorn shrubs, there is now an open diverse meadow that processes stormwater runoff. The thousands of plants needed for this bioswale were planted by hundreds of volunteers who now have a connection with this restoration site and the biodiversity that continues to thrive there.

Retention and Detention Ponds

Large-scale approaches to dealing with stormwater runoff typically include retention and detention ponds. These are areas set aside to collect stormwater runoff in large volumes. Retention ponds (also referred to as wet ponds) are engineered to retain standing water between rain events. In this way, when rain happens, the influx of new runoff moves through a retention pond and is unlikely to resuspend the sediment that collects on the bottom of the pond. A detention pond (or dry pond) is engineered to slow down the drainage of stormwater, usually drying out in between rain events. This delayed runoff helps reduce the surge of peak flow that enters a main waterway, spreading the volume out over time, and diminishing the erosive force in the main channel.[10]

Both retention and detention ponds lessen the threat of flooding in downstream communities after major rain events.

PCS has been working for multiple years now with the Kent County Drain Commission (KCDC) on a large retention basin called Kreiser Pond in the Silver Creek subwatershed of Plaster Creek. This retention pond was originally excavated to accommodate excess runoff from Silver Creek during times of heavy precipitation. The partnership with KCDC began in 2011 when they asked us to help with plans to expand the size of Kreiser Pond. We worked with KCDC to modify the basin so it would hold more water. KCDC provided the excavation work, and PCS provided the native vegetation to help capture stormwater. We also enhanced the surrounding area with native plantings, largely in response to local neighbors who complained about the huge population of giant ragweed that had proliferated. This site has become an important outdoor classroom for local schools and a valuable focus point for educational tours and volunteer workdays for tree planting with local residents. Over time school groups and neighbors alike have reported a dramatic increase in the diversity and abundance of birds and insects in this urbanized greenspace.

Permeable Pavement

Another green infrastructure strategy that we promote allows stormwater to percolate into the ground even while it is on a hard surface. Permeable or pervious pavement is a new approach to urban planning where hard surfaces are engineered in a way that water can pass through their surface into a catchment area below. This green infrastructure option does not have the biodiversity benefits of rain gardens and bioswales, but it can be extremely effective at reducing runoff while still allowing hard surfaces for parking lots or roadways.[11] One of the churches we partner with has a permeable parking lot that has served as an example for other locations in the watershed. Permeable pavement is becoming an important strategy for minimizing runoff and retaining stormwater on site. In 2022 PCS received an exploratory grant from EGLE to develop detailed plans and identify possible sites for retrofitting parking lots with permeable surfaces. This appears to be a very promising future direction for our work.

Floodplain Restoration

Healthy floodplains are absolutely essential to having a healthy creek. Floodplains are natural landscape features that border most waterways and collect overflowing water during times of high volume. Once water enters a floodplain it slows down, and when water moves more slowly, it cannot carry as much sediment. Therefore, floodplains are areas where suspended sediment drops out of moving water and where floodplain plants reduce water volume through their important work of transpiration. The water that emerges below a healthy floodplain will be both cleaner and of lower volume than the water that entered the floodplain upstream.

With high peak flows erosion happens not only from stream banks, but also from along the bottom of a stream. This type of erosion results in a downward cutting that causes a creek to become progressively lower relative to the surrounding land, which means even more volume is needed before the creek can overflow its banks and enter a floodplain. When less water enters a floodplain, more water is transported downstream, stimulating erosion in other places. Additionally, many floodplain habitats have been converted into residential neighborhoods that are directly damaged by periodic flooding. Retention walls and berms are often constructed to keep water out of former floodplains, which only passes that volume and energy downstream where it will cause additional erosion in a damaging negative feedback loop.

Floodplain restoration is the largest and most ecologically complex type of green infrastructure project we have undertaken in the Plaster Creek watershed. Our first floodplain restoration project was in the upstream reaches of the Plaster Creek watershed at Shadyside Park. When the park was developed the floodplain at this site had been cleared and planted into lawn. Erosion was decimating this area, and the stream had cut downward, resulting in steep drop-offs to the creek adjacent to playground areas frequented by children. The restoration plan we developed with a local civil engineering group involved hiring an excavating company to decrease the height of these banks, essentially contouring a new floodplain that the creek would overflow into more frequently. In partnership with the Kent County Parks Department, we planted this new floodplain with over seventy thousand native plants, including more than two hundred trees along the top of the slope for additional soil protection, enhanced percolation, and to support more biodiversity. Today heavy rains will fill this entire floodplain with water, creating what looks to be a temporary pond. When this happens the water that disperses out of the creek channel into the new floodplain encounters native plants and it slows down. The slower water can't keep as much sediment suspended, and so the floodplain has become an important space where sediment is taken out of the creek. One extremely gratifying outcome of this restoration project is the gravel bars that have appeared in the main channel. Prior to this project the substrate in the main channel was sand and topsoil that had washed down from upstream agricultural areas. Today this sand and topsoil are accumulating in the floodplain, and the main channel's gravel bars can support a much healthier community of stream insects and fish. On a recent visit we were delighted to watch a large water snake hunting these gravel bars, a scene that would have been highly unlikely prior to the implementation of this project.

Growing Native Plants for Restoration Work

Over the years we have developed a protocol for germinating, transplanting, and raising the native plants that are needed for watershed restoration. Each year PCS staff collect seeds from more than four hundred different species. Originally these seeds came from remnant natural populations in West Michigan, but as we have installed more green infrastructure projects, these restored sites have themselves become important seed sources for our work. To induce the seeds to germinate, we have found it works best to store them in cloth bags in a refrigerator until mid-November, when we put them outdoors for about three months of winter weather. We mix the seed bags with soil, mimicking the natural conditions that native seeds would normally experience. In mid-February we bring the bags into our greenhouse, thaw them, and begin planting the seeds into open flats of potting mix soil. We have found the best germination occurs when the seeds aren't covered with soil. Instead, we just spread them out on top of the soil, being sure to keep the soil moist and warm. Most species will germinate within two weeks after they have been planted.

This process works for approximately 80 percent of the seeds that are collected. Each year we try treatment variations for species that don't seem to germinate well with this general approach. One of these alternative treatments utilizes a series of raised beds into which we directly plant the seeds in the fall. This way the seeds are not spending the winter inside cloth bags, but instead they

FIGURE 13. The first step in propagating native plants for restoration is collecting seeds.
PHOTOGRAPH BY GAIL GUNST HEFFNER.

are directly in the soil. Some of these raised beds have very rich topsoil, some have sand, and some are a mix of sand and topsoil, and we are trying different species in these different soil types. One group of seeds that are always challenging to germinate are those that occur inside fleshy fruits. These fruits are usually eaten by birds or mammals and then passed through digestive tracts that subject them to all kinds of chemical exposures. Trying to unlock the secrets of some of these hard-to-germinate species has been a great research activity for students in Biology 250 or for those doing internships with PCS. Over time we are creating a highly useful data set on seed germination treatments for West Michigan native plants.

After a few weeks of growth, the successfully germinated seedlings are transplanted into thirty-eight-cell plug flats. This is time-consuming work, and to keep up with the pace of projects we have in the summer, we need over one hundred flats transplanted per week (about 4,500 individual plants). This work is particularly conducive to volunteer assistance and is often done by groups of volunteers, PCS staff, and summer college and high school students cooperatively. Transplanting seedlings is a great example of an activity that while tedious, can be lots of fun when undertaken by a group of people. Once plug flats are filled with

FIGURE 14. After seeds sprout in the greenhouse, seedlings are transplanted and eventually moved outside before installation in green infrastructure projects.
PHOTOGRAPH BY GAIL GUNST HEFFNER.

new seedlings, we keep them in our four-season greenhouse where they receive lots of tender loving care. After several weeks, these flats are moved to one of our two "cold-frame" or three-season greenhouses. These greenhouses are a step closer to real-world conditions with ambient temperatures similar to the outdoors, and where swinging doors are kept open to expose seedlings to wind, which helps to strengthen them. After spending a couple weeks in the cold-frame greenhouses, we move the flats outdoors into our range, which is a shade-netted area of raised pallets. Here the seedlings are subjected to natural outdoor temperatures, wind patterns, and rain. The only protection they receive is the netting that blocks about 50 percent of direct sunlight. When there isn't rain, they receive supplemental watering. After a few weeks in the range the flats are ready to be moved out to project sites for out-planting. This system keeps us supplied with plants for green infrastructure projects throughout the summer and into the fall. What began in the early 2010s as a small operation has now become a successful process for growing thousands of native plants per year. Our plant propagation work requires concerted effort, but it is a magnet for drawing community volunteers.

Helping to Heal People's Relationship with the Earth

Working with native species that have been germinated from locally collected seed adds a great deal of meaning to our PCS work. In most cases, when we are installing a garden or bioswale with native plants, we know the specific local sites where these plants came from. When we collect seeds from remnant natural habitats that have been around for centuries, we are tapping into plant lineages that date back to days when the Ottawa first inhabited these lands. Controlled burning, a practice modeled by Indigenous people, has become an important tool for us in promoting the success of restored habitats while discouraging nonnative invasive species. We have also been inspired by the stories of Chief Blackbird and the historical accounts of the beauty of the Black Hills, which itself has become an important source of native seeds for our plant propagation work. By bringing native plants previously tended by the Ottawa back to our West Michigan landscape, we are honoring the sustainable way the Ottawa lived. This decolonizing approach is one way to put the concept of reconciliation ecology directly into practice.

The palette of projects available to help Plaster Creek ranges from floodplain restorations that can take years to plan and install, to rain gardens that by contrast seem tiny in scale. Yet every example of capturing stormwater, allowing it to soak into the ground, and letting the native plants do their good work of processing that water and enhancing diversity makes a difference. By intentionally including watershed residents in this reconciling work, we are growing better relationships, human and more than human. These examples of hands-on restoration can be implemented in any watershed or landscape. Green infrastructure implementation contributes to reconciliation ecology and helps to heal people's relationship with the earth. People and creation can return to a coexistence that promotes mutual flourishing.

CHAPTER 10

Loving Our Downstream Neighbor—A Call for Environmental Justice

My surprise caught my attention. I (Gail) was walking with a small group of Plaster Creek Stewards (PCS) staff along a highly industrialized section of Plaster Creek in the downstream reaches of the watershed. We were noting that the creek looks different here compared to other sections—more channelized, lots of broken concrete, steeply cut banks, and lots of trash. This section of the stream makes it easy to believe that Plaster Creek is the most contaminated waterway in West Michigan. We were talking about how high levels of bacteria (though not visible) brand Plaster Creek unsafe for even partial body contact, making it hazardous for swimming or even touching.

And then we rounded a bend and there before us were two people fishing in Plaster Creek. I didn't expect to see them. I didn't expect to find anyone interacting with the water along this section of the creek. These two people appeared to be a grandfather and his young grandson relishing a quiet moment together—one generation teaching another generation the skill of fishing. It could have been a scene from a classic American childhood. But they were *fishing in Plaster Creek*.

In that moment I made a number of assumptions. I assumed they lived near the creek because they were African American and African American communities are prevalent in this part of the city. I assumed they were low-income because the man was fishing rather than working on a weekday. And I assumed they did not know the creek was contaminated with multiple bacterial pollutants. I knew they were putting themselves at risk, and I felt an internal tension. Do I speak up and say something about the contaminated creek? Do I interrupt their quiet time together with disturbing information?

In the instant that my mind wrestled with whether to speak up or remain silent, I also knew this was not an isolated incident. People are drawn to water—to its sights and sounds, to the way it reflects light and creates shadows, to its cool feel on the skin. In the Bible water is intended as a provision and as a delight. Psalm 46 reminds us that "there is a river whose streams make glad the city of God" (v. 4). Yet here in Grand Rapids there is a river whose streams cause harm.

Observing firsthand the surprising sight of the boy and his grandfather interacting with this urban creek in a way that could bring them injury woke me up to what has often been invisible to me. Some people, particularly many Black and brown people, do not enjoy the benefits of a vibrant, healthy place to live. People like me—white, educated, and middle-class—who do have the privilege of living in healthy places, often don't realize this privilege is not available to everyone. Witnessing with my own eyes people who live in my city enjoying the calm and beauty of the flowing water, without adequate knowledge of how this might put them in harm's way, made the issue more real. It put a face on the reality that people of color in the United States are disproportionately impacted by environmental degradation. And it made me ponder new questions: Why are some neighborhoods safer, cleaner, and more desirable than others? Why do Black and brown people in the United States experience more environmental risks than white people? What can be done about this inequity? And it reminded me again that communities are interconnected and interdependent, especially when considered within the context of a watershed. What happens in one place always affects how things happen in another place. To this day, I still think about the conflicted emotions I felt seeing people fishing in Plaster Creek, and I regret that I didn't engage them in conversation about the risks they were facing.

The interdependency we all experience in our lives is sometimes obvious and sometimes catches us by surprise. We are always upstream from some and downstream from others, no matter where we live or work. This is true for water in watersheds, but it is also true in the way goods and services, products and waste, are consumed and dispersed in our daily lives. Recognizing this interdependence is crucial to the work of reconciliation ecology. Typically, we care about what happens upstream from us and the way it may impact our lives, but we think less about our impact on those downstream from us. This lack of attention to downstream impacts can lead to environmental injustice. Environmental injustice has been documented as an outgrowth of environmental racism. First, we'll consider how race intersects with environmental issues and we'll examine environmental racism in general. Next, we'll consider how leaders of color organized a national environmental justice movement in response to environmental racism. Finally, we'll turn our attention to the Plaster Creek watershed and the relationship between upstream and downstream, illuminating the connection to environmental justice. We'll hear stories from the oral history project to show how awareness of upstream–downstream connections varies widely among watershed residents. We then describe our approach of fostering upstream–downstream connections as an important initial step for promoting reconciliation ecology.

Environmental Racism

Concern for a healthy and safe environment has been a topic in an expansive body of literature for more than sixty years. But only since the early 2000s have scholars systematically explored how race and ethnicity are related to environmental concerns. An examination of the racial structure in the United States has led researchers to uncover differential economic, social, political, and even environmental rewards to groups along racial lines. Sociologist Eduardo Bonilla-Silva writes

> When race emerged in human history, it formed a social structure (a racialized social system) that awarded systemic privileges to Europeans (the peoples who became "white") over non-Europeans (the peoples who became "nonwhite"). Racialized social systems, or white supremacy for short, became global and affected all societies where Europeans extended their reach. . . . A society's racial structure [is] the totality of the social relations and practices that reinforce white privilege.[1]

Racialized societies, such as the United States, are *organized* by a racial hierarchy. This view emphasizes that racism is more than personal prejudice against one people group by another. Racism is also structural and institutional and has been documented in all aspects of American life.[2] Environmental racism is one example of institutional racism.

Environmental racism is a combination of prejudice and the power to implement decisions and policies that defend, protect, and enhance the social positions and quality of life of whites at the expense of people of color.[3] Environmental racism also includes processes that disproportionately result in minority and low-income communities facing environmental harms and limited environmental benefits.[4] As such, environmental racism exists in subtle and not-so-subtle ways throughout the United States, resulting in people of color being more burdened by pollution, contamination, and other environmental problems when compared to white people.

Communities of color experience more exposure to environmental hazards and risks that create health problems because of the unequal environmental burden these communities bear.[5] Communities of color have also been targeted as sites for incinerators, landfills, garbage dumps, and other waste facilities. An early study, *Toxic Waste and Race*,[6] conducted in 1987 by the Commission for Racial Justice, found that race was the single most important factor (i.e., more important than income, home ownership rates, or property values) in the choice of location for toxic waste sites. In other words, environmental inequities are not primarily the result of economic factors. "Institutional racism influences local land-use policies, industrial facility siting, and where people of color live, work, and play."[7] It is not a mere coincidence that communities of color end up getting all the garbage dumps and waste facilities. This is environmental racism.

Addressing Environmental Racism by Promoting Environmental Justice

People of color began organizing to address environmental racism in the 1970s and 1980s. These initial organizing steps laid the groundwork for an environmental justice (EJ) movement that blossomed by the 1990s and early 2000s. An EJ framework was adopted to uncover the assumptions that contribute to unequal environmental protection in our society.[8] The EJ framework argues that all individuals have the right to be protected from environmental degradation and adopts a public health model of prevention to eliminate the threats before harm occurs. The EJ framework also shifts the burden of proof to polluters or others who do harm, and finally it redresses disproportionate impact through targeted action and resources. Environmental justice asserts that all people and communities are entitled to equal protection under the law for environmental, health, employment, education, housing, transportation, and civil rights. The EJ movement uncovers underlying assumptions and conditions that contribute to and produce differential exposure and unequal protection. Seeking environmental justice has become a central concern for all those who want to address and eliminate environmental racism.

The U.S. Environmental Protection Agency defines environmental justice as "the fair treatment and meaningful involvement of all people regardless of race, color, national origin, or income with respect to the development, implementation, and enforcement of environmental laws, regulations, and policies."[9] Environmental benefits and burdens must be shared equitably. No people group should bear a disproportionate share of environmental risks or consequences. One important premise of the EJ definition is that those who are most impacted need to be included in the consideration and decision-making about options to address the problem. Philosopher Gretel Van Wieren writes,

> What voices are not at the table and why? Are there ways in which decision-making processes and procedures are developed and enacted that marginalize certain individuals and groups? Who decides in the first place who will participate, and according to what criteria? And how and why is this or that ecosystem or particular area of land chosen for restoration in the first place? To these ends, careful and sustained attention to the *process* of and *procedures* related to assisting the recovery of ecosystems is required when justice concerns are considered.[10]

In other words, environmental justice means that the people most impacted by environmental threats or risks are able to make their voices heard and share in decision-making that will improve their lives and communities. Too often people of color have not been taken seriously when they speak up about environmental health and sustainability.[11]

In 1991 the first People of Color Environmental Leadership Summit was held in Washington, D.C. Indigenous leaders present at this summit were not satisfied with catch-all language for all people of color groups and pressed for a greater level of inclusion for Indigenous concerns, framing environmental justice in terms of colonial histories of oppression and domination. Different conceptions of justice exist in the EJ movement, and Indigenous leaders argue that there are important distinctions between Indigenous people and other people of color. Indigenous scholar and author Dina Gilio-Whitaker explains,

> Too often Indigenous conceptions of justice—and Indigenous ways of understanding land and human relations with it—are obstructed or not recognized at all. . . . Indigenous nations in North America experience numerous barriers to their participation in the governance of environments. . . . The very thing that distinguishes Indigenous peoples from settler societies is their unbroken connection to ancestral homelands. Their cultures and identities are linked to their original places in ways that define them. . . . In Indigenous worldviews, there is no separation between people and land, between people and other life forms, or between people and their ancient ancestors. . . . Potawatomi scholar Kyle Powys Whyte refers to these interconnections as systems of responsibility. . . . Whyte notes that environmental injustice occurs when systems of responsibility between humans and the land are disrupted through the processes of colonization.[12]

Part of the problem in addressing environmental injustice is that it is too easy for most people with privilege who are in positions of power to focus merely on their own self-interest and to disregard dangerous situations others may face. Because these environmental threats are often distant or invisible, they are seldom recognized as environmental injustice and thus they are ignored by many white people. Very few Americans have any concept of how their decisions, actions, or behaviors can impact positively (or negatively) those around them.

Upstream–Downstream Awareness and Action in the Plaster Creek Watershed

Writer Norman Wirzba argues that what we don't see, we don't care about. He is arguing essentially that people have developed an "ecological amnesia" because of how we have learned to live in the world:

> Cities have existed for a very long time, of course, but today's cities are historically unique because of their large size, which tends to insulate inhabitants from

> agricultural and ecological realities. This means that the people living in them have no understanding or appreciation for the ecological contexts and responsibilities that make their living possible. Today's forms of urban and suburban life make it likely that people will not appreciate where their food and energy come from and what processes have been used to make them available. They may not understand how easily ecological systems can come to ruin. This is problematic because what people do not see and understand they will less likely value and protect.[13]

This is true for watersheds too. What people don't see, they don't care about. When people living downstream in a watershed fail to understand the life experiences of people living upstream in a watershed, it is easy to point fingers and blame them for the problems experienced in the downstream areas. Similarly, when people living in the upstream sections of a watershed fail to see and understand the life experiences of those living in the downstream sections, their actions can create disastrous effects, even if it is more through ignorance than malicious intention. Wendell Berry offers words of wisdom on this:

> People who live at the lower ends of watersheds cannot be isolationist—or not for long. Pretty soon they will notice that water flows, and that will set them to thinking about the people upstream who either do or do not send down their silt and pollutants and garbage. Thinking about the people upstream ought to cause further thinking about the people downstream. Such pondering on the facts of gravity and the fluidity of water shows us that the golden rule speaks to a condition of absolute interdependency and obligation. People who live on rivers might rephrase the rule in this way: Do unto those downstream as you would have those upstream do unto you.[14]

In the downstream reaches of the Plaster Creek watershed, occasional signs warn residents that it is dangerous to wade, swim, or even touch Plaster Creek as it flows through their neighborhoods. We asked conversation partners in the Plaster Creek oral history interviews what they knew about upstream and downstream relationships in this watershed; their responses varied widely, and some were quite striking. Some of our conversation partners showed little awareness of anything beyond their own immediate small world. Others had a vague but intuitive sense of the relationship between upstream and downstream, vocalizing a simple awareness that their lives are impacted by the people who live upstream from them. A few conversation partners described a deep recognition that their actions impact those who live downstream and articulated an ethical responsibility to take better care of the water not just for their own sake but for the sake of others as well.

One of our interviewees suggested that most people don't think about downstream impacts because they can't see a river or creek from where they live. "Most people don't even think they affect anything. . . . They live in their own little world, and even people who can see the river every day don't acknowledge it. So, if you're far enough away that you can't see the water . . . upstream-downstream doesn't matter. [People assume], 'I don't affect it because I can't see the water anywhere.'"[15]

Exploring public perceptions of the Plaster Creek watershed, we asked, "Do you ever think about where water goes after it leaves your property?" Most had little to no awareness of what happens to water when it leaves their property or their local park or school. One elderly individual who grew up in a rural section of the watershed explained it like this: "I didn't know where Plaster Creek went. I did know that it came into the Grand River. But our little world was just from a little north of 68th Street to maybe two miles south beyond that. I didn't know what happened to it after it left us."[16] Another respondent replied, "I guess I've never really thought about it. No. You kind of live in your own little world, right? You think about where it's coming from . . . because your kids are playing in it and then . . . it goes *somewhere*."[17]

A middle-aged man, whose family lived for multiple generations near Plaster Creek in different sections of the watershed, reminisced, "We used to think that if we were upstream in this big woodsy area, we thought that the creek kind of came out of like a pure woods where you could almost drink it or something. And then I was shown these pictures of way upstream, with cows standing in the water, and the creek going through farms. So there is probably a lot more that went on upstream than we ever knew about."[18]

Some of our conversation partners described being aware that what happens upstream does affect them, and they commented particularly on the polluted nature of Plaster Creek. Some respondents described bacterial contamination coming from upstream dairy or horse farms; some respondents described seeing a sheen of oil on top of the water; others described a chemical odor. One respondent has noticed *all* of these issues in her observations of Plaster Creek over the years she has lived near the creek:

> We were concerned with where [the water] was coming from because . . . we knew that it was coming from the horse pasture, and we were getting a lot of farm residue and stuff in there. So that concerned us, because it was right where the kids were playing. . . . When they played at the park, we could see that it wasn't just the normal color. . . . Sometimes it would be really, really gold. Rusty. And sometimes it would just have a chemical smell, especially after it rained. . . . And sometimes it would have that sheen to it on the top. It wasn't . . . normal.[19]

It is perfectly understandable and appropriate to care about the water your own children are playing in. But how can that concern be extended to care for other people's children who are playing in the creek downstream? How do we foster a genuine responsibility for the common good and not just our own children?

Another conversation partner from a rural, now suburbanizing section of the Plaster Creek watershed described how his awareness has grown over the past twenty years. He described how upstream areas affect downstream areas in this way:

> Because I live in the country, I look at it from the perspective, maybe, of the farmers. And the farmers don't pay attention to what's going on downstream. They know they have to keep the creek cleaned out (and I'm talking in general from the two or three little tributaries that I'm most familiar with). . . . They need to keep the brush cut down so that their land stays dry, so that they are able to do their farming. That is their focus. I don't really see any efforts that I am aware of, that farmers are worried about runoff, either from the fertilizers that they are using or from the "natural" fertilizer. There's a lot of cattle in the Dutton area where the waste is flowing into the creek. So I guess I don't see the farmers, the landowners being really aware of what's going on out here in the country affecting the urban setting in Grand Rapids as the water flows through. . . . You know, I don't see people intentionally trying to harm the waters. But I don't see a whole lot of awareness per se that what we are doing out here at the headwaters is affecting the people in Grand Haven. But Plaster Creek flows into the Grand River, into Lake Michigan, and we end up drinking it. Twenty years ago, I never paid attention to that, but realizing today that I am called to be a steward of God's whole creation. What I am doing in my little spot is affecting other people. . . . In my area I don't think the suburban dwellers realize what we are doing or not doing is really affecting the people farther downstream.[20]

Because watersheds are nested, what happens in the Plaster Creek watershed affects the Grand River, which affects Lake Michigan, which affects all the Great Lakes, all the way to the St. Lawrence Seaway and to the Atlantic Ocean. We are all interconnected. Some of our interviewees articulated a richer understanding of this relationship between upstream and downstream.

> I now know that when you see all the sediment in there, it is not just *that* creek. It is going to Lake Michigan. So, I understand the connections now and how all those pollutants that are on the streets—the oils and things leaking out of cars and the trash and whatever—that doesn't just wash away. It goes somewhere downstream. It goes to somebody's section of the creek that *they* visit. It affects the wildlife out in the Grand River and the water quality of Lake Michigan even.[21]

Part of understanding the relationship between upstream and downstream is acknowledging personal complicity and not merely passing the responsibility on to others. One respondent lamented that it's easy for downstream people to place responsibility for the problems of Plaster Creek on the upstream folks, not realizing downstream areas can be causing some of their own problems.

> Downstream [people]—they blame their problems on upstream. They're not understanding what their localized issues might be, causing some of their own problems. I think it's, "Oh, look, it's the people upstream that are causing the problems and not where we are"—not realizing by paving the area that used to be open or putting in new driveways or houses, that this causes more imperviousness, causes more runoff. I don't think they realize that—they think the only problem is still coming from upstream.[22]

Shifting Worldviews

We have seen evidence among some residents that concern for Plaster Creek and the Lower Grand River watershed is growing. Some of our conversation partners described how their perspective and worldview have shifted. The issue of environmental justice has become clearer to them, and they have been motivated to take action to promote reconciliation. One middle-aged conversation partner talked about living his whole life near Plaster Creek and how his view of the creek has changed over time.

> I grew up by it. I see the impact that it has on the area where I enjoy living. I enjoy the country. . . . I've lived here, I've gone to a church here all my life. I guess what really touches me is—if you were talking to me about a creek that flowed through Rockford or Cedar Springs, it wouldn't have that impact on me at all, because it doesn't affect me personally. Now that I am a stakeholder, Plaster Creek flows through my property and all this history that is over the last forty or fifty years, all these things come together. [To most] people in general, it's just a creek, it's always there and it flows. . . . It is the big picture, but it's also the little picture tied together. That is why I am concerned about Plaster Creek.[23]

A few of our conversation partners had a much fuller sense of the interconnectedness of people who live within the same watershed. A former employee of the Michigan Department of Environmental Quality shared an interesting history of Plaster Creek as they tried various ways to restore the damage being done to it.

> Plaster Creek was a real significant watershed in our learning as a program in the late eighties, early nineties—that helped set policy for the future. . . . It was very interesting to me to see how the early studies in the eighties about hydrology . . . [shifted the thinking from] the old way of doing business, which was to get the water away as fast as you can, in total disregard for what happens downstream. In my twenty-one years of working in the Grand Rapids district and caring about Plaster Creek, one of the things that was so important to me was the diverse ethnic culture. . . . It was the lower economic and certain ethnic groups who really don't have much political say that were being impacted. . . . So here we have great kids under the greatest social pressure and low economic [status] and with no voice, and they are the ones being the most impacted.[24]

A local pastor described his growing understanding of the upstream–downstream connection:

> When you are throwing stuff into a creek and it is going away from you, you never think about the consequences. But when it is coming toward you and you just can't stop it, you really care about what's in that creek. . . . You are completely subject

> to whatever the upstream person is putting in there because the creek only flows one way. Unless you change the person's heart upstream, there is nothing stopping what's coming toward you. That's helplessness and that's unjust.[25]

One interviewee described in detail his experience with two different tributaries that drain into Plaster Creek—one in a more suburban area and another in a more urban area. His experience of interacting with two different sections of the watershed highlights the stark contrasts that exist between upstream and downstream and points to a need to make the issues more explicit for the public. Restorative change can't happen unless people develop eyes to see the problems within their own section of their watershed. As a child he grew up in a suburban section of the Plaster Creek watershed and had rich learning experiences playing outside near the Indian Creek tributary. "We played in the woods on both sides of the creek . . . and the times we had down there, just being able to walk around and discover and explore, I will always have that. That was a great part of growing up."[26] He went on to describe being a mischievous teenager and often going with friends underground into the storm drains ("we called them sewer tunnels") along the Silver Creek tributary that flows under the city of Grand Rapids. One time late at night he and his friends had been exploring the storm drains underground, and when they climbed out, they were surprised to find themselves in a neighborhood quite different from their own. Here they had an eye-opening experience:

> We had reached an older section of the storm drains where it went from being concrete to brick. . . . We continued walking further and further and eventually the novelty wore off, so we climbed out. . . . We pulled up into an area with some light industry, some older office buildings, some residential. I knew that, at least at that time, we were in a neighborhood where a couple of white kids ought not to be at 11:00 at night. So we decided to walk home. As we walked up Jefferson to Hall Street and turned onto Hall towards home, there was a group of some tough looking guys. As we walked past, we wanted to just keep a low profile and get home. They started to trash talk us and when we got to the corner of Hall and Madison, we heard some really fast footsteps behind us, and I felt a bash on the back of my head. . . . I ran into the street and that's kind of a blur when all this was happening, but I remember seeing a couple of people beating up on a friend of mine.

> There was a party going on across the street, and the people there shouted off our [attackers] and they ran away. The people from the party yelled, "What the f—are you doing here?" so we had to explain what we had been doing. And about that time, we realized our third friend was missing. We last saw him right at the time the attack happened, and now he was nowhere to be found. The people at the party were talking with us when we saw a police cruiser coming towards us on Hall, so we flagged him down. We had to answer rounds of questions like "what are you doing here?" and "why were you in the storm drains?" We were put in the back of the police cruiser (we were very worried about our friend) and the police took us home. We had to wake our parents, explain what had happened and then call the parents of our missing friend. . . . You can imagine the gut-wrenching feeling for his parents. Before the end of that phone conversation, our missing friend walked in. It turned out that he ran all the way north on Madison, all the way to Lake Drive and then ran all the way down Lake Drive on adrenaline the whole way back home and didn't stop until he got there. So his parents were able to say, "He just walked in. He's safe." So . . . I had a bump on my head for another week and none of us sustained major injuries. But yeah, the things kids do.[27]

The comparison of these two experiences—the first as a young child playing in an upstream section of the watershed and the second as a teenager exploring the downstream section of the watershed—is quite striking. These two stories offer important insights for the careful reader. Our conversation partner's experience of growing up in the upstream section of the watershed where it was less developed and in a more natural state created opportunities for him to experience independent play as a child and freedom to explore, discover, and learn about the world—both its people and the place. Yet the children growing up in the urban downstream section of the watershed didn't have the same opportunities. Why not? The creek in their section of the watershed was buried underground, and there was no chance to interact with the water and the creatures that live in and near the creek. Our conversation partner's experience as a teenager interacting with youth living in the downstream reaches of the watershed was not positive. Race and class differences led to an exchange of anger and violence, which did not happen in a vacuum. Larger societal forces of inequality and injustice led to both unhealthy ecological places and to unhealthy personal interactions.

What we see from these two experiences is that one section of the watershed was deemed less important than the other. In the downstream urban section, land was needed for housing or industry, so the creek was buried, placed in a storm sewer, and almost forgotten, essentially erased from the landscape. In the other section the creek was allowed to remain in its more natural state, playing a significant role in a child's life, enabling him to become an adult who values and cares for the environment. We are not glorifying undeveloped land nor suggesting that all urban development is wrong. But careful decisions need to be made about how to protect and preserve the water and landscapes in cities so that urban dwellers are not disproportionately burdened by pollution and contamination compared to suburban and rural residents. Policymakers as well as the public need to pay attention to long-term impacts of their decisions and actions and not assume some places and people are less important and, therefore, expendable.

Motivating Behavior Change to Promote Environmental Justice

For places that care about long-term sustainability and generational survival, decision-makers will need to pay particular attention to issues of social, economic, and environmental equity. Sociologist Michael J. Lorr argues that urban sustainability in North America is likely to continue at the surface level of addressing environmental problems under the rubric of "greening" cities at the expense of participatory planning, environmental justice, and ecological democracy.[28] This is a risk in Grand Rapids if people of color are not included in planning and decision-making that affects their neighborhoods. For example, as Grand Rapids undertakes a major river restoration project important questions need to be considered: How will people of color, whose neighborhoods have often been overlooked in the past, not be displaced when improvements spark new economic activity? How will the people who have a long history living in their neighborhoods (sometimes multigenerational) not become victims of gentrification and priced out of their homes and jobs, as neighborhoods become greener, more desirable, and more expensive to live in? Whose dreams will come true, and who will be left behind by the plans for river revitalization? Policymakers have a moral responsibility to learn about the history of a place, to take seriously who has lived here in the past, and to connect with and learn from current residents to know how to promote *equitable* flourishing in that place. It is not coincidental that this discussion of gentrification sounds similar to our earlier discussions of colonization. In many ways the same mentality that European colonists brought to new lands in North America are exhibited by privileged persons in positions of power when considering "urban revitalization" or "suburban development."

Environmental justice becomes a question of whose interests count. Decision-makers are obligated to consider the interests of all people, not just the wealthy or the powerful. And community leaders must also consider the following questions: What will *prompt* people to consider the interests of others to be as important as their own? What will *persuade* people to work for environmental justice? What will *provoke* people to become involved, take moral action, exercise self-restraint where needed, to contribute to the common good?

Part of prompting people to consider the interests of others as important as their own is to encourage them to name their own self-interest, "What's in it for me?" To engage the public in making behavior change, people need to understand and be able to articulate their own self-interest, while also recognizing that their self-interest is embedded within the interests of the common good. One of our conversation partners said it like this,

> People don't change unless they really have a belief, a higher belief in the greater, bigger good. That has to be out of their core values or otherwise they'll be unwilling to change. So, you always answer the question, "What's in it for me, why is it important for me to make that change?" That's sometimes hard to do when the impacts are not being felt by them. The impacts are all being felt downstream.[29]

Raising awareness of the impacts is an important first step, and people are more apt to take restorative action when they know people personally who have been negatively impacted by environmental contamination. In an article about moral education and social justice Roger Bergman quotes philosopher Gabriel Marcel, who explains that personal encounter is fundamental for people wanting to enact social justice.

> How is a commitment to the difficult work of social justice provoked in the first place? and How is that commitment sustained over a lifetime? The philosopher Marcel provides a pointed answer to the first question: "Through personal encounter. Nothing else ever changes anyone in any important way" (as cited in Maguire, 1985, p. 78). Want to provide a new openness to questions of social justice? Then offer opportunities for personal encounter with the victims of injustice.[30]

Being able to interact firsthand with others who have different life experiences creates the potential for empathy to develop. And empathy can motivate people to take action for change. Getting to know real people, whether that be neighbors or fellow watershed residents living in other sections of the watershed whose lives are impacted by environmental injustice, can foster genuine empathy, out of which can emerge motivation to care about and work for the restoration of degraded urban landscapes.

PCS has worked to build awareness, empathy, and motivation among residents by intentionally fostering relationships between upstream residents and downstream residents. We host education and action events each year and invite people from all parts of the watershed to participate. These gatherings have been a way to practice reconciliation ecology and to demonstrate that restoring Plaster Creek is not only in people's individual self-interest but also in the community's self-interest. One example was the installation of a large green infrastructure project in an upstream county park. Local elementary, middle, and high schools from upstream and downstream in the watershed brought students and teachers to help. College students, local residents and families, congregations, and local businesses provided teams of volunteers to assist. People of all ages and backgrounds from upstream and downstream throughout the Plaster Creek watershed worked side by side for many months on this project that helped to heal the Plaster Creek watershed ecologically and socially. Personal encounters make a critical difference for motivating involvement in reconciliation ecology.

Working to promote environmental justice is slow and long-term work—building trust, mutual listening, trying to involve people from different backgrounds in the planning and decision-making process. In recent years there has been progress to address environmental justice. PCS is one of a number of organizations working to build coalitions of demographically distinct groups in support of environmental justice in West Michigan. Local organizations such as the Healthy Homes Coalition, Amplify, LINC UP, and the C4 initiative (Community Collaboration on Climate Change) are among those who are working to share leadership and power to address injustices and lessen the burden of pollution in BIPOC neighborhoods in Grand Rapids. There is still much work to be done by us all, but momentum seems to be building.

Communities that want to promote lasting change and genuine urban sustainability will find ways to include grassroots people (families, children, school groups, congregations, condominium associations) in ecological restoration. This

FIGURE 15. Upstream and downstream watershed residents work side by side to install native plants into a floodplain restoration site.

PHOTOGRAPH BY GAIL GUNST HEFFNER.

type of mobilization will increase the likelihood that equity and environmental justice will be fostered. PCS contributes to sustainable urban development by seeking equity and social justice and not merely advocating for a greening of cities and watersheds. Creating upstream–downstream partnerships among local schools and among faith communities, providing opportunities for neighbors and families to work together side by side, and partnering with other justice-seeking organizations are concrete ways to promote environmental justice and to practice reconciliation ecology.

CHAPTER 11

Engaging Faith Communities

It was a warm spring evening the first time we were invited to talk about the Plaster Creek watershed with members of the At-Tawheed Islamic Center, which serves an ethnically diverse Muslim community in West Michigan and whose property includes a segment of Little Plaster Creek. A month earlier we had been introduced to two of the leaders of the Islamic Center at a luncheon organized by the Kaufman Interfaith Institute at Grand Valley State University, centering on the theme of Interfaith Service. After we spoke about our work, two men stayed around to chat. They invited us to educate their community about the problems with Plaster Creek and offer ideas of what the Islamic Center could do to take restorative action.

Several things stand out from our first meeting at the At-Tawheed Islamic Center. The hospitality and gracious welcome from their community is unforgettable. The delicious and abundant food, their warmth and kindness even with the naïve mistakes we made: Dave thought he needed to take his shoes off when first entering the building, but later realized he was the only person in socks downstairs during the meal; Gail tried to shake hands when greeted by a gentleman at the door, and he politely shook his head "no" (we later learned it is considered disrespectful for men to shake hands with women). What is especially memorable about this first meeting was the quiet attentiveness and interest their members showed as we explained the current condition of Plaster Creek and then their enthusiastic response when we suggested possible actions we could take together.

It didn't take long for the Islamic Center to organize their first restoration project—a rain garden to capture stormwater draining off their parking lot. The

FIGURE 16. People of diverse faith backgrounds help care for Plaster Creek.
PHOTOGRAPH BY GAIL GUNST HEFFNER.

partnership that has developed between the At-Tawheed Islamic Center and Plaster Creek Stewards (PCS) is an example of reconciliation between Christians and Muslims, between upstream and downstream, and between old and young, men, women, and children—it has enriched us all. We have learned *about* and *from* each other; we gave a talk together at an environmental conference about our interfaith alliance; we have collaborated on three restoration projects at the Islamic Center property with more being planned; and now At-Tawheed has introduced us to a second Muslim community, the ICC Behar Mosque, which has become a partner with PCS on a recent grant-funded project to further promote the work of reconciliation ecology together.

The Role of Religion in Fostering Reconciliation

PCS was initially launched in response to a request from a Michigan Department of Environmental Quality (MDEQ) staff member to help reach out to members of the faith community who were resistant to the government. What began in

2009 as a summer workshop for a few local congregations has now blossomed into partnerships throughout the Plaster Creek watershed with many communities of faith working together to take restorative action—reconciliation ecology embodied. Congregations have the potential to be influencers and leaders in the vision for restoring the earth. Philosopher Gretel Van Wieren writes, "Religion plays an integral role in forming cultural values and worldviews, which in turn shape a society's ethical orientation toward the natural world."[1]

PCS as an initiative of Calvin University situates itself within the Reformed tradition of historic Christianity, which has a high regard for the creation. However, most faith traditions no matter how diverse acknowledge the importance of caring for the natural world. Though faith communities may emphasize different aspects of the human–earth relationship, there is a common understanding of brokenness and the need to work for wholeness and healing. And yet, over the past decades environmental groups have made minimal effort to engage with faith communities, and faith communities have been largely inactive.

As Indigenous author Dennis Martinez writes, "This world is incredible. The spirituality behind the material phenomenon that we see is simply breathtaking. It's been ignored, and it's been ignored to our peril."[2] In recent years, however, scholars and environmental leaders have begun to challenge people of faith to recognize and acknowledge their role in creating the brokenness in which our current environmental crises exist, and to honestly face what is needed to reimagine a different way forward. Author Ched Myers argues,

> The church will embody a moral equivalent to these times neither by advocating for minor reforms nor by offering a new rhetorical lexicon. Rather, it needs to promote pastoral and theological disciplines that are on the one hand *radical*, diagnosing the root pathologies within and around us while also drawing deeply on the roots of our faith traditions, yet which on the other hand are *practical*, empowering deliberate steps toward significant change. Our task as Christians is nothing less than working to help turn our history around—which is, as it happens, the meaning of the biblical discourse on repentance.[3]

While recognizing some of the "pathologies" that have led to our current problems, we can draw on the strengths of our faith traditions as a source of motivation to care for the earth. The Doctrine of Discovery was used as a legal rationale for the U.S. government to expel Indigenous people from their land based on the belief that Indigenous religions and cultures were inferior to European Christianity.[4] A number of Christian denominations and faith communities have made public statements critiquing the Doctrine of Discovery and providing an important starting point for the work of reconciliation ecology.[5] Honest acknowledgement of the pain caused by theologies of entitlement and conquest is a critical first step in addressing the brokenness among people groups as well as between humans and the natural world.

Van Wieren further argues that despite the damage that Christianity has caused by colonizing and oppressing both people and the earth, there is still an important role for Christians to play in healing past and current traumas.

> It is important to note that religion in general and Christianity in particular have not always proven to be a helpful source for promoting earth care. In fact, quite the opposite: Western Christianity's history of colonization and domination of peoples and nature in God's name makes one wonder whether it, or any other religion with a colonizing destructive past for that matter, is redeemable in terms of its ability now to function as a genuine earth faith. . . . Many ecological theologians . . . contend that there are resources embedded deep within Christianity (as well as other religious traditions) that can be retrieved and reformed in order to defend earth and to help form holistic visions for living more justly and peaceably with one another and with the earth.[6]

People of faith are increasingly challenged to expand their vision, acknowledging that God cares for the fullness of creation, not only humans. Communities of faith are poised to reimagine a new way forward in seeking reconciliation, finding ways to live in mutually fulfilling relationships with others, working for the flourishing of all creatures and communities. Van Wieren continues,

> Although scholars may disagree over precisely which parts or wholes of the natural world ought to be cared for, and according to which reasons, the fundamental idea that earth is sacred in some sense and therefore worthy of reverent respect and care pervades Christian environmental thought. Moreover, Christian environmental ethicists tend to emphasize the notion that human beings have been created with a capacity for living in mutual, fulfilling relation with others, including other creatures and creation as a whole. They also tend to share the conviction that certain classes of people, and their ecologies, have been treated unjustly by

more privileged or powerful groups in society and that the healing of earth will also require the healing of relationships between human beings.[7]

It is difficult, often uncomfortable, to admit some of us have benefited from the same history that has caused others immeasurable pain. For many European Americans it is complicated to see, let alone honestly acknowledge, how privilege and entitlement have made our lives easier. Yet reconciliation is not possible without an honest acknowledgement of past wrongs. Many religious writers argue that reconciliation is only needed between people and God, but that's as far as reconciliation extends. There is less understanding and emphasis on the need for reconciliation between people groups, and between people and the natural world. Fred Bahnson and Norman Wirzba write convincingly about this narrow view of reconciliation held by many people of faith in the dominant American society in their book, *Making Peace with the Land: God's Call to Reconcile with Creation.*

> Today's church suffers from a reconciliation deficit disorder. The cause of this disorder is an impoverished imagination. As Christians, we have a hard time imagining that God desires all creatures—human and nonhuman, living and nonliving—to be reconciled with each other and with God. For a variety of reasons, we have come to think that God cares primarily, perhaps only, about us.[8]

We notice a contrast between the practice of faith and spirituality among European American Christians and the practice of faith and spirituality among Indigenous people in North America. Many Christians view the work of restoring ecological health to the earth including our watersheds as *peripheral* to their faith expression. But Indigenous writers often emphasize a fundamental intersection between ecological restoration and Indigenous spirituality and see care for the earth as central to their faith practice. In an interview, Daniel Martinez, a tribal leader involved in ecological restoration, spoke eloquently that people need a spiritual connection if there is any hope to heal the earth.

> What is important is to get the right people involved in the right places doing the right things for as long as they can, and for future generations to build on that idea. . . . And, the ceremonies; keep going to the ceremonies, keep the prayers and the ceremonies up. This is extremely important that people have that spiritual connection. We also need to expand that kind of spirituality into

> the natural world as well. . . . We need to retain the same spiritual appreciation and respect for the natural world, and not go for short-term economic fast track gains at the expense of long-term ecology and economy. So, there is no separation between spirit and matter. . . . The ceremonies can be a touchstone . . . a vehicle for reaching that consciousness and experience of spirituality because it is going to carry over into how you treat other people. . . . You have that spirit of love inside you. All world religions, *all world religions* have preached that, that's nothing new.[9]

So much can be gained if we open ourselves to listen and learn from one another. While there will never be complete agreement—religiously, culturally, politically—creating space for people to pursue spiritual connections with respect and honesty is an important aspect of reconciliation ecology.

Listening to the Voices of Watershed Residents

During the interviews with participants in the Plaster Creek Oral History Project, conversation partners were asked if they felt the faith community had a role to play in the restoration of Plaster Creek. Several of our conversation partners who described themselves as people of faith spoke broadly about "stewardship" or "creation care," terms commonly used by Christians in describing humanity's relationship with the earth.

> I think that we, as stewards of the creation God has given us, have a responsibility to make people aware of these issues and give people an opportunity to help restore it. . . . I think that churches and members of the faith community do have an important role in restoring the ecosystem . . . [finding] ways to connect our members to it, so we can build that sense of connection to our natural environment and our responsibility towards it within our own church—so that we can act in appropriate ways toward restoring that which God has given us responsibility for.[10]

> And the bigger picture behind it . . . [is] the Christian virtue of caring for and tending to creation, I mean, back when we had the mandate in the Old Testament to be fruitful and multiply but also to care for this creation we've been entrusted with, that's preeminent.[11]

One of our conversation partners articulated a deficit in her work with state government because it failed to connect with people's sense of purpose or values. She expressed the unique contribution the faith community could make:

> One of the things that I've learned over the years, especially as it relates to trying to get public awareness and changed behavior through outreach, is that *real change occurs when you can tap into people's core values*. Even with the Nonpoint Source program that I was promoting, it was deficient because through all the surveys and everything, it was directed at what people thought. You'd get an intellectual response; you would not get a heart response. You can talk to people's heads without even realizing behavior is based on how people feel, not how people think. . . . So much of what the state Nonpoint Source program was trying to do . . . [was] not really tying it into the real core values and creation care.[12]

Other conversation partners affirmed an ethical motivation, perhaps without a religious motivation, to care for the natural world. As in any conversation there are times when respondents stumble over how to articulate their ideas, yet what is clear is the responsibility they believe people have to care for the earth and to care for other people, as we see in this comment.

> I was just thinking that ethic of stewardship is . . . you know, doesn't necessarily have to be a religious, um, belief, it should be just sort of a . . . a . . . I don't know, a . . . state of being. Knowing what impacts you make—not only to the world but to other people.[13]

In some of the interview transcripts respondents described the importance of being a good steward of God's creation yet admitted they haven't done much concretely to take this seriously. It was interesting to note when an inconsistency between rhetorical narrative and lived experience occurred. Some even admitted the disconnect between their words and actions. Here is one such example:

> I think as Christians we have a responsibility to care for God's creation and we can do it in a lot of different ways. Certainly, polluting the creek is not taking care of God's creation. . . . Unfortunately, not too many people think of that. And you are looking at one right now that doesn't think too much of that. I haven't thought about Plaster Crick for years until we were here and . . . I looked down

> at the crick which then brought back a lot of memories. But I haven't looked at the crick or thought about it, because I live miles away from it. So it never occurs anymore in my thoughts. But certainly, as Christians we have a responsibility to care for God's environment, for God's creation, without any question. We shouldn't abuse it, and we certainly shouldn't pollute it in any way. When I go to Grand Haven—where the Grand River enters Lake Michigan—and if you are up on a hill and you look down . . . there's a large area there that's brown and . . . it's horrible to see that going into Lake Michigan. I don't know what people think. Like I said before, what happens to all that pollution we put in there? I mean, it just doesn't magically disappear. I mean, it pollutes the body of water. And, well, I guess, I'm not one that should criticize or talk about that, because I have not ever done anything to correct that either.[14]

This participant articulates a Christian responsibility to care for the earth, but he also admits that not many people think to follow it, including himself. He openly confesses how he hasn't thought of Plaster "Crick" for many years and therefore hasn't taken much action to prevent pollution. These comments demonstrate a disconnect between what many people say they believe and how they live or act.

Part of the reason we're writing this book is to motivate people, including people of faith, to pay attention and take action to heal the brokenness found in their places—to align their actions with their beliefs. No one is ever neutral—we are either moving in the direction of bringing healing or we are moving in the direction of causing more harm, even if we are not conscious of this. One helpful starting point for aligning behavior and belief is to raise awareness of the problem and then provide low-stress, high-reward opportunities to get involved—to help people connect their actions to their beliefs, to connect knowing and doing in concrete ways. One conversation partner described his congregation's growing involvement:

> I would say there was little to no awareness of the creek or our church's proximity to the creek until we got involved with Plaster Creek Stewards. We have a number of parishioners who just live . . . right along the creek. . . . What is really cool is that since we got involved with the Stewards, we've adopted this creek. This creek that had already adopted us in some ways . . . the awareness is growing without a doubt.

> It just feels so right that the church is involved on the ground level here. There is a lot of energy around that. We've tried to make the congregation aware of what's going on and there's been write-ups in our newsletters and on our website about the rain gardens coming in, about this partnership, about what's coming up in the future. . . . We did a sermon series about ecological stewardship. So awareness is increasing. And the creek is more and more becoming ours and vice versa. Just a lot of opportunities we have as a church to engage the neighborhood because we find that a lot of folks who we'd say, "Come to our church picnic," and they'd say, "No, thanks." . . . But when "Oh, you're going to clean up the creek? I want to do that. Can I come with you?" And then it is something that we are doing alongside our neighbors . . . where everybody is the same and . . . we get to illustrate God's love for creation, and his love for this neighborhood. So that is a really cool way to connect with our neighbors.[15]

Since congregations are often trusted partners in the community, they are well positioned to serve as a hub for information, educating people about how to heal their relationship with creation. One of our conversation partners, who didn't self-identify as a person of faith, nevertheless affirmed the role of the faith community in networking and connecting people to care about the natural world.

> The faith community in West Michigan is so strong and makes West Michigan what West Michigan is. . . . And I think that maybe these faith communities could be kind of a stepping point, as a networking point to the education and relationship that this community has with the creek. That could be a stepping stone—to get out to the community, the information, things like that.[16]

Throughout the years of PCS work, we have interacted with many congregations, giving educational presentations, implementing green infrastructure on site, and providing ideas and resources for those congregations interested in promoting watershed restoration. Many of these faith communities have been long-term partners in our work, and our volunteer base has expanded with members of these various congregations. Reaching out to faith communities continues to be an important, generative part of our work in reconciliation ecology.

FIGURE 17. Site of an old Grand Rapids landfill being converted into native gardens at Sherman Street Church.

PHOTOGRAPH BY DAVID P. WARNERS

Fruitful Congregational Partnerships

In 2018 the National Wildlife Federation (NWF) reached out to PCS for assistance to bring their Sacred Grounds program to West Michigan. Sacred Grounds works with houses of worship to link faith practices and caring for the environment. The NWF website describes the program in this way:

> The mission of the Sacred Grounds program is to promote the installation of native plant gardens that connect people to nature and provide access to nature for all. Particularly in urban communities, Black, Indigenous, and People of Color (BIPOC) have less access to nature and safe green spaces than white folks in the same cities. Native plants are not only a foundation for healthy ecosystems and wildlife, but also play an important role in mental, physical, and social health by providing opportunities for people to connect to nature in their neighborhoods and communities. Native plants can also help to manage stormwater and reduce flooding, support local food cultivation, improve water quality, and enhance community resilience. Through the Sacred Grounds program, participants both learn to plant and install their own native plant garden, while educating and engaging the community and contributing to a network of accessible natural spaces and habitats.[17]

In the spring of 2019 PCS began what has become an ongoing, collaborative partnership with the National Wildlife Federation. We developed a pilot program for Sacred Grounds in West Michigan by engaging houses of worship in the Plaster Creek watershed. Since then, PCS has led educational presentations for over thirty teams from local congregations, conducted site assessments, and developed site designs for green infrastructure projects on the property of participating houses of worship. We have assisted volunteers with implementing and installing rain gardens and pollinator gardens on site. And we have hosted follow-up maintenance workshops so that the congregations can learn how to maintain these green infrastructure projects after installation.

To become a certified Sacred Grounds house of worship, congregations need to accomplish three goals: gather a team of congregational leaders who provide direction and ongoing support for the project, educate the congregation and engage the larger community, and install a native plant garden at their house of worship. The Sacred Grounds project dovetails and supports similar goals that

PCS has put in place—particularly education and on-the-ground restoration. The pilot program PCS conducted was successful, and now our partnership with the Sacred Grounds program has expanded to include houses of worship throughout the Lower Grand River Watershed in West Michigan.

One of the congregations in the Plaster Creek watershed, Church of the Servant, has done an especially notable job of taking seriously its responsibility to care for their place. This faith community has initiated a unique project they have named "Refugia." Their hope is to help the congregation connect their indoor worship space, which is designed to dignify the ordinary, with their outside property to exhibit a vision for creation care—from the migratory birds that pass through to the creatures that live in their shared space to the members of the congregation and community.

The word "refugia" expresses a particular relationship between place and purpose. Biologists apply the term to describe places that have been protected from surrounding harsh conditions where organisms and relationships are able to persist. Refugia nurture essential ecological interactions and become the foundation of resilient communities that emerge from a crisis. This concept has been expanded upon by Debra Rienstra in her beautiful book, *Refugia Faith*.[18] As a side note, refugia might not have been needed had European Americans not disturbed the thriving ecological interactions that existed before they arrived. Nevertheless, the Refugia project at Church of the Servant is an exciting response to current conditions and warrants attention and celebration. In addition to being a "refuge" (a safe place), the congregation's vision is to create a place where native plants, birds, and butterflies flourish, where edible native plants grow, and where people learn healthy interactions with the broader creation in which they are embedded. This congregation includes white, educated European Americans as well as many refugees from around the world, and they have collaborated on various aspects of the Refugia project together. The Refugia project includes walking trails, a protected wetland, a wildlife corridor, a restored prairie, a community garden space for refugees and other neighbors, rain gardens and a bioswale to capture stormwater, and a large solar array to generate electricity. The Refugia project therefore serves multiple purposes, allowing for human thriving within a larger context of ecological thriving that witnesses God's purpose for the fullness of the whole creation.

Conversations are also beginning within the congregation to develop a land acknowledgement statement to honor the Indigenous people who lived sustainably on this land for millennia before Europeans arrived. The Refugia project is an innovative example of a congregation that is allowing itself to be *changed* by its relationship to the land and by others who share the land with them. This congregation is a living example of reconciliation ecology in process where they are developing their property in ways that support relationships that nurture hope and resilience. The Refugia project is an embodiment of what Bahnson and Wirzba encourage when they write,

> Reconciliation with the land means learning to see the land as part of God's redemptive plan and acknowledge God's ongoing presence there. That will require putting ourselves in proximity to the land and staying there long enough to be changed.[19]

This faith community is modeling the concept of shalom by celebrating the many other life forms God created to exist along with humanity, thereby promoting mutual flourishing. "Shalom" is a Hebrew word that in the Bible is usually translated into English as "peace." However, its meaning is far richer: shalom points toward a way of living in which all things (human and nonhuman) are interacting together in harmony. Shalom foreshadows a hopeful future, yet also breaks through our present reality with tangible examples of what is to come.

You may wonder about the cost of the Refugia project and whether it is only possible for wealthier or well-resourced congregations. Much of the Refugia work has been done by congregational volunteers to keep costs low. And there is ongoing conversation in West Michigan to create opportunities for energy upgrades and other creation care projects targeted to low-income congregations so they can benefit from new technologies and funding possibilities.[20]

Another conversation partner, a pastor whose congregation has collaborated with PCS for more than a decade, was particularly passionate about the role of the faith community in caring for Plaster Creek.

> [The faith community] should and could play a primary role. I think that the church should be the leader in environmental stewardship. I think we should set the standard. I wish that there was no EPA because the churches were doing their job. I wish the EPA would dissolve because it was useless, because the local congregations were making it happen—the fact that we need to have this discussion is to the shame of the church. . . . I think the church should be embarrassed that the government has had to step in and to do some things that the church should

> have been doing all along. . . . I think that if the church sees itself correctly, we will look at the environment differently. I am so excited that all of this is falling into this congregation's lap . . . helping us reengage in something we should have been engaged in all along. And it is giving us a head start in becoming a congregation that loves the creek and is known for loving the creek, and which sets the tone for how to love the creek.[21]

Accomplishments and Ongoing Work with Faith Communities

When PCS was launched in 2009, we developed a vigorous action plan for the first three years. Some of those ideas unfolded as planned and even went beyond our original vision. Other plans were dropped because we lacked either time, funding, or other resources to complete those aspects of the plan. But it is quite interesting to note that at one of those very early planning sessions, as we brainstormed ideas for beginning the work of watershed restoration, we identified that engaging the faith community in the Plaster Creek watershed was an important starting point. Here's a small excerpt from a 2008 Calvin College Faculty Development Workshop report:

> How can we partner with local faith-based groups?
>
> 1) Craft a plan to approach the faith community in the Plaster Creek watershed beginning with our denomination; include a theological foundation for creation care, develop worship resources, and create opportunities for people to take specific action.
>
> 2) Work with the denominational headquarters to develop it as a demonstration site for caring for the watershed—including unpaving impervious surfaces, adding rain gardens and rain barrels, stream clean-ups, reforestation, prayer gardens.

More than a decade after launching PCS, it is exciting to realize that we have accomplished most of those original plans. We have partnered with more than forty communities of faith within the Plaster Creek watershed, and members from diverse congregations have become involved in the work—some through adult education, some through their youth groups, some through installing green infrastructure on their properties or at their homes. The headquarters of the Christian Reformed denomination (which is aligned with Calvin University) has actually become a demonstration site for on-the-ground restoration strategies—installing multiple pollinator gardens, a bioswale, a restored prairie, rain gardens, and many trees. Communities of faith have been far more receptive to our efforts than we anticipated, and opportunities for partnerships have grown beyond what we initially imagined.

Yet there is still so much to do—many more people to reach, more watershed land to be restored, more stormwater runoff to be intercepted, and much more reconciliation work to do between people groups with different racial and ethnic identities, religious perspectives, worldviews, and life experiences. The work is underway and ongoing. For the people who have become involved in the restoration of Plaster Creek, personal experiences can be transformative. The literature attests to this as do the stories told through the Plaster Creek Oral History Project. Some writers describe this sense of transformation in religious terms of renewal and healing.

> What is the religious dimension in the transformation and renewal that many restoration practitioners reference; and what sorts of religiously symbolic action may restoration perform? . . . Restorationists at times utilize religious language to refer to the personal experiences of healing, renewal, communion, and dependency in relation to nature that are generated through the restorative act. [Eric] Higgs writes that a "special communion forms when people literally dig into the earth to reverse a tide of degradation, atone for past actions, seek a new way of relating to things other than humans, or enjoy the pleasure of good company and good work."[22]

This description is also a confirmation of the importance of praxis—being able to imagine *and* implement, reflect *and* take action—for reparation and reconciliation to occur. One of our conversation partners also affirmed being changed by the creek as he has become involved in the restoration work. And he credits this transformation to the movement of God's spirit in the world.

> And so, things become less simple and more complicated and more intimate. And that's how our relationship with God develops, I think. And it seems that that's how God is making our relationship with this creek develop. Where it starts off as this really easy breezy kind of thing, but then well, guess what . . . you can try to change the creek, but the creek is also going to try to change you. And I think that is one of the ways God is being powerful in this situation. We can't be stewards of Plaster Creek and be the same as we've always been. If we want the creek to change, we have to change. And that just screams to me how the Holy Spirit works in our lives. It's this constant progression.[23]

Not all those involved in reconciliation ecology recognize the possibilities and opportunities of working with local congregations. The potential for congregations to become a hub for praxis—of reflection and action—is often overlooked by those within the congregation *and* by those in the environmental community. Reimagining what is possible and a willingness to step outside of traditional understandings is required. As Ched Myers articulates in *Watershed Discipleship*,

> It is both theologically sound and politically radical to propose, therefore, that we Christians ought to recenter our citizen-identity in the *topography of creation* rather than in the *political geography of dominant cultural ideation*, in order to ground our discipleship practices in the watershed where we embody our faith.[24]

Myers later goes on to admit his arguments are seen as marginal in many North American churches. Nevertheless, he maintains that faith communities are poised to practice how to love and care for our unique places and where we can allow the social and natural landscapes to shape us.

> Obviously, understanding Christian discipleship fundamentally in terms of a commitment to heal the world by restoring the social and ecological health of our watersheds is still marginal in our North American churches. . . . In so many ways local congregations are ideally situated to become centers for learning to know and love our places enough to defend and restore them. But we must first reinhabit our watersheds as *church*, allowing the natural and social landscapes to shape our symbolic life, mission engagements, and material habits.[25]

In the years since we began PCS, people of all ages and from diverse religious and cultural backgrounds have joined the effort. For some people working with PCS has provided a concrete way to align their spoken religious beliefs to their lived behavior. Helping faith communities make upstream–downstream connections within our watershed has led to new relationships and new understandings about similarities and differences that exist among us. These efforts have also fostered a growing respect for what can be accomplished when we work collectively rather than in isolation. Gathering diverse groups of people together to learn about the watershed and then providing opportunities for them to work side by side on restoration projects has been productive and encouraging. Yet challenges remain—both learning to listen to others' perspectives and experiences and taking the time to build trust in order to engage the broad diversity that exists in this watershed. These are important steps in the reparation and restoration processes that ultimately lead to reconciliation between people groups and between people and the earth.

CHAPTER 12

Shaping Future Environmental Leaders

Friday, June 24, 2022, was a busy day at Sherman Street Church, even though it wasn't a Sunday. This inner-city church (built in 1907) has been converting its traditional landscaping to native plantings, including the steep bank at the back of its property. The bank has cement troughs that served as garbage conduits, leading down to one of Grand Rapids' former city dumps, now occupied by the church parking lot. Through a partnership with Plaster Creek Stewards (PCS) this community-focused congregation is cultivating beauty and diversity out of an old dump site.

That Friday we were clearing weedy vegetation from the bank and extending a native garden that had been planted through Sacred Grounds funding from the National Wildlife Federation. This work was undertaken by PCS summer staff and two groups of high school students, one employed by PCS and the other employed by a partner nonprofit, Friends of Grand Rapids Parks. The activity was a balance of hard work, laughter, conversations, and good will.

Toward the end of the day, I (Dave) was working near the top of the bank and noticed an elderly woman motioning for me to come over. As I approached, I saw that she was holding a piece of paper and pen. My first thought was that she was unhappy because we had removed some invasive shrubs and vines from the fence line that separated her property from the garden area. But she greeted me with a smile, introduced herself, and asked about the work that was happening. As I explained what we were doing, her smile grew. She said she had put the fence up and let the vines grow because in the past there were street gangs running through the parking lot, up the slope, and through her yard. And they frightened her. But now, she loves the open view, especially seeing all these young people working on the gardens together. Then, reaching out with the paper and pen, she asked me to give her an address where she could send a check. She said the money wouldn't come for a couple months because she has some bills to pay first, and it might not be very much, but she really wanted to support this work. Engaging youth in the challenging work of reconciliation ecology can be one important way of renewing social relationships in the watershed and reconnecting young people with the natural world.

Childhood Experiences with Nature

Childhood experiences influence and shape us as adults. Think about your own childhood. What is your first memory of being outdoors, of playing outside rather than inside? What do you remember about the landscape of your childhood, the hills and valleys or the flatness around you, where water collected or where it flowed? What do you remember about the seasons changing, the uncertainties of the weather, the birds and animals who shared the landscape with you? Richard Louv writes, "Passion is lifted from the earth itself by the muddy hands of the young; it travels along grass-stained sleeves to the heart. If we are going to save . . . the environment, we must also save an endangered indicator species: the child in nature."[1] The memories of our childhood call out unique experiences for each of us, especially as we try to recall memories of what may have been long forgotten. How people view their landscape, whether urban or rural or more natural, and whether they pay attention and notice it when they are adults is influenced in part by the experiences they had as children.

Literature on child development suggests that children need a healthy relationship with the natural world for their own health and psychological maturation. Meaningful interactions with nature increase children's emotional affinity toward nature, their ecological beliefs, and their likelihood of engaging in pro-environmental behaviors.[2] This chapter examines the child–nature relationship and the influence of childhood experiences in creating future environmental leaders. We

FIGURE 18. Youth of all ages help each other plant native habitats to protect the creek.
PHOTOGRAPH BY GAIL GUNST HEFFNER.

explore the literature on human development and also hear from participants in the Plaster Creek Oral History Project who describe their childhood experiences interacting with the natural world—stories of discovery, of adventure, of risk, of exploration. Many of the stories reveal a common experience for children regardless of the differences of race, religion, gender, or culture. This chapter highlights another hallmark of PCS's work—that engaging youth in reconciliation ecology can have multiple benefits.

Child–Nature Connections and Healthy Human Development

A strong child–nature connection has been shown to benefit the child in terms of physical health,[3] the development of personal and social capabilities,[4] improved test scores, and reduced behavioral problems such as attention-deficit/hyperactivity disorder.[5] While many factors contribute to a person's health, sense of purpose, and sense of belonging, a positive relationship with nature can be a contributing factor for healthy human development. Increasingly researchers describe a broad range of benefits of outdoor play for children as well as positive long-term effects on adults who have meaningful interactions with the natural world, including stress reduction, attention restoration, social connectedness, and improved mental health.[6]

> As awareness of humanity's relationship with the environment has increased in the past few decades—buoyed of late by the larger popular concern about climate change—so has empirical evidence for nature's psychological benefits. . . . Back in 1865, Olmsted [landscape architect Frederick Law Olmstead] thought exposure to natural environments would prevent a "softening of the brain," "irascibility," and "melancholy." Nearly 150 years later, scientists now know that nature has a remarkable ability to restore attention, that it soothes aggression, and that it may even ease mild depression.[7]

A significant understanding of nature's positive effect on the human mind has come through studies of attention, leading to the development of attention restoration theory. The theory originated in the 1980s with Stephen Kaplan and associates who found that exposure to nature had a profound restorative effect on the brain's ability to focus.[8] Conversely, some writers are describing what has been lost in recent decades as children play outside less and less and spend more time in front of screens and with inanimate objects. A new phrase has emerged (though it is not a medical definition) to describe this cultural shift: nature-deficit disorder.

> Nature deficit disorder describes the human costs of alienation from nature, among them: diminished use of the senses, attention difficulties, and higher rates of physical and emotional illnesses. The disorder can be detected in individuals, families, and communities. Nature deficit can even change human behavior in cities, which could ultimately affect their design, since long-standing studies show a relationship between the absence, or inaccessibility, of parks and open space with high crime rates, depression, and other urban maladies.[9]

Participants in the Plaster Creek Oral History Project described their childhood delight and pleasure from outdoor exploration, but often didn't think about the risks they faced. Looking for crayfish, finding toads, and trying their hand at fishing without the assistance of parents or other adults were described by many respondents as some of their favorite memories of childhood. Most parents (from the 1930s to the 2000s) issued warnings about the creek; some parents followed through and were vigilant watching their children when they were near the creek; other parents allowed more freedom. In general, children who grew up between the 1930s and 1950s were given much more freedom to explore without parental supervision. However, even as early as the 1940s, some parents in the upstream agricultural regions of the watershed didn't want their children swimming in Plaster Creek. One of our conversation partners who grew up during that time in the upstream reaches of the watershed described how his memories revolve around swimming in Plaster Creek and trying to keep out of the sight of "the parents."

> The folks never liked us to go swimming in it, but the park crews cleaned out an area of Dutton Park one year. . . . That left a nice little swimming hole about four feet deep. . . . That was right near the start of the creek, so the parents didn't complain as much there. They'd rather have us swim there before the water ran through all the barnyards. . . . The parents kept hassling us, they'd say, "You'll get polio, you'll get amnesia [*sic*], don't go in there." But I'm sure they knew we did *a lot*. I think they kind of encouraged us to go out to the park. There was no lifeguard, no official swimming, but it was cleaner water. . . . That's where the creek started, then it went through the pig farm and the pastures. A lot of kids used to swim in there and probably very few had the permission of the parents.[10]

Another conversation partner who lived downstream in an urban area also remembers using Plaster Creek for fishing, swimming, and other forms of recreation.

> We'd go down as far as Buchanan, which is quite a bit downstream. . . . One thing we used to do, we had rafts. And then we kind of graduated from rafts to plastic boats. . . . They were like about this long, just one-person little deals. And when it rained hard, we would have our parents drop us off by the rec center and then we'd float the creek down. And it was really pretty exciting because when that creek gets up there in flood stage, I mean, anything can happen. That current was pretty nasty.[11]

There were noteworthy historical and cultural shifts occurring during the twentieth century, and the decade in which our interviewees grew up influenced the messages they received from adults. What was considered acceptable in one generation was not necessarily acceptable in the next generation. As an example, several of our older conversation partners mentioned swimming naked in Plaster Creek as children. One interviewee told us, "In 1898, there was an ordinance that said that boys could swim naked in the creek. However, in 1918 it was changed. That was now inappropriate. Boys were no longer allowed to do that."[12] Archival photos from the Grand Rapids Public Library show naked children swimming in Plaster Creek in the early 1900s. Surprisingly this was during the period when Plaster Creek was being used as a conduit for human waste removal. Another conversation partner born in the early 1930s offered this humorous childhood memory of swimming and enjoying Plaster Creek.

> Our mothers were willing to let us go for half a day, take a lunch, play down there, build forts down there whatever we wanted to do. And then come back for supper. And ironically, we would swim in the nude. Now in today's world, that just would not go. But at that time, mothers knew it and it was okay. . . . I remember one time we were fishing off of Buchanan Street by the railroad trestle—my brother and I and another kid and a neighborhood girl. We were fishing and we didn't catch anything. It was a hot day and we finally decided to go swimming and she swam in the nude too. And we didn't think anything of it . . . [long pause] . . . Oh, we probably thought something about it![13]

Children wearing bathing suits to swim in local creeks is only one small example of shifting cultural norms. Perspectives on what is deemed safe or dangerous have shifted over time as well. Two of our conversation partners we learned later were father and son. They grew up in different sections of the Plaster Creek watershed with very different experiences because of differing parental rules. The father (who spoke above about nude swimming as children) continued vividly recalling his memories from the 1940s and how different the cultural norms were in those days because parents and teachers were more lenient.

> In the forties we'd swim down there, we'd fish down there, we'd hunt for turtles and crayfish, and we'd take our lunch down there, build forts down there, we spent a lot of time playing down there. And it may have been contaminated at that time, but we didn't know it. Culture was very different at that time. . . . We had an hour and half lunch hour. We'd play softball or whatever for an hour and then we'd run down to the creek and take a dip before we came back for class. And

> teachers accepted that, I mean, we ran off the playground and went swimming. Not a big deal. I mean, what did I say? Culture was so different then. Are you picking me up on that? My parents were just happy to let us play at the creek. It was not a threat to them.[14]

By the 1950s, those who grew up in the urban downstream sections of the watershed were becoming aware of industrial dumping while those in the rural upstream sections of the watershed remained vaguely aware of potential bacterial contamination from farms. Fast-forward twenty-five years to the late 1960s and the son of the last respondent talked about the rules his parents had for their children playing in Plaster Creek.

> Plaster Creek was kind of our hangout. So we did a lot down there. . . . We all had hatchets. . . . You cut some trees down, build a fort. And we did some ice skating on the creek one winter until somebody fell in and almost drowned. So our parents put an end to that. In the summer we did water rafting. . . . As far as swimming, the rule was—my parents said, "You can wade but you can't swim," so we could wade up to our waist and *of course*, it wasn't much to swim from there. But we tried not to go underwater a lot because people said you'd get lockjaw. So, on our way home we would kind of work our jaws to make sure they didn't stick![15]

In some ways his childhood experience of Plaster Creek was not much different from his father's (rafting, building forts, fishing). But in other ways, his experience was quite different. His parents were aware of the polluted nature of the stream by this time and expressed concern for their children's safety by setting rules of no underwater swimming. Although we can recognize some generational differences between this father and son, both of their childhoods preceded the Clean Water Act in 1972, which made industrial dumping illegal and led to water-quality monitoring finally becoming the norm. Both of these men grew up in a time when the waters of Plaster Creek were not fully safe for child's play (as is true today), though the reasons for the contamination differ.

The key point is that freedom to explore outdoors as children and to learn independently without adult supervision is critical to the formation of ecological commitments as adults. "Childhood exposure to nature on one's own and with friends positively predicts both adulthood environmental citizenship and commitment to nature-based activities."[16] A conversation partner who grew up in a suburban section of the watershed in the 1980s remembered playing at Plaster Creek:

> Being able to go places by myself or with friends . . . helped me develop relationships. There wasn't really a set pattern of things to do. . . . Nobody was programming it for us. We didn't have a schedule from anybody, wasn't planned, we just went and explored without some kind of objective in mind. And I think that the time that we had down there and the time with friends helped me appreciate the natural world in a firsthand way that I would not have been able to do otherwise. . . . That independent time, that time with friends out there both helped me come to an appreciation of that and those were formative times for those friendships.[17]

Gender differences also emerge as distinct when adults recall their connection with the natural world as children. Both male and female conversation partners describe the feeling of adventure and exploration they experienced as children playing near Plaster Creek. Yet there are clear differences in the stories remembered and shared in these interviews. For example, a number of boys describe their encounters near the creek as experiences of freedom and growth, in contrast to girls who describe their experience as mysterious or forbidden.

Observe the difference the following female conversation partners expressed describing their childhood memories of playing near Plaster Creek. These three female conversation partners remember their experiences with Plaster Creek as formative, but for them growing up in the 1950s, Plaster Creek had the draw of a forbidden place. Each one described an element of risk in this childhood exploration, with threats perceived as real.

> We liked to go down there. And our mother was always nervous about us being there, so we often went there without telling her that that's where we were. So it had the sense of the forbidden. . . . When I was young, we were on those trails, and we helped make those trails with our feet. We did a lot of observation as children, knowing where certain flowers were growing in the woods around Plaster Creek. We would make forts, you know how children always do that, so we would do that. And we would sometimes get *really* brave and cross logs and go to the other side of Plaster Creek, but not for very long![18]

> When we got old enough my girlfriends and I would float down the creek in a little blue plastic boat—and we'd float down the creek and tip over frequently. . . . All the kids in the neighborhood played down there. Everyone built camps during the summer. We all had our camps. And the game was that you really had to hide your camps—otherwise, other neighborhood kids would find them and wreck them. So it was kind of territorial almost, except that you were trying to hide your camp so that no one would find them and ruin them. And if you found someone else's you always took what you wanted.[19]

> We moved to Grand Rapids when I was in fourth grade and my parents built a house [in the suburbs]. . . . My girlfriend and I and maybe my sister would start to explore the area. There were ravines and at the bottom of the ravine was a creek [a tributary to Plaster Creek]. We discovered on this creek that there was this place that had a sandy shore and it felt like a beach. So, we took off our shoes and waded in the creek. . . . The water looked very pretty and dappled, and the sandy bottom looked clear and clean. I was *very* thirsty, and said, "I think I want to get a drink." My girlfriend responded with, "My mother said you can't drink out of that creek, it's dirty. There are bugs in it." So, I looked at it, I didn't see any bugs. . . . Then I saw this old Coke bottle, so as they packed up and started walking off, I cleaned up that Coke bottle and filled it up. I didn't see any bugs. So . . . glug, glug, glug. I drank a good half of it, and I felt so much better. Then I threw the Coke bottle away—didn't want to show the others—and then I caught up with them. So we kept exploring and whatever we did that day and we finally got home. I didn't tell anybody. . . . Then that night I was *so* anxious, "Am I going to get sick?" But I finally fell asleep. The next day, I was fine. Didn't get sick that week so I thought, "It must be okay." [Laughs] We had a lot more good times of exploring![20]

Boys, on the other hand, tell quite adventurous stories of climbing through and exploring the large matrix of storm drains under one section of Grand Rapids. One respondent talked about creating their own torch to light their way as they explored inside the storm drains.

> You could pour torch fluid in a pop bottle and put a cloth in it—basically a Molotov cocktail that you don't throw—and you'd light the way. . . . We'd go

> down there and we'd each have one flashlight and about three of these Molotov cocktails and we'd explore that way. . . . Every so often your foot would catch the edge of the water where it is slimy and somebody would slip and the bottle would smash. All the fluid would leak out into the stream and then catch fire and the whole stream would light up with this huge fire. We just thought it was funny although we'd lose a light in the process. We didn't try to do it on purpose. But that's my most vivid recollection of going down there.[21]

This conversation partner spoke about going underground often enough that they mapped a four-mile section of storm "tunnels" underneath Grand Rapids. He recalled one frightening experience for his brother and two friends as they were exploring the storm drains and a huge rainstorm began above unbeknownst to them. Stormwater runoff began rushing into the storm drains, and the boys were trapped inside the drain, holding on together to the metal rungs of a ladder leading to a manhole cover (which was locked from above) while the water rose and rose.

> You've got the tunnel and then every so often there would be this kind of almost like an underground tower with little steps inside with a manhole on top. And the three of them were cramped up into that little five-foot square area there . . . watching the water rise just below them. . . . They were thinking, "If it overflows into the street, we are dead." And it went all the way up, filled the tunnel, so they were completely trapped and . . . the manhole cover, they couldn't push it up, it was sealed for whatever reason. . . . They were probably hanging up there for thirty minutes before they finally saw the stormwater start to recede.[22]

Some of our male conversation partners were aware of the risks involved in such exploration, but others seemed oblivious to the dangers. We heard adventurous stories from both women and men who grew up within the Plaster Creek watershed, yet they describe very different types of risk and danger. Some of these differences are probably due to the influence of male and female socialization at the historical period of their growing up.

Exploring the dynamics of family, culture, religion, and education is beyond the scope of this book, but gender differences can clearly be detected, and this has an impact on the freedom children were given to play outside. The salient feature of the child-nature experience is the amount of freedom to explore that children are offered in their outdoor play as described by researchers who have studied children's exposure to nature as predictive of adult environmental citizenship.

> With freer play, children have much deeper interactions with nature and hence cultivate stronger and more enduring connections with nature. These findings, in light of the differences between free and structured play, are additionally insightful because commitment to nature-based activities is not only associated with improved health but also with enhanced environmental citizenship.[23]

Children need freedom within safe boundaries to explore the world. Respondents who had memories of Plaster Creek from childhood happily recalled their experiences, oftentimes with laughter and sometimes with embarrassment about what they actually did as children along Plaster Creek. What was striking is they used language that revealed a sense of affection for what the creek meant to them during their formative years.

Affection and Learning to Care for Our Place

Improved health is not the only benefit a person receives from robust interaction with the environment as children. Important life lessons are learned as well. Some theorists have written about the importance of feeling an attachment to a place and have used attachment theory to describe the benefits of feeling connected to a particular place. Richard Louv writes,

> Surely children need a quality attachment to land not only for their own health, but in order to feel compelled to protect nature as adults—not only as common-sense conservationists, but as citizens and as voters. . . . In the world of child development, attachment theory posits that the creation of a deep bond between child and parent is a complex psychological, biological, and spiritual process, and that without this attachment a child is lost, vulnerable to all manner of later pathologies. I believe that a similar process can bind adults to a place and give them a sense of belonging and meaning. Without a deep attachment to place, an adult can also feel lost. . . . Attachment to land is not only good for the child, but good for the land as well. . . . If a geographic place rapidly changes in a

> way that demeans its natural integrity, then children's early attachment to land is at risk. If children do not attach to the land, they will not reap the psychological and spiritual benefits they can glean from nature, nor will they feel a long-term commitment to the environment, to the place.[24]

When a child gets to know a particular place well, often a deep affection develops. What we have affection for, we want to take care of. Learning to care for a place has the potential to contribute to a child's sense of self while also sustaining the natural world. Environmental education advocate David Orr emphasizes that

> The child must have an opportunity to "soak in a place, and the adolescent and adult must be able to return to that place to ponder the visible substrate of his own personality." Hence, knowledge of a place—where you are and where you come from—is intertwined with knowledge of who you are.[25]

One conversation partner who grew up in the 1960s and has lived his entire life in different sections upstream in the watershed described some of his most vivid memories then and now of Plaster Creek. Noticing the fish in Plaster Creek as a child began as a curious inspection and has continued to be a lifelong observation. One year he discovered a surprising thing.

> As I think back, I was actually living on 60th Street at that time, and I believe Plaster Creek or one of the tributaries flowed through the property and I can remember as a little kid going back on the farmland, in the water, and playing in the creek. I was a little boy—and it's water and it's fun to play in. That's my earliest memory back in the early sixties. And then through the school years, they'd take school groups to Shadyside Park in Dutton. The creek crawls through the park and I remember watching the little fish swimming in the stream. Every time I've ever been to Shadyside Park since then, I'm over there looking for the fish! Because it's just something I remember from being young and being in elementary school. . . . In the late nineties, early 2000s you had to look a lot harder to find any fish. In the last few years, they are there again! Last year we were out by our creek—our kids love it—and I'm cutting some dead trees and harvesting them. I look down in the water and there's a fish! Over the years, we've seen *little* minnows in our section. So, I think, "No, that can't be a fish. There hasn't been a fish like

> that in this creek for thirty years." So, I get my wife and we look, and this thing must have been a twenty-seven- to twenty eight-inch trout. It was huge! And we could not figure out where this thing came from. . . . This was one humongous fish trying to go upstream.[26]

One of the advantages of interviewing folks who have lived in a particular place long term is that we can gain insight into how things have changed over time. Not all changes are negative; some changes are positive. This conversation partner's knowledge of his particular place, his observations and attention over a long period of time, offers a unique vantage point on the Plaster Creek watershed. The fact that he observed a large fish in Plaster Creek after many years of only seeing minnows reveals something of the resilience of the natural world. But it also points to how his connection to the natural world has been formative. Because he noticed and observed changes to the world close to him, he developed a long-term commitment to care for the earth.

Childhood experiences with nature not only influence our life at that moment but often have a lasting effect on how we view the world and our place in it. One female conversation partner, who grew up downstream in a suburban area, spoke eloquently about why Plaster Creek matters to her and why she cares about it. This is the place where she learned to notice the world.

> It is where I learned—and it was a kind of learning by osmosis—but it was your territory and . . . I wanted to know what I was seeing. And it affected me. [My sister and I] were in a business for many years and now we are both doing plants. And I really think Plaster Creek had something to do with that. 'Cause that's where we learned to love it. I learned the power of observation and figuring out how to do things even when your parents said "No." It's a skill we all have to learn, right? And working together with other kids. There was a whole sense of awe about what nature was and . . . you could explore it for yourself. This sense of being able to go out and see it and do it and make observations about it.[27]

These stories illustrate Richard Louv's emphasis on the significance of connecting to a place. When children are detached from the natural world, there are broad ripple effects. Conversely when children are connected to nature, much can be gained.

Nature-deficit disorder can be recognized and reversed, individually and culturally. But deficit is only one side of the coin. The other is natural abundance. By weighing the consequences of the disorder, we also can become more aware of how blessed our children can be—biologically, cognitively, and spiritually—through positive physical connection to nature. Indeed, the new research focuses not so much on what is lost when nature fades, but on what is gained in the presence of the natural world.[28]

Lifelong Impact of Childhood Experiences with Nature

Today's kids are made aware of the current global threats to the environment by teachers, parents, and news reports. Growing up with this knowledge can be frightening and overwhelming. If young people today are to develop a sense of agency to make restorative changes, an important first step is their own physical contact and intimacy with nature. "Self-exposure to nature during childhood was associated with improved adulthood commitment to nature-based activities and with enhanced environmental literacy and political-ecological citizenship behaviors during adult life."[29] This connection was affirmed among conversation partners who articulated that developing a sense of agency for environmental care goes back to meaningful interactions they had with the natural world as young children. This is no small thing.

One conversation partner described the benefit of his Indigenous background that taught him traditional ecological knowledge that he later combined with technical scientific knowledge when he attended university. But it was his early experiences learning about the natural world from elders that have impacted him for life.

> The rivers were highways. . . . Grand Rapids to our tribe at one time was like our Garden of Eden, because down there you had the rapids, which were charged—they could put oxygen back in the water which did good for all the animals, fish, mammals, birds, whatever. . . . There were animals for sustenance, clothing; there were plants for medicines, for foods. In Grand Rapids downtown there was everything that a person needed to survive. . . . I was really fortunate to grow up when I did because to have older Indian people teaching me, even

> though later I went to college and learned the whole technical sense of the things I already knew.[30]

Two other conversation partners who grew up in the 1980s describe vividly how their experiences playing outside in their youth have been instrumental in shaping their future understanding. The first described how his times with friends playing by the creek created opportunities to develop competencies and confidence that have been impactful for life. The second conversation partner acknowledged that although as a child he didn't fully realize the problems the creek was facing, the memories and fun he experienced when young gave him a foundation of basic understanding that he could recall to make sense of concerns he learned about as he grew to adulthood.

> We will always have those times in the woods. . . . It was part of becoming an adult for me and part of coming of age. These were things that were planned and done by us, as kids. . . . There's just things that kids can think up and try to do when given some freedom and opportunity. The kinds of memories that come from experiences like that. You know, there's something about being outside. . . . The subtotal of these experiences contributed to my formation as a person and my learning how to *have* a friend, *be* a friend. Being outside was the ideal and best place for those kinds of experiences to happen. And much of that happened right by the creek. Those experiences . . . can all be formative for us because the more we are able to go outside and do things and accomplish things and figure things out and have these experiences, we are the ones who are responsible for them. I believe there is a direct correlation between that and the level of competence and confidence we have as adults.[31]

> As a kid, you like the trees falling down over the creek because then you can climb over them and it's the bridge, the natural bridge crossing—one of the fun things we would do as a kid. Now I know why those trees were falling and still are falling over the creek. . . . It's all the runoff from the urban environment where there is all this pavement.[32]

Young people also need diverse learning opportunities if we hope they will become future leaders in reconciliation ecology. One of our conversation partners recalled a learning experience as a high school student in the mid-1970s that transformed the way he thinks about the *connectedness* of the natural world. His school held an Environmental Week when he was a ninth grader. He was required to research a topic of interest, and he chose to study the impact of the pesticide DDT. Here's an excerpt from his interview.

> I read *Silent Spring* when I was fifteen years old and found the prose was just astounding. It just takes you from one place and puts you in another, because she was the first scientist that was thinking broadly about the impact of watersheds and watershed management and the connectedness. If anything was clear in that week, it was the connectedness. One guy gave a lecture, a slideshow. He had photographs of a parking lot and all the dust in the parking lot and how when it rains all the dust in the parking lot goes down that drain and that drain goes into a sewer and the sewer goes into a creek . . . So he actually started in a parking lot and then started filming all the watershed changes and then ends with an aerial photograph of the Grand River flowing into Lake Michigan. And of course, you have it flowing thick with silt and it is surrounded by the blue water of Lake Michigan. I *still* remember this as clear as can be and he said, "What you are doing in that parking lot is affecting what's happening twenty-five miles away where the Grand River flows into Lake Michigan. And if you improve the management of water at this upland site and this parking lot, then what the water does when it hits Lake Michigan will not be so devastatingly bad." You could just see it was just nasty. But for some reason, that lecture when I was fifteen years old, just stuck in my mind. It is like, yeah, there is no place in the landscape where you are not impacting water quality.[33]

These conversation partners confirm that their childhood experiences, including free play outdoors, learning from elders, and school experiences that stretched their imaginations, have shaped them into adults who work to heal the degradation of the earth.

Developing Future Environmental Leaders

In the fall of 2012 PCS leaders were invited to an Urban Waters national training held in Washington, D.C., at the headquarters of the Environmental Protection Agency (EPA). There we were introduced to policymakers and practitioners working to restore urban waters throughout the United States. We learned about organizations in Washington, D.C., and Atlanta who had initiated youth development programs for water protectors and earth keepers. Their vision was inspiring, and this motivated us to develop our own youth development initiative.

In the summer of 2013, we launched the Plaster Creek Stewards Green Team to provide at-risk urban youth with education and research experience in watershed ecology and restoration, job skill development in green infrastructure installation and maintenance, and interaction with faculty and college student assistants. The educational programs we had been doing in watershed schools provided an opening to invite high school students to apply for the Green Team. We prioritized high schools in the Plaster Creek watershed whose students may not have been considering higher education as an option for their future. We worked to recruit students who might benefit from mentoring by college students, hoping to demystify the college experience and increase their future likelihood of pursuing education beyond high school.

In keeping with our focus on upstream–downstream connections we expanded the Green Team in 2015 to include students from the nearby Rogue River watershed. Both the Plaster Creek watershed and the Rogue River watershed are nested within the much larger Lower Grand River watershed. Green Team students in the upstream Rogue River watershed tend to be rural or suburban and predominantly white, while Green Team students in the downstream Plaster Creek watershed tend to be urban and members of racial and ethnic minorities.

The learning experiences for the Green Teams from these two subwatersheds have been rich and broad. Students learn how to work as part of a team to accomplish goals; they learn about watershed issues and their relevance to environmental justice; they learn about the role of green infrastructure in low-impact development; and most importantly they experience cross-cultural engagement by working across racial and cultural differences that usually divide communities. Part of the Green Team experience includes diversity and inclusion training to raise awareness and develop a common language to discuss equity issues. At least weekly throughout the summer the two Green Teams meet together for classroom instruction on watershed ecology and work side by side installing green infrastructure in one of the two watersheds. At the end of each Green Team experience, a day is set aside for Green Team participants to shadow Calvin students who are involved in summer research. This experience introduces the high school students to scientific research and the possibilities college offers for

FIGURE 19. Plaster Creek Stewards Green Team installing a green infrastructure project.
PHOTOGRAPH BY GAIL GUNST HEFFNER.

them. Helping the high school Green Team students make watershed connections, learn about upstream–downstream interactions, and develop a vision for their own educational future are all important aspects of preparing young people to become environmental leaders.

Initial funding for the Green Team program came from the Michigan Colleges Alliance and later from the EPA Urban Waters division. Local foundations and businesses contributed to the expansion of the program. In recent years the Green Team program has garnered broad grassroots support from individuals, local partners, and Green Team alumni. This summer program has been operating for more than a decade, and many Green Team students have now graduated from high school and continued on to college. This unique learning experience has influenced many of the Green Team participants as they chose their fields of study and/or future vocations. A survey of former Green Team students asked what they most remember about their experience and how their understanding of their relationship to the natural world has changed. One Green Team alumna responded:

> I remember [our leader] introducing us to some of the plants in the nursery in my first year with the Green Team. He explained each plant's different abilities, needs, and preferences—elucidating the fact that all plants were different, like they had a personality, and would provide different things to a rain garden or forest. Most distinctly, I remember him showing us a leggy plant called boneset that was used by Native Americans to help bones heal. I was like, "What?? Plants can heal?? Medicine can grow?!" Since then, I have continued to be fascinated by medicinal plants and traditional healing systems that operate in vastly different methods and philosophies from our conventional Western medical system. As a current medical student, I am hoping to pursue research in how different cultures make meaning around wellness, illness, and healing. . . . Our health is closely tied to the health of the natural world.[34]

Her understanding of our human interdependence with the natural world and the connections between upstream and downstream has impacted the way she understands her place in the world.

> Coming to understand that water is always a shared resource made me aware of the power my actions have to change the water experienced by those downstream. We all have a duty to steward the water in front of us; my pollution affects someone else's water downstream. And I depend on my upstream neighbors to steward their water. It was a visceral application of the Golden Rule that has made me come to understand how inextricably tied we are to the experiences of the rest of humanity, not just regarding our water. . . . Green Team helped me begin to realize, at quite a young age, that nature and humanity were created to be in relationship with each other. We will always be dependent on the natural world; self-sufficiency feels like an illusion.[35]

Hearing these words from a former Green Team student, who can articulate so clearly how her experience with the Green Team has impacted her understanding, her education, and her vocational choices, points to the importance of engaging youth and helping them actually *see and experience* human–nature relationships.[36]

Young people can be introduced to reconciliation ecology in various ways. Free play outdoors for children sets the stage for more structured experiences in school and community settings as children grow into adulthood. Every time young people are encouraged to interact with creation, better understand how it works, document its condition with research, help it to heal by taking reparative action, the critically important relationship between people and nature grows. The Green Team program meaningfully engages the next generation of watershed stewards and is an example of how to develop future environmental leaders and earth keepers by connecting matters of environmental and social justice.

CHAPTER 13

An Invitation to the Work of Reconciliation Ecology Everywhere

In the years since we began Plaster Creek Stewards (PCS) in 2009, many community members across age and gender, race and ethnicity have gathered for education sessions and have toiled with us in hot weather and cold, in rain, in sunshine, and even in snow. Sometimes the work is tedious, sometimes difficult, while other times it hardly feels like work at all. Overall, we have found that work undertaken with others to improve the world we share is joyful work. One very creative idea emerged this year from a young couple who has been actively involved with PCS for many years. In honor of the husband's fortieth birthday, they purchased forty trees and invited their friends and family to help plant these trees along a tributary of Plaster Creek near their home. Not only did this celebration result in forty new trees helping to increase biodiversity, capture stormwater, and absorb carbon, this event introduced new people to the work of PCS and reconciliation ecology in a fun and celebratory way.

An Unfolding Story

The new story of the Plaster Creek watershed continues to unfold. When we began our watershed work, we had *some* idea of the problems that existed. We knew degradation was being caused by unexamined assumptions leading to damaging lifestyles. We recognized injustices existing in our place. Yet what we have learned along the way about the present and the past has been more unsettling and much more challenging than we ever envisioned. As white European Americans, we were naïve about the history of this place and did not fully grasp how much our ancestors contributed to the environmental damage we are experiencing. Watershed restoration is only one aspect of the ecological and social healing that is needed on our planet. Radical change is needed if we hope to avert a grim future. Yet watershed restoration is a good place to begin, because no matter where you live everyone lives in a watershed. This final chapter is an invitation for readers to consider how to practice the hopeful work of reconciliation ecology in their own place.

Learning from Indigenous Worldviews

Because worldviews shape ways of living, they have far-reaching impacts. Environmental degradation is often a symptom of underlying worldview assumptions that encourage human greed, convenience, and valuing the natural world only for the resources it provides. Because many assumptions are unconscious and taken-for-granted, it is difficult to challenge them. Yet a paradigm shift is possible—one that changes the way people interact with each other and live within the land. Native American scholar Daniel Wildcat writes,

> The most difficult changes required are not those of a physical, material, or technological character, but changes in worldviews and the generally taken-for-granted values and beliefs that are embedded in modern, Western-influenced societies. In this respect, what humankind actually requires is a climate change—a cultural climate change, a change in our thinking and actions—if we are to have any reasonable expectation that we might mitigate what increasingly appears to be a period of dramatic plant and animal extinction.[1]

While much can be learned from Indigenous worldviews, we highlight three key assumptions to create a foundation for implementing watershed restoration through reconciliation ecology.

First, Indigenous worldviews see *humans as part of the natural world*, not outside of it or separate from it. This requires a shift from thinking we are the pinnacle of importance. We must replace our urge to conquer and control with a focus on learning how to live carefully within our places, more in harmony with the earth. How can we best fit into the natural world? We need both systemic change *and* individual change—incentivized policies that encourage people to drive less, walk more, eat more from the local economy, and reduce consumption. Learning how to live in a community in ways that support our neighbors and increase biodiversity are achievable goals. These approaches have implications for how we care about local waters. For example, municipalities can learn how the land absorbed rain in presettlement times and then choose options that more carefully mimic the environmental services the land formerly provided. Residents can learn to use and reuse rainwater, instead of sending it into the nearest creek as quickly as possible.

Second, part of learning to live in harmony with the earth is to recognize that *humans are in relationship with the nonhuman world* and can learn to interact in mutually dependent symbiotic ways that enable all to thrive. The gifts of the natural world were not intended just for humans. Many Indigenous traditions focus on "finding ways to live . . . within environments, instead of expending the energies modern humans expend to changing environments," as Wildcat suggests.[2] This frame of reference opens opportunities for recognizing our kinship with the nonhuman world and the gifts it offers to us.

Supporting policies that create and preserve land (i.e., parks and preserves) and working to ensure that all neighborhoods have healthy green spaces are ways to recognize our kinship with the natural world. Surrounding our homes, schools, and houses of worship with plants that originated in Europe or Asia is a subtle way to perpetuate colonialism and can damage North American biodiversity. But incorporating native plants into local landscapes is a step toward decolonization. Native insects and birds will return, and healthier, more reciprocal relationships will emerge.

Third, learning to *live within an environment necessarily places limits on human autonomy* and stands in contrast to the belief in unlimited frontiers exhibited by settler colonists and their descendants. Recognizing our human limits could spur us to *live with restraint*, not taking more from the natural world than what we can give in return. Living within boundaries fosters humility, creativity, and the potential for rich flourishing to occur.

These three elements of Indigenous worldviews can help shift our thinking away from "one size fits all" to asking different kinds of questions about what is needed for people and other creatures to thrive in each particular place. As Wildcat argues, much can be learned from Indigenous cultures who created ways of living to match their unique landscape and environment.

> We might do well to ask ourselves how residing in places might foster life enhancement—not so much making places our own but allowing places to give us homes. . . . If American society will take Native cultures seriously, we can examine how Indigenous tribal cultures, unlike the increasingly homogeneous global consumer culture, maintain a tangible and meaningful connection between where a people live and how they live. The result will be useful knowledge about how living within a biosphere with diverse landscapes and environments . . . requires people- and place-specific investigations.[3]

Living in a place of water abundance or a place of water scarcity should influence how we live in the landscape. How do we protect water and not overuse it for nonessential needs? How do we guarantee that healthy waters will be available for future generations?

For white Americans who have lived unquestioningly (and often unconsciously) within a settler colonial worldview for decades, challenging our own assumptions is difficult. We may not even realize how these assumptions permeate our thinking and affect our relationship with the earth. Reconciliation ecology offers one way to reframe how people live in relationship with the natural world and can contribute to the work of decolonization.[4] Admittedly, decolonization is an expansive and challenging endeavor for communities who have lived with historical dissonance for decades. Yet the challenge is to move beyond making "superficial changes without realizing the depth and difficulty of the learning that is necessary to interrupt systemic colonial patterns that are perceived as normal, natural and in many cases, benevolent."[5]

For insights from Indigenous ways of living to take root, European Americans will need to listen respectfully and with openness to the life experiences of Black, Indigenous, and People of Color (BIPOC) in our communities and submit ourselves to learn from them as an important part of reconciliation ecology. Indigenous writer Taiaiake Alfred encourages non-Indigenous people to become allies in the healing of the natural world.

> They [non-Indigenous people] can play a part in the decolonization of this land simply by disassociating themselves from the privileges that are built into being

> part of the settler society, softening the stifling grip mainstream society has on Indigenous existences. Forgoing the need to be right, to be in charge, and to possess. . . . For all of us, Indigenous and settler alike, there is only self-questioning and embracing this commitment: Listen to the voices of our Indigenous ancestors channeled through the young people of our nations, learn from Indigenous culture how to walk differently, and love the land as best you can.[6]

If healing and restoration are to happen, developing relationships of trust between diverse people groups is imperative. And building reconciled relationships will take time, humility, patience, forgiveness, and hard work, if trust is to grow. The emerging commitment to live into a new and better future comes out of the brokenness of the past but can lead to future collaborations that will promote healing.[7] While it is impossible to change every American's worldview, our hope is for enough people to be persuaded until a tipping point is reached. Working for reconciliation ecology can contribute to a transformed future.

Implementing Reconciliation Ecology

In our experience, learning how to implement reconciliation ecology has involved a continuous process of recognizing problems, acknowledging our complicity, and committing to reparative action to heal the damage that's been done. While the brokenness between humans and the natural world is expansive and daunting, we can approach restoration and healing as more than an obligation. It is also an invitation to reflect on what is possible, to creatively imagine new directions, and to actively repair damaged relationships. "When we all take these steps to heal, we can both address the harms of the past, and stop the cycle of harm that continues because of the lasting legacy of colonization."[8] For those interested in promoting reconciliation ecology personally and collectively in their place, we offer some suggestions for how to begin.

Recognition

Get to know your place. What features of the natural landscape are unique to where you live? How is your home place similar to and also different from other places? Notice what has been maintained and preserved and what has been damaged and degraded over time.

What watershed do you live in and who resides there with you? By identifying who shares your home place, you begin to recognize whose lives are intertwined with yours. Raising awareness is a first step to healing degradation. We each have the potential to influence others either positively or negatively. Ponder who is in your sphere of influence and consider how to enlist them in the quest for reconciliation.

Pay attention to water. Does your place suffer more frequently from excess flooding or drought conditions? Are the nearby rivers, streams, lakes, and oceans a source of clean water or a conduit for contaminated water? What other species have been influenced by the changes that have occurred in your watershed over time?

Notice where rainwater collects or where it flows during a rainstorm. One of our conversation partners in the Plaster Creek Oral History Project suggested, "One thing an average resident or citizen could do is watch their property during a rainstorm and find out where the rainwater goes."[9] Once you know, you can learn how to protect and care for that water.

Acknowledging Complicity

Learn about the peoples native to your home place and what has been happening to them during the past two hundred years. Learn about the immigrants who came to your place and what drew them there. Who has thrived in your place? Who has been marginalized? Who has had the power to enact change and who has been blocked from participating in decisions that affect their lives? Louise Erdrich, a Pulitzer Prize–winning novelist, writes, "Our history marks us. Sometimes I think our state's beginning years haunt everything: the city's attempt to graft progressive ideas onto its racist origins, the fact that we can't undo history but are forced to either confront or repeat it."[10] Erdrich is referring to her home state of Minnesota, but the same can be said for Michigan and most places in North America. We must face the parts of our history that disgrace or embarrass us, knowing that if we don't confront them, the pain and suffering of the past will be repeated.

Only when we honestly acknowledge what the history of colonization has done in the United States can we begin to undo its damage. This is true broadly, but it is also true in local watersheds.

> Central to a watershed ethos should be a commitment to restorative justice for all those displaced in the past and marginalized in the present. The land itself is an historic subject whose story must be learned. The current health of a place must be assessed from the perspective of both land and people who have experienced degradation. . . . In particular, we must learn the legacy of Indigenous communities—whether disappeared, displaced, or "inconveniently" present. Though many traditional lifeways were casualties of conquest and colonization, our collective survival depends upon learning how First Nations lived sustainably.[11]

And so the PCS team takes every opportunity to tell watershed residents the stories of our past—the stories of gypsum and waterfalls, walleye, boarding schools, and buried streams. These stories recount how Ken-O-Sha was a healthy, life-supporting stream that enhanced the lives of birds and bears, fish and people but later became the life-threatening Plaster Creek. And these stories remind us that we are capable of so much more than erasing beauty and contaminating streams. Today watershed inhabitants are becoming inspired to live better within the land, in ways that promote the beauty and diversity that formerly characterized this watershed.

A land acknowledgement statement is a preliminary step that an organization or institution can take to acknowledge past and present harm to people and to the earth. We lament that many of the injustices that have happened in the Plaster Creek watershed cannot be undone. But through a more accurate understanding of the history of our watershed, we honor the presence of Indigenous people. As an organization, PCS has developed a land acknowledgment statement that reads,

> The Plaster Creek Watershed occupies a portion of the ancestral home of the Hopewell people (Goodall Focus), and more recently the Anishinaabe Three Fires Confederacy of Ojibwe, Ottawa, and Potawatomi nations. We are grateful for the way these early inhabitants cared for the land and loved it. We are informed by their teachings and strive to honor their example through ongoing education and restoration work.[12]

In every community across the United States, there are environmental justice issues at play. One way to begin the work of reconciliation is to identify and learn about local environmental justice issues by getting to know the people and places most impacted by them. People with privilege have a responsibility to acknowledge injustice wherever it occurs and work to address it, in partnership with those most affected by environmental injustice. Concerted effort is required to move beyond words to specific actions to promote reconciliation ecology in every place.

To heal the broken relationship we have with the land means to acknowledge what we have done to cause the damage and then refrain from doing additional harm. Learning new behaviors, new practices, new ways of thinking about the land are all important steps in the healing process.

Restorative and Reparative Actions

Discover who is doing environmental restoration in your local community and get involved by volunteering or providing financial support. Do your local environmental groups offer educational opportunities for community members to learn about the past and current history of the issues facing your community? Move from thinking about the problems to taking specific action to address the problems.

Colleges and universities could be a resource for local communities who are trying to address environmental degradation. Tapping into faculty expertise in community-based research can help local communities identify and address specific local problems. Additionally, colleges and universities benefit greatly from the insights and experiences of community members if they take the time to listen and learn. Often translation is needed between colleges and communities. This is similar to the translation needed between traditional ecological knowledge and scientific ecological knowledge. Both have valuable contributions to make, and learning how to listen to each other to foster true understanding is no small task.

Faith communities are another potential resource for organizing people to practice reconciliation ecology in their local place. Congregations from diverse backgrounds can be invited into this work of restoration. Beginning with the land on which the congregation gathers for worship, houses of worship can demonstrate to the larger community how to care for the natural world. Part of this work involves getting to know who lived within the land in the past, what led to their displacement, and taking steps to be reconciled with the descendants of past dwellers.

Reaching out to youth and providing mentoring or internship opportunities is an investment in the future. Young people need both knowledge and practice in implementing needed restorative changes. As young people grow in experience, they will develop a sense of agency that they can, in fact, make their places better. Follow the example of Indigenous elders who take seriously passing on their knowledge and experience to the next generation by volunteering with local schools or youth programs.

Urban development will continue in the United States; we will not ever return to presettlement times. The question is how to develop cities in ways that protect and safeguard water. In the last two decades new methods of designing and constructing sustainable urban settlements have introduced low-impact development (LID) techniques and green infrastructure (GI) to minimize negative impacts on stormwater drainage. Some communities are implementing innovative techniques to capture, retain, and reuse rainwater within their particular watershed to meet the need for flood prevention and improve water quality. Citizens as well as local officials can learn about the native landscapes that were present in their place before European settlement. Efforts to bring back native plants through landscaping, LID practices, and other green infrastructure projects can significantly contribute to a more beautiful and biodiverse future.

Our ultimate task is to help people connect with each other and develop affection for their place. We affirm what Indigenous writer Daniel Wildcat advocates: "We are trying to reconnect, in a deep spatial and spiritual sense, to the places where we live and the life systems that support us."[13] When asked what can be done to restore the Plaster Creek watershed, one of our conversation partners began his train of thought with specific actions that could be taken but eventually ended by saying what he felt was the single most important action for promoting reconciliation.

> I think one of the ways . . . you can help to "save the creek," so to speak, is by helping people connect with it better . . . [so] they take more stake in it. When they can connect with it, they enjoy it, they figure out the value it has and they want to do something about it. . . . Helping people to connect with those green spaces and the importance of them is going to be probably the single best thing we can do to save the creek.[14]

FIGURE 20. Doing hard work together can be a joyful experience.
PHOTOGRAPH BY GAIL GUNST HEFFNER.

Each Small Place Is a Part of the Mosaic of the Whole

This beautiful, diverse, yet wounded world is itself made up of many small mosaic pieces, and each one, if tended well, can contribute to the flourishing of the whole. As we collectively work to improve the places in which we live, we *can* learn how to better fit in. The relationship of humanity with Plaster Creek is a subplot of the human presence on earth. And our response today in *this* place is but one contribution to the global challenge of sustainability. When our response here coalesces with similar responses in places elsewhere, a hopeful future emerges. We affirm what writer Barry Lopez wrote in his final, impassioned book:

> We must invent overnight, figuratively speaking, another kind of civilization, one more cognizant of limits, less greedy, more compassionate, less bigoted, more inclusive, less exploitive. . . . At the heart . . . is a simple but profound statement: "I object." I have studied what we have done to the planet and I object. I object to the exploitation of, and the lack of respect for, human laborers. I object to the frantic commercialization of the many realms of daily life. I object to the desecration of what is beautiful. . . . I object to society's complacency. . . . [It's] an invitation, instead to reimagine our future, to identify a different road than

the one that the prophets of technological innovation, or global climate change itself, are offering us. It's the road to our survival.[15]

By hearing the story of Plaster Creek, we hope readers will be inspired to address the plight of their own places, which will help save our common, imperiled planet. And as we work collectively in our various places, take time to celebrate the small wins. It has taken the Plaster Creek watershed two hundred years to achieve the degraded condition it is in today. It will likely require several more decades of concerted effort for lasting improvements to be realized. Yet we are witnessing a growing interest among West Michigan residents to learn how they can contribute to improving this place. As momentum continues to build, we are cultivating a hope that one day the walleye will return to spawn in Plaster Creek. And then perhaps the creek's name could appropriately be changed back to Ken-O-Sha, Water of the Walleye, honoring the Indigenous people of our place and the reconciliation that is underway.

Notes

PREFACE

1. In this book we use the name "Ottawa" instead of "Odawa" because "Ottawa" is how most Indigenous members of this group refer to themselves.
2. Blackbird, *History of the Ottawa and Chippewa*, 28–29.
3. Belknap Writings and Correspondence, Captain Charles Eugene Belknap Collection.
4. Quoted in Brown, "The Watershed Approach," 1.
5. Myers, *Watershed Discipleship*, 11, 17.
6. Orr, *Ecological Literacy*, 129.
7. Rosenzweig, *Win-Win Ecology*; Francis, "Perspectives on the Potential for Reconciliation Ecology in Urban Riverscapes."
8. Warners, Ryskamp and Van Dragt, "Reconciliation Ecology"; Bouma, Huizenga, and Warners, "Assessing a Reconciliation Ecology Approach to Suburban Landscaping."
9. Each participant in the Plaster Creek Oral History Project agreed to be interviewed and signed a consent form. To safeguard their identity, no names or aliases have been used in the book. When a quote is used, the transcript is identified by number and page from which the quote comes (e.g., PCOHP #16, 22 means the quote comes from page 22 of the 16th transcript for the Plaster Creek Oral History Project).
10. Gyasi, *Homegoing*, 226–27.
11. Brickell, "London and the River Lea," 41.

INTRODUCTION

1. Rosenzweig, *Win-Win Ecology.*
2. Treuer, "Return the National Parks."
3. Warners, Ryskamp, and Van Dragt, "Reconciliation Ecology."
4. Bahnson and Wirzba, *Making Peace with the Land*, 17.
5. Many other countries have instituted Truth and Reconciliation Commissions, including Sierra Leone, Guatemala, Liberia, Australia, and Chile. An article in *Yes! Magazine* describes Canada's Truth and Reconciliation Commission, highlighting benefits the United States could achieve by acting similarly: Stacey McKenna, "A Way Out of a Dark Past," *Yes! Magazine*, November 3, 2020, https://www.yesmagazine.org/issue/what-the-rest-of-the-world-knows/2020/11/03/canada-truth-reconciliation.
6. Tutu, *No Future without Forgiveness*, 270.
7. Tutu, *No Future without Forgiveness*, 271.
8. PCOHP #72, 11.
9. Maathai, "Marching with Trees."
10. Bahnson and Wirzba, *Making Peace with the Land*, 31.
11. Berry, *It All Turns on Affection.*
12. Mann, "1491: New Revelations." Mann's insights were first published in an *Atlantic* article in 2002, followed by a more detailed book in 2005. See also Stokes Brown, *Big History.*
13. Cronon, *Changes in the Land.*
14. Cronon, *Changes in the Land*; Cleland, *Rites of Conquest*; Jennings, *The Founders of America.*
15. Cleland, *Rites of Conquest*; Cronon, *Changes in the Land.*
16. Jennings, *The Christian Imagination*, 8.
17. Three excellent books by historians that detail how injustice played out in the Great Lakes region are Richard White's *The Middle Ground* (1991), Charles E. Cleland's *Rites of Conquest* (2001), and Michael Witgen's *An Infinity of Nations* (2012). Theologian Willie Jennings describes how racism toward Indigenous people was immersed within Christian faith in an interview by Dustin Dwyer, "An Idea on the Land." Jennings discusses the origins of racism within Christianity more broadly in *The Christian Imagination.*
18. Dwyer, "An Idea on the Land."
19. Berry, *A Small Porch*, 79.
20. Wildcat, "Climate Change and the Indigenous Peoples," 514.

21. Freire, *Pedagogy of the Oppressed*, 51.
22. Freire, *Pedagogy of the Oppressed*, 72.
23. Perhamus and Joldersma, "Dismantling White Supremacy," 7.
24. Moore and Nelson, *Moral Ground*, 468.

CHAPTER 1. KEN-O-SHA'S GEOLOGIC PAST AND THE PLASTER CREEK WATERSHED TODAY

1. See Tunison, "Flood Damage Report"; Craig, "Rivers Run High as More Rain Lurks"; Anderson, "Mich. City Declares Emergency as Flooding Continues"; McMillin, "104-Year-Old April Rainfall Record Shattered in Grand Rapids"; Vande Bunte, "2013 Flood."
2. We acknowledge the work of Clint Smith in *How the Word Is Passed*, where we first encountered the phrase "discovered ignorance," which aptly describes how we came to understand the problems in the Plaster Creek watershed.
3. Schaetzl, "Gypsum."
4. Young and Stearley, *The Bible, Rocks and Time*, 341–64.
5. Adams et al., *Gypsum Deposits in the United States*, 18.
6. Mayer, *Lehre vom Gyps*.
7. Weston, "Observations on Alabaster or Gypsum as a Manure," 421–22.
8. Cole, *Grand Rapids Flora*, 17.
9. Large wetland areas (including current-day Hudsonville and Jenison located west of Grand Rapids) were particularly attractive to Dutch immigrants, who had plenty of experience working wet soils using ditches, canals, and dikes.
10. Krajick, "Defending Deadwood."
11. Cronon, *Changes in the Land*, 116.
12. Cleland, *Rites of Conquest*, 47–49.
13. Herb et al., "Thermal Pollution."
14. Hopkins, *Introduction to Plant Physiology*, 37.
15. Allan, Castillo, and Capps, *Stream Ecology*.
16. Meeker, Elias, and Heim, *Plants Used by the Great Lakes Ojibwa*; Catton, "The Real Michigan," 7–8.
17. Garfield, "The Peoples Play Grounds."
18. Dillenback and Leavitt, "Wyoming."

19. Today this location is occupied by Roosevelt Park near the intersection of Clyde Park and Grandville Avenue in Grand Rapids.
20. Granger and Ball, quoted in Grimsley, *The Gypsum of Michigan and the Plaster Industry*, 44.
21. "Gypsum Mines," Grand Rapids Historical Commission, http://www.historygrandrapids.org/article/2330/gypsum-mines.
22. Grimsley, *The Gypsum of Michigan and the Plaster Industry*, 105.
23. Schaetzl, "Gypsum."
24. Grimsley, *The Gypsum of Michigan and the Plaster Industry*, 98.
25. For Michigan's Water Quality Standards, see EGLE, "Michigan's *E. coli* Water Quality Standards."
26. "Clean Water Act," U.S. Environmental Protection Agency, https://www.epa.gov/tmdl.
27. Cronon, *Changes in the Land*, 13.

CHAPTER 2. EARLIEST WATERSHED INHABITANTS AND THE ARRIVAL OF THE OTTAWA

1. Hilton et al., *History of Kent County*, 127.
2. Coffinberry and Strong, "Explorations of Ancient Mounds."
3. As clarification, our use of the name "Anishinaabeg" refers to the group of people that included Ottawa, Ojibwe (also known as Chippewa), and Potawatomi; the word "Anishinaabe" is used as an adjective when describing something associated with the Anishinaabeg. A similar word, "Anishinaabemowin" refers to the language of the Anishinaabeg, which had various dialects among the Ottawa, Ojibwe, and Potawatomi.
4. Rincon, "Earliest Evidence for Humans in the Americas"; Ghose, "Humans May Have Been Stuck on Bering Strait."
5. Logan, *Oak*.
6. Cleland, *Rites of Conquest*, 17.
7. Meeker, Elias, and Heim, *Plants Used by the Great Lakes Ojibwa.*
8. Cleland, *Rites of Conquest*, 22.
9. Quimby, "The Hopewell Indians," 26.
10. Cleland, *Rites of Conquest*, 18.
11. Quimby, "The Hopewell Indians," 27; Belknap, *The Yesterdays of Grand Rapids*, 45.
12. From Belknap, *The Yesterdays of Grand Rapids*, 44: "The men who gathered curios reaped considerable financial benefit from their sales to museums." Belknap himself,

though only a boy at the time, reports selling "quite a bit of silver ornament that I had collected" to Alfred Preusser, the local jeweler, whose family promotes the business today as being "Michigan's oldest jeweler" (http://www.preusserjewelers.com/).

13. Halsey, "The Converse Mounds," 3.
14. Quimby, "The Hopewell Indians," 29.
15. Cleland, *Rites of Conquest*, 44–58; White, *The Middle Ground*, 62.
16. Baxter, *History of the City of Grand Rapids*, 12.
17. Quimby, "The Hopewell Indians," 30.
18. Blackbird, *History of the Ottawa and Chippewa*, 23; Cleland, *Rites of Conquest*, 27. For another description of the Anishinaabeg in Michigan, see Clifton, Cornell, and McClurken, *People of the Three Fires*.
19. Hoffman, "The Mide'wiwin."
20. Clifton, Cornell, and McClurken, *People of the Three Fires*, 8–11; White, *The Middle Ground*, 19; Cleland, *Rites of Conquest*, 182–83.
21. Marsh, "Dekanahwideh." This Six Nation Confederacy including Mohawk, Oneida, Onondaga, Cayuga, Seneca, and Tuscarora was founded with broad goals of promoting peace, establishing civil authority, promoting righteous living, and preventing their lands from becoming invaded. The Great Law of Peace is widely recognized as a significant example of formal government legislation designed to protect and promote an early manifestation of democracy. The founding fathers of the United States likely borrowed from this Iroquois model in crafting the U.S. Constitution. See Schaaf, "From the Great Law of Peace to the Constitution" and Jensen, "The Imaginary Connection."
22. White, *The Middle Ground*, 11–49.
23. Cleland, *Rites of Conquest*, 103.
24. Clifton, Cornell, and McClurken, *People of the Three Fires*, 27.
25. Baxter, *History of the City of Grand Rapids*, 24; Cleland, *Rites of Conquest*, 44.
26. Cleland, *Rites of Conquest*, 44–58; White, *The Middle Ground*, 62.
27. Belknap, *The Yesterdays of Grand Rapids*, 51. See also Hudson's Bay Company. "The Canoe."
28. Belknap, *The Yesterdays of Grand Rapids*, 48–51.
29. White, *The Middle Ground*, 185; Blackbird, *History of the Ottawa and Chippewa*, 45; Baxter, *History of the City of Grand Rapids*, 43. See also Fischer, "L'Arbre Croche (Waganakising)."
30. Feest, "Andrew J. Blackbird and Ottawa History," 119.
31. Feest, "Andrew J. Blackbird and Ottawa History," 123.

32. Cleland, *Rites of Conquest*, 72.
33. Cleland, *Rites of Conquest*, 122.
34. Jennings, *The Founders of America*, 184.
35. Belknap Writings and Correspondence, Captain Charles Eugene Belknap Collection.
36. Belknap, *The Yesterdays of Grand Rapids*, 163–64.

CHAPTER 3. INTERACTIONS BETWEEN THE OTTAWA AND EUROPEAN IMMIGRANTS

1. Map included on a commemorative plaque in downtown Grand Rapids, honoring the two hundredth anniversary of the 1821 Treaty of Chicago.
2. A map and additional information can be found at Schaetzl, "Indian Land Cessions and Reservations."
3. These words come from the written comments delivered by the president of the Ottawa Nation and handed to Gail Heffner after the event. For more on the Treaty Commemoration event, see Downtown Grand Rapids Inc., "200th Anniversary Commemoration."
4. Clifton, Cornell, and McClurken, *People of the Three Fires*, 2.
5. Wildcat, *Red Alert!*, 138.
6. Moore, *History of Michigan*, 32; Butterfield, *History of Brulé's Discoveries and Explorations.*
7. White, *The Middle Ground*, 23.
8. Baxter, *History of the City of Grand Rapids*, 23; Hilton et al., *History of Kent County*, 23–27.
9. Witgen, *An Infinity of Nations*, 112.
10. For more information, see Cook, "Ontonio Gives Birth."
11. Cleland, *Rites of Conquest*, 78; Baxter, *History of the City of Grand Rapids*, 24–26.
12. Jennings, *The Founders of America*, 171; White, *The Middle Ground*, 50–93.
13. For more on this reciprocal influence, see White, *The Middle Ground.*
14. "Finding Aid for the Rix Robinson Collection," 10–12. Some historical accounts report the first LaFramboise trading post was located where the Flat River and Grand River converge (present day Lowell, Michigan). Rix Robinson moved that post to Ada soon after he took over the Lowell post in 1821 and likely operated both posts simultaneously.
15. "Rix 'Uncle Rix' Robinson," Find a Grave, January 24, 2004 (created by graver), https://www.findagrave.com/memorial/8313479/rix-robinson.

16. "Finding Aid for the Rix Robinson Collection," 5.
17. "Rix 'Uncle Rix' Robinson."
18. Written instructions to McCoy included: "Inculcate proper sentiments toward the Government, . . . strive to induce the Indians to engage in agriculture and the rearing of domestic animals," and "persuade them to stay at home." Quoted in Baxter, *History of the City of Grand Rapids*, 50. Also see Cleland, *Rites of Conquest*, 222.
19. Baxter, *History of the City of Grand Rapids*, 50.
20. Hilton et al., *History of Kent County*, 174–75.
21. Belknap, *The Yesterdays of Grand Rapids*, 137.
22. Baxter, *History of the City of Grand Rapids*, 50.
23. Clifton, Cornell, and McClurken, *People of the Three Fires*, 25; Baxter, *History of the City of Grand Rapids*, 28.
24. Belknap, *The Yesterdays of Grand Rapids*, 45–47.
25. Baxter, *History of the City of Grand Rapids*, 9.
26. After two years at the Thomas Mission, McCoy was hired as agent for the U.S. government to facilitate movement of Great Lakes Indians to "Indian Lands" west of the Mississippi. McCoy supported the Indian Removal Policy promoted by Lewis Cass. McCoy desired to lead a utopian Indian community free of the negative influences of white traders and alcohol. Cass heralded McCoy as "a man devoted to the moral and physical improvement of the Indians, and to their final location, where they can be secure against evils, which have reduced and threatened to destroy them." For more, see Baxter, *History of the City of Grand Rapids*, 9.
27. Baxter, *History of the City of Grand Rapids*, 48; Clifton, Cornell, and McClurken, *People of the Three Fires*, 26.
28. Baxter, *History of the City of Grand Rapids*, 32.
29. Campau plotted the land for future development using Indian trails as major roads, while his neighbor to the north, Lucius Lyon, used a geometric English grid system. This is why current day Monroe Street runs along a diagonal (formerly an Indian path) while all the streets north of Pearl were situated at right angles by Lyon. For more see Belknap, *The Yesterdays of Grand Rapids*, 27–30.
30. Chief among these diseases was likely smallpox, but also chickenpox, influenza, and leptospirosis; For more, see Marr and Cathey, "New Hypothesis for Cause of Epidemic among Native Americans."
31. In the late 1500s, scientist Thomas Harriot wrote about disease spread: "Within a few days after our departure from everie such towne, the people began to die very fast, and

many in short space . . . which in truth was very manie in respect of their numbers. This happened in no place . . . but where we had been." Quoted in Jennings, *The Founders of America*, 168.

32. Hilton et al., *History of Kent County*, 138.
33. Blackbird, *History of the Ottawa and Chippewa*, 8–9; see also Feest, "Andrew J. Blackbird and Ottawa History," 117.
34. Mann, "1491: New Revelations"; see also Koch et al., "Earth System Impacts."
35. For more see, "Indian Lands," *Becoming American: The British Atlantic Colonies, 1690–1763*, National Humanities Center, http://nationalhumanitiescenter.org/pds/becomingamer/growth/text7/indianlands.pdf.
36. Review of *Documents and Proceedings*, 77.
37. Jackson, "Fifth Annual Message."
38. Baxter, *History of the City of Grand Rapids*, 9.
39. Hilton et al., *History of Kent County*, 161.
40. For more, see EJI, "Congress Creates Fund to 'Civilize' Native American People."
41. Parkman, "Some Comments on the Indians," 49.
42. Cleland, *Rites of Conquest*, 199. Contemporary historian Robert Swierenga also claims the two broad cultural groups were "incompatible" and "not suited to live together." See "The Dutch and the Ottawas: A Unique Cultural Interchange," Dutch-American Heritage Day, Pinnacle Center, Hudsonville, MI, November 20, 2008, http://www.swierenga.com/DutchandOttawaDAHD1108.html.
43. Mann, "1491: New Revelations."
44. Jennings, *The Founders of America*, 171.
45. Mann, "1491: New Revelations."
46. Gilio-Whitaker, *As Long as Grass Grows*, 112–14; Blackbird, *History of the Ottawa and Chippewa*, 48; Cleland, *Rites of Conquest*, 186–92.
47. For more, see Swierenga, "The Dutch and the Ottawas."
48. Cleland, *Rites of Conquest*, 150.
49. Cleland, *Rites of Conquest*, 212.
50. Cleland, *Rites of Conquest*, 213.
51. Cleland, *Rites of Conquest*, 214–15.
52. Although Cass publicly decried the use of alcohol in treaty negotiations, the supply list for this ten-day event included 39 gallons of brandy, 91 gallons of wine, 41 ½ gallons of fourth proof spirits, 10 gallons of whiskey, and 6 gallons of gin. At one point in the negotiations, Campau claimed he was owed trading debts and secretly convinced Cass to pay him out of the treaty budget. When other traders learned about this

covert agreement they were furious because they also claimed trade imbalances. This disagreement boiled over and led to a vicious fight in which Campau was described as poised to kill another trader named Jacob Smith if bystanders had not intervened. For more see Cleland, *Rites of Conquest*, 216–18.

53. Cleland, *Rites of Conquest*, 217.
54. Cleland, *Rites of Conquest*, 220.
55. Cleland, *Rites of Conquest*, 221–25.
56. Baxter, *History of the City of Grand Rapids*, 60.
57. Baxter, *History of the City of Grand Rapids*, 31.
58. White, *The Middle Ground*, 226.
59. Robinson passed away January 13, 1875, in Ada, still sound in mind but physically worn out. Today, Robinson Road leaves Grand Rapids, heading eastward along the old Indian trail that connected the village at the rapids of O-wash-ta-nong with the Indian Village of Chief Hazy Cloud, where his daughter Se-be-quay and her husband Rix Robinson lived together for over fifty years. "Rix 'Uncle Rix' Robinson."
60. The U.S. government also agreed to pay the Ottawa $30,000 annually for twenty years, a $5,000 annuity for education for twenty years, $3,000 for missions, $10,000 for agricultural equipment, $3,000 for medicine and health care, and $2,000 for tobacco, along with $150,000 for provisions. An additional $3,000 was to be split among the Indian leaders, and $300,000 would offset Indian debts to traders. For more, see Feest, "Andrew J. Blackbird and Ottawa History," 121.
61. Cleland, *Rites of Conquest*, 198–223.
62. Blackbird, *History of the Ottawa and Chippewa*, 97–99; Feest, "Andrew J. Blackbird and Ottawa History," 120.
63. U.S. failure to carry through on treaty promises was a consistent pattern. George Manypenny, negotiator of multiple treaties while commissioner of Indian Affairs, expressed frustration with his government's actions: "Had I known then, as I now know, what would result from these treaties I would be compelled to admit that I had committed a high crime." See Cleland, *Rites of Conquest*, 228.
64. A map and more on treaties can be found at Michigan History Center Staff, "A Short History of Treaties."
65. Grand Rapids Board of Trade, *Grand Rapids as It Is*, 2.
66. Tuttle, *History of Grand Rapids with Biographical Sketches*, 54–55.
67. A resilient band of the displaced Great Lakes Ottawa still live in Oklahoma. For more see "Ottawa Tribe of Oklahoma," Southern Plains Tribal Health Board, 2022, https://www.spthb.org/about-us/who-we-serve/ottawa-tribe-of-oklahoma/.

68. For more, see "Tribal, Ottawa of Oklahoma," Grove Oklahoma, https://www.cityofgroveok.gov/building/page/tribal-ottawa-oklahoma.
69. For more, see Boomgaard, "Grand River Bands of Ottawa Indians Continues Fight."
70. Jennings, *The Christian Imagination*, 157.
71. For more, see EJI, "Congress Creates Fund to 'Civilize' Native American People."
72. For more, see Pember, "Death by Civilization."
73. For more, see "History and Culture: Boarding Schools," Northern Plains Reservation Aid, http://www.nativepartnership.org/site/PageServer?pagename=airc_hist_boardingschools.
74. For more, see Stateside Staff, "Harbor Springs Boarding School."
75. Baxter, *History of the City of Grand Rapids*, 34.
76. Cleland, *Rites of Conquest*, 78; Baxter, *History of the City of Grand Rapids*, 28, 46; Belknap, *The Yesterdays of Grand Rapids*, 18; Clifton, Cornell, and McClurken, *People of the Three Fires*, 25; Jennings, *The Founders of America*, 181; Hilton et al., *History of Kent County*, 216–17; Tuttle, *History of Grand Rapids with Biographical Sketches*, 10.
77. Hilton et al., *History of Kent County*, 183.

CHAPTER 4. EUROPEAN SETTLEMENT IN WEST MICHIGAN AND THE IMPACT ON PLASTER CREEK

1. For more information, see "Michigan Census," FamilySearch, https://www.familysearch.org/en/wiki/Michigan_Census.
2. For more information, see "Grand Rapids, Michigan Population History, 1870–2021," BiggestUsCities.com, https://www.biggestuscities.com/city/grand-rapids-michigan.
3. For more information, see "Grand Rapids: Economy," City-Data.com, https://www.city-data.com/us-cities/The-Midwest/Grand-Rapids-Economy.html.
4. For more information, see Pohl, "Michigan: The Hands that Feed You."
5. PCOHP #81, 6.
6. PCOHP #66, 13–14.
7. PCOHP #18, 2.
8. Proulx, "Swamped."
9. PCOHP #18, 3.
10. PCOHP #55, 6.
11. Walsh et al., "Urban Stream Syndrome"; Francis, "Positioning Urban Rivers within

Urban Ecology."

12. PCOHP #28, 6.
13. PCOHP #63, 5.
14. For more on the history of burying creeks and streams, see Buchholz and Younos, *Urban Stream Daylighting*, 5.
15. Brown, Keath, and Wong, "Transitioning to Water Sensitive Cities," 7.
16. PCOHP #33, 15–16.
17. PCOHP #61, 8–9.
18. Ferrier, "Water Resource Recovery Facility History Document," 2.
19. Tarr, "The Separate vs. Combined Sewer Problem," 136–37.
20. C. Drury, "Article V,—A Revised List of the Coleoptera Observed Near Cincinnati, Ohio, with Notes on Localities, Bibliographical References, and Description of New Species," *Journal of the Cincinnati Society of Natural History* 20 (1901–6): 109, qtd in Hedeen, *The Mill Creek*, 108.
21. Lydens, *The Story of Grand Rapids*, 196.
22. More information on sewage in the Plaster Creek Watershed can be found in the Grand Rapids Historical Commission's book, *Glance at the Past.*
23. Burian and Edwards, "Historical Perspectives of Urban Drainage," 13.
24. For more on this history, see Buchholz and Younos, *Urban Stream Daylighting*, 6.
25. Tarr, "The Separate vs. Combined Sewer Problem," 151–52.
26. See the "Annual Report for the Grand Rapids Wastewater Treatment Plant" written by Superintendent Otto Green in one of the historical inserts within his 1970 *Annual Report*, 22–23.
27. PCOHP #18, 7.
28. PCOHP #18, 4.
29. PCOHP #26, 2, 7.
30. PCOHP #16, 1.
31. PCOHP #60, 6, 7, 8.
32. PCOHP #26, 6.
33. For more on this residential development, see Samuelson et al., *Heart and Soul.*
34. PCOHP #55, 7–8.
35. For more on this history, see Boissoneault, "The Cuyahoga River Caught Fire."
36. For more, see "History of the Clean Water Act," EPA, https://www.epa.gov/laws-regulations/history-clean-water-act.
37. For more, see "Point Source: Pollution Tutorial," National Oceanic and

Atmospheric Administration, https://oceanservice.noaa.gov/education/tutorial_pollution/03pointsource.html.

38. For more, see "Basic Information about Nonpoint Source (NPS) Pollution," EPA, https://www.epa.gov/nps/what-nonpoint-source.
39. For more on the combined sewer separation project in Grand Rapids, see "Sewer Improvement Project," City of Grand Rapids, https://www.grandrapidsmi.gov/Government/Departments/Environmental-Services/Wastewater-Treatment/Sewer-Improvement-Project.
40. PCOHP #24, 1–2.
41. PCOHP #18, 10.
42. PCOHP #63, 6.
43. PCOHP #72, 11.
44. PCOHP #18, 14.
45. PCOHP #55, 13.
46. PCOHP #18, 7–8.
47. PCOHP #63, 1.
48. PCOHP #72, 5–6.
49. PCOHP #8, 12.
50. PCOHP #15, 1–2.
51. "The term *low impact development* (LID) refers to systems and practices that use or mimic natural processes that result in the infiltration, evapotranspiration or use of stormwater in order to protect water quality and associated aquatic habitat." For more, see "Urban Runoff: Low Impact Development," EPA, https://www.epa.gov/nps/urban-runoff-low-impact-development.
52. For more information on low-impact development (LID), also see "What Is LID? Five Principles of Low Impact Development," Contech Engineered Solutions, https://www.conteches.com/stormwater-article/article/111/what-is-lid-five-principles-of-low-impact-development.
53. For more information on green infrastructure, see "What Is Green Infrastructure?," EPA, https://www.epa.gov/green-infrastructure/what-green-infrastructure.
54. PCOHP #18, 9.
55. PCOHP #72, 6.
56. PCOHP #63, 9.
57. PCOHP #55, 2.
58. PCOHP #81, 1.
59. Berry, "Think Little."

CHAPTER 5. WORLDVIEW CONTRASTS AND ECOLOGICAL FALLOUT

1. Blackbird, *History of the Ottawa and Chippewa*, 100.
2. Grand Rapids Board of Trade, *Grand Rapids as It Is*, 20.
3. Sire, *The Universe Next Door*, 17.
4. Berry, "Think Little."
5. Davidson-Hunt et al., "Iskatewizaagegan (Shoal Lake) Plant Knowledge."
6. Pierotti and Wildcat, "The Science of Ecology," 96.
7. Wildcat, *Red Alert!*, 64.
8. Indigenous people understood other life forms as relatives and recognized they were in relationship with these relatives; these two words have the same root in English, from *relacioun*, indicating a "connection, correspondence" and from *relationem*, meaning "a bringing back, restoring" and a sense of being connected by "kindred and affinity"; *Online Etymology Dictionary*, s.v. "relation (n.)," https://www.etymonline.com/word/relation; *Online Etymology Dictionary*, s.v. "relationship (n.)," https://www.etymonline.com/word/relationship.
9. An Anishinaabeg creation story recounts that Kitche Manitou made plant beings of four kinds—flowers, grasses, trees, and vegetables—placing them where they would be most beneficial to achieve harmony. Animal beings were created next, each with their own powers. Kitche Manitou then called all the animals together to tell them next he would be creating the grandchildren (people), and he wanted help in raising them. "What will you do for the grandchildren?" he asked. The deer and moose said they could provide meat, others promised what they could to help raise the grandchildren well. Finally, after hearing from everyone, Kitche Manitou created human beings who were last in the order of creation, and the most dependent on all the others; Jones, "Shaking Tent."
10. Johnston, *Ojibway Heritage*, 12–13.
11. There are many variant names for Nanabozho including Nanabush, Wenebozho, and Menabosho.
12. Johnston, *The Manitous.*
13. Rheault, *The Way of Good Life.*
14. Baxter, *History of the City of Grand Rapids*, 46.
15. The Anishinaabeg also had a set of principles called the Grandfather Teachings that emphasized the virtues of respect, honesty, wisdom, bravery, truth, humility, and love. For more, see Blackbird, *History of the Ottawa and Chippewa.*

16. Cleland, *Rites of Conquest*, 59.
17. *Inter caetera*, Papal Encyclicals Online, https://www.papalencyclicals.net/alex06/alex06inter.htm.
18. "The Doctrine of Discovery, 1493," The Gilder Lehrman Institute of American History, https://www.gilderlehrman.org/history-resources/spotlight-primary-source/doctrine-discovery-1493.
19. Murphy, "Decolonizing Environmentalism."
20. Cleland, *Rites of Conquest*, 65–72, 96–97. For an interesting account of responses by Anishinaabeg to early missionary efforts, see Stoehr, "Salvation from Empire."
21. Cleland, *Rites of Conquest*, 54–58.
22. Cronon, *Changes in the Land*, 97–98; Jennings, *The Founders of America*, 184.
23. Kimmerer, *Braiding Sweetgrass*, 52.
24. Quaife, *The Western Country*, 21, quoted in Cleland, *Rites of Conquest*, 101.
25. Baxter, *History of the City of Grand Rapids*, 43.
26. Cleland, *Rites of Conquest*, 67.
27. Schlender, *Plants Used by the Great Lakes Ojibwa*, preface.
28. Kimmerer, *Braiding Sweetgrass*, 178.
29. Kimmerer, *Braiding Sweetgrass*, 53.
30. Kimmerer, *Braiding Sweetgrass*, 55.
31. Kimmerer, *Braiding Sweetgrass*, 53.
32. Goudzwaard, *Capitalism and Progress*, 49.
33. Cleland, *Rites of Conquest*, 44.
34. Cleland, *Rites of Conquest*, 67.
35. Cleland, *Rites of Conquest*, 48–49.
36. Cleland, *Rites of Conquest*, 242.
37. Cleland, *Rites of Conquest*, 67.
38. Jennings, *The Christian Imagination*, 227.
39. Kimmerer, *Braiding Sweetgrass*, 17.
40. Hilton et al., *History of Kent County*, 172.
41. Roos et al., "Native American Fire Management."
42. The Little Traverse Bay Bands of Odawa Indians have several references to the special relationship that the Ottawa have had with water: "Environmental Services," https://ltbbodawa-nsn.gov/departments/natural-resources-department/environmental-services/.
43. Belknap, *The Yesterdays of Grand Rapids*, 51.
44. Steinberg, *Nature Incorporated*, 16.

45. Hilton et al., *History of Kent County*, 172.
46. Cronon, *Changes in the Land*; Witgen, *An Infinity of Nations*; Gilio-Whitaker, *As Long as Grass Grows.*
47. Wildcat, *Red Alert!*, 64–65.
48. Wildcat, *Red Alert!*, 61.
49. Bahnson and Wirzba, *Making Peace with the Land*, 28–29.
50. Wildcat, *Red Alert!*, 85.
51. Guatemalan scholar Néstor Medina suggests the Indigenous notion of *buen vivir* (translated as "the good life") captures the contrast between Native American worldviews and European American worldviews. For more, see Medina, "You are Me and I am You," 36.
52. Kimmerer, *Braiding Sweetgrass*, 329.

CHAPTER 6. THE EMERGENCE OF PLASTER CREEK STEWARDS

1. Boyer, "The Scholarship of Engagement," 11.
2. Reardon, "Participatory Action Research," 57.
3. Gamson, "Higher Education and Rebuilding a Civic Life," 26.
4. Freire, *Pedagogy of the Oppressed*; hooks, *Teaching to Transgress.*
5. Heffner and Beversluis, *Commitment and Connection*, xv.
6. PCOHP #27, 1.
7. For more on PCS, see https://calvin.edu/plaster-creek-stewards/.
8. Van Wieren, *Restored to Earth*, viii, 2.
9. For more on River Network, see their website: https://www.rivernetwork.org/.
10. For more on the Urban Waters Learning Network, see their website: https://urbanwaterslearningnetwork.org/.
11. For more, see TetraTech, *BMP Planning to Address Urban Runoff.*
12. For more on rainscaping, see the PCS page on rainscaping, https://calvin.edu/plaster-creek-stewards/restoration/rainscaping/, or LGROW's page on rainscaping, https://www.lgrow.org/rainscaping.
13. PCOHP #55, 9.
14. PCOHP #28, 9.
15. Former research student, email conversation with author, October 18, 2021.
16. Two national programs inspired the creation of the Plaster Creek Stewards Green Team—Groundwork Anacostia River DC and the West Atlanta Watershed Alliance. For

more on Anacostia River DC, see "Youth and Community Engagement Changes Places and Lives," https://urbanwaterslearningnetwork.org/resources/youth-community-engagement-changes-places-lives/. For more on West Atlanta Watershed Alliance, see https://www.wawa-online.org/.

17. PCOHP #33, 15.
18. PCOHP #27, 8.
19. Van Wieren, *Restored to Earth*, 6.

CHAPTER 7. DEVELOPING ENGAGED CITIZENS THROUGH PLACE-BASED EDUCATION

1. Middle school science teacher, personal email with author, October 4, 2020.
2. Heffner and Beversluis, *Strengthening Liberal Arts Education*, 15.
3. Freire, *Pedagogy of the Oppressed*, 25.
4. Orr, *Ecological Literacy*, 130.
5. Orr, *Ecological Literacy*, 129.
6. Sobel, *Place-Based Education*, 9.
7. Orr, *Ecological Literacy*, 126.
8. Zwinger, *Into the Field*, vii.
9. Bjelland, "From Stewardship to Place-Making and Place-Keeping."
10. Berry, *Home Economics*, 52.
11. Bonzo and Stevens, *Wendell Berry and the Cultivation of Life*, 184.
12. Heffner and Warners, "Educating in Places, Not Spaces."
13. PCOHP #28, 6.
14. PCOHP #69, 1, 3.
15. PCOHP #71, 4–5.
16. PCOHP #71, 5.
17. PCOHP #71, 6–7.
18. PCOHP #71, 16.
19. PCOHP #60, 6.
20. PCOHP #69, 20.
21. PCOHP #28, 5.
22. For more on the 2021 improvements, see Wynder, "Grand Rapids Celebrates Reopening of Ken-O-Sha Park."
23. See "2012 Jefferson Lecture with Wendell Berry," National Endowment for the

Humanities, April 25, 2012, https://www.neh.gov/news/2012-jefferson-lecture-wendell-berry.

24. Middle school science teacher, personal email with author, October 5, 2020.
25. Middle school science teacher, personal email with author, October 4, 2020.
26. Middle school science teacher, personal email with author, October 4, 2020.
27. The watershed puzzle is a flexible activity for students of all ages, who draw a map showing various land uses. After "developing" their watershed, the group talks about interactions of land/water/humans and concludes with making adjustments to their designs to include protection for water and downstream neighbors.
28. High school teacher, personal email with author, October 5, 2020.
29. For more, see Groundswell's homepage: https://www.gvsu.edu/groundswell/.
30. For more, see Herman et al., *Floristic Quality Assessment.*
31. For more, see https://calvin.edu/plaster-creek-stewards/education/presentations/.
32. Louv, *Last Child in the Woods*, 158.
33. Bonzo and Stevens, *Wendell Berry and the Cultivation of Life*, 189.
34. Orr, *Ecological Literacy*, 131.

CHAPTER 8. ASSESSING THE PROBLEMS WITH APPLIED RESEARCH

1. Robbins, "Native Knowledge."
2. For a mainstream introduction to TEK, see "Forming a Relationship with Mother Earth," National Park Service, https://www.nps.gov/subjects/tek/index.htm.
3. For Indigenous perspectives on TEK, see Alessa, "What Is Truth?" and Pierotti, *Indigenous Knowledge.*
4. Kimmerer, *Braiding Sweetgrass*, 175–79.
5. The four classes are Evolution and Ecology (Biology 160), Cell Biology and Genetics (Biology 161), Plant and Animal Physiology (Biology 230), and Research Methods (Biology 250).
6. "Summer Research Poster Fair," Calvin University, https://calvin.edu/events/poster-fair/.
7. For more on HEC-HMS, see the U.S. Army Corps of Engineers, https://www.hec.usace.army.mil/software/hec-hms/.
8. To access this report, "Plaster Creek Hydrology Study," see https://calvin.edu/go/PC-hydrology.

9. To watch the video, see Plaster Creek Stewards, "Beautiful, Useful and Free Rain Gardens for Plaster Creek."
10. Michigan water quality standards can be found in EGLE, "Michigan's *E. coli* Water Quality Standard."
11. For more information, see https://greatlakesecho.org/2015/07/30/mi-company-uses-dogs-to-sniff-out-water-pollution.
12. The research report is DeJong, "Plaster Creek Bacterial Monitoring and Source Tracking Project."
13. The published paper is Singh et al., "Relative Success of Native Plants in Urban Curb-Cut Rain Gardens."
14. The summary report is Singh and Warners, "Overview of PCS Transpiration Dataset."
15. For a copy of the research poster, David E. Martinez Vasquez, Martin L. Vanderschoot, and David Warners, "Stomatal Conductance and Reed Canary Grass Suppression Traits of Native Michigan Trees," see https://calvin.edu/go/tree-transpiration.
16. The published paper is Vander Meer et al., "Indicator Species Characterization and Removal."

CHAPTER 9. RECONCILING THE HUMAN–NATURE RELATIONSHIP THROUGH ON-THE-GROUND RESTORATION

1. "*Carex virescens*," at Reznicek, Voss, and Walters, *Michigan Flora Online.*
2. To view this historical record, use the Specimen Search at Reznicek, Voss, and Walters, *Michigan Flora Online*, entering "*Carex virescens*" for "Scientific Name" and selecting Kent County.
3. Stivers and Crow, "Emma Jane Cole."
4. Crow, "Emma Cole's 1901 *Grand Rapids Flora.*"
5. A description of this project is Crow and Warners, "The Legacy of Late-19th-Century Emma Jane Cole." See also Calvin University, "Historical Field Botany."
6. Cole, *Grand Rapids Flora*, xiii–xiv: "Since the district has become more thickly settled, it is undergoing rapid transformations. Much of the swamp land is being drained, cleared, and utilized; forests are being deprived of their valuable timber, and uplands converted into farms. The woodlands at present consist mostly of the 'wood-lot' reserved by the farmer. From the standpoint of systematic botany, this district is unfortunate in having so little territory which is not capable of cultivation."
7. For more, see "What Is Ecological Restoration?," Society for Ecological Restoration,

https://www.ser-rrc.org/what-is-ecological-restoration/.

8. Two different rain garden calculators are provided by PCS, https://calvin.edu/plaster-creek-stewards/restoration/rainscaping/, and the Rain Garden Alliance, http://raingardenalliance.org/right/calculator.
9. For more, see Jensen and Muladore, "The Grayling Stormwater Project 2007 Update."
10. For more, see "What's the Difference between Detention and Retention?," Forsite Group, https://www.foresitegroup.net/post/what-s-the-difference-between-detention-and-retention.
11. For more, see Upper Midwest Water Science Center, "Evaluating the Potential Benefits of Permeable Pavement."

CHAPTER 10. LOVING OUR DOWNSTREAM NEIGHBOR—A CALL FOR ENVIRONMENTAL JUSTICE

1. Bonilla-Silva, *Racism without Racists*, 9.
2. For examples of American structural racism in housing, education, and religion, see Massey and Denton, *American Apartheid*; Kozol, *Savage Inequalities*; Emerson and Smith, *Divided by Faith*; Lelyveld and Correspondents, *How Race Is Lived in America.*
3. Bullard, "Environmental Justice."
4. Taylor, *Toxic Communities.*
5. Bullard, *Dumping in Dixie*; Bullard, "Environmental Justice"; Bullard, *Quest for Environmental Justice*; Taylor, *The Environment and the People*; Taylor, "The Evolution of Environmental Justice Activism."
6. Commission for Racial Justice, *Toxic Wastes and Race.*
7. Bullard, Johnson, and Torres, "Atlanta Megasprawl," 22.
8. Taylor, "The Rise of the Environmental Justice Paradigm."
9. "Environmental Justice," EPA, https://www.epa.gov/environmentaljustice.
10. Van Wieren, *Restored to Earth*, 24.
11. Heffner, "Making Visible the Invisible," 151.
12. Gilio-Whitaker, *As Long as Grass Grows*, 23–24, 27.
13. Bahnson and Wirzba, *Making Peace with the Land*, 29.
14. Berry, "Watersheds and Commonwealth," 135.
15. PCOHP #63, 8.
16. PCOHP #32, 7.
17. PCOHP #34, 8.

18. PCOHP #9, 6.
19. PCOHP #34, 8.
20. PCOHP #54, 13.
21. PCOHP #28, 8.
22. PCOHP #55, 2.
23. PCOHP #54, 15–16.
24. PCOHP #72, 3.
25. PCOHP #27, 7.
26. PCOHP #3, 5.
27. PCOHP #3, 2–3.
28. Lorr, "Defining Urban Sustainability," 25.
29. PCOHP #72, 9.
30. Maguire, "The Feminist Turn," 78, quoted in Bergman, "Teaching Justice after MacIntyre," 7.

CHAPTER 11. ENGAGING FAITH COMMUNITIES

1. Van Wieren, *Restored to Earth*, 9.
2. Martinez, "American Indian Cultural Models," 118.
3. Myers, *Watershed Discipleship*, 4–5.
4. See Gilio-Whitaker, *As Long as Grass Grows*, 37, 56–57; Myers, *Watershed Discipleship*, 5, 34–35.
5. See Myers, *Watershed Discipleship*, 36; see also "Synod Repudiates Doctrine of Discovery," Christian Reformed Church, June 17, 2016, https://www.crcna.org/news-and-events/news/synod-repudiates-doctrine-discovery.
6. Van Wieren, *Restored to Earth*, 7–8.
7. Van Wieren, *Restored to Earth*, 25.
8. Bahnson and Wirzba, *Making Peace with the Land*, 21.
9. Martinez, "Native Perspectives on Sustainability," 17–18.
10. PCOHP #28, 10–11.
11. PCOHP #18, 17.
12. PCOHP #72, 5.
13. PCOHP #55, 13–14.
14. PCOHP #26, 15.
15. PCOHP #27, 2.

16. PCOHP #29, 7.
17. For more, see "Healthy Habitats and Healthy Communities Go Hand in Hand," National Wildlife Federation, Sacred Grounds, https://www.nwf.org/SacredGrounds/About.
18. Rienstra, *Refugia Faith*.
19. Bahnson and Wirzba, *Making Peace with the Land*, 55.
20. For more, see "Sacred Spaces Clean Energy Grant," Christian Reformed Church, https://www.crcna.org/climate-witness-project/energy-stewardship/sacred-spaces-clean-energy-grant.
21. PCOHP #27, 9–10.
22. Higgs, "What Is Good Ecological Restoration?," 342, quoted in Van Wieren, *Restored to Earth*, 21.
23. PCOHP #27, 5.
24. Myers, *Watershed Discipleship*, 15.
25. Myers, *Watershed Discipleship*, 210.

CHAPTER 12. SHAPING FUTURE ENVIRONMENTAL LEADERS

1. Louv, *Last Child in the Woods*, 158.
2. See Collado, Staats, and Corraliza, "Experiencing Nature in Children's Summer Camps."
3. See Floyd et al., "Park-Based Physical Activity," and Hartig et al., "Nature and Health."
4. See Chawla, "Childhood Experiences," and Chawla, "Benefits of Nature Contact."
5. See Seltenrich, "Just What the Doctor Ordered."
6. See Frumkin et al., "Nature Contact and Human Health."
7. Jaffe, "This Side of Paradise."
8. For more, see Kaplan, "The Restorative Benefits of Nature"; Mayer et al., "Why Is Nature Beneficial?"; and Kaplan and Berman, "Directed Attention as a Common Resource."
9. Louv, *Last Child in the Woods*, 34.
10. PCOHP #32, 1, 3, 5.
11. PCOHP #9, 3.
12. PCOHP #13, 3–4.
13. PCOHP #8, 3.
14. PCOHP #8, 3.
15. PCOHP #9, 1–2.

16. Asah et al., "Mechanisms of Children's Exposure to Nature," 826.
17. PCOHP #3, 5, 7.
18. PCOHP #47, 1.
19. PCOHP #60, 2.
20. PCOHP #35, 1–2.
21. PCOHP #66, 2.
22. PCOHP #66, 7.
23. Asah et al., "Mechanisms of Children's Exposure to Nature," 811–12, 828.
24. Louv, *Last Child in the Woods*, 155–57.
25. Orr, *Ecological Literacy*, 130.
26. PCOHP #54, 1, 5.
27. PCOHP #47, 6.
28. Louv, *Last Child in the Woods*, 34–35.
29. Asah et al., "Mechanisms of Children's Exposure to Nature," 831.
30. PCOHP #81, 11.
31. PCOHP #3, 6–7.
32. PCOHP #28, 6.
33. PCOHP #4, 15–16.
34. Former Green Team participant, personal email with author, August 28, 2021.
35. Former Green Team participant, personal email with author, August 28, 2021.
36. For more, see the video at "Green Team," Calvin University, calvin.edu/plaster-creek-stewards/green-team/.

CHAPTER 13. AN INVITATION TO THE WORK OF RECONCILIATION ECOLOGY EVERYWHERE

1. Wildcat, *Red Alert!*, 5.
2. Wildcat, *Red Alert!*, 77.
3. Wildcat, *Red Alert!*, 114–15.
4. For helpful resources on decolonization, see Jimmy and Andreotti, *Towards Braiding*.
5. Jimmy and Andreotti, *Towards Braiding*, 8.
6. Alfred, "Don't Just Resist."
7. See Warners, "Walking through a World of Gifts."
8. Villanueva and Giovale, "Healing from Colonization."
9. PCOHP #55, 13.

10. Erdrich, *The Sentence*, 72.
11. Myers, *Watershed Discipleship*, 18.
12. See "Commitment to Justice," Plaster Creek Stewards, https://calvin.edu/plaster-creek-stewards/commitment-to-justice/.
13. Wildcat, *Red Alert!*, 133.
14. PCOHP #28, 9.
15. Lopez, *Embrace Fearlessly*, 24–26.

Bibliography

Adams, George I., et al. *Gypsum Deposits in the United States.* Washington, DC: Department of the Interior, U.S. Geological Survey, Government Printing Office, 1904.

Alessa, (Na'ia) L. "What Is Truth? Where Western Science and Traditional Knowledge Converge." In *The Alaska Native Reader: History, Culture, Politics*, edited by M. (Shaa Tl'aa) Williams, 246–51. Durham, NC: Duke University Press, 2009.

Alfred, Taiaiake. "Don't Just Resist. Return to Who You Are." *Yes! Magazine*, April 9, 2018. https://www.yesmagazine.org/issue/decolonize/2018/04/09/dont-just-resist-return-to-who-you-are.

Allan, J. David, Maria M. Castillo, and Krista A. Capps. *Stream Ecology: Structure and Function of Running Water.* New York: Springer International, 2021.

Anderson, Alisha. "Mich. City Declares Emergency as Flooding Continues." *USA Today.* April 22, 2013.

Arbogast, A. F., J. R. Bookout, B. R. Schrotenboer, A. Lansdale, G. L. Rust, and V. A. Bato. "Post-Glacial Fluvial Response and Landform Development in the Upper Muskegon River Valley in North-Central Lower Michigan, U.S.A." *Geomorphology* 162, nos. 3–4 (December 2008): 615–23.

Asah, Stanley T., David N. Bengston, Lynne M. Westphal, and Catherine H. Gowan. "Mechanisms of Children's Exposure to Nature: Predicting Adulthood Environmental Citizenship and Commitment to Nature-Based Activities." *Environment and Behavior* 50, no. 7 (2018): 807–36. https://doi.org/10.1177/0013916517718021.

Bahnson, Fred, and Norman Wirzba. *Making Peace with the Land: God's Call to Reconcile with Creation.* Downers Grove, IL: InterVarsity Press, 2012.

Baxter, Albert. *History of the City of Grand Rapids, Michigan (with an Appendix—History of Lowell Michigan).* Grand Rapids, MI: Munsell, 1891.

Belknap, Charles E. *The Yesterdays of Grand Rapids.* Grand Rapids, MI: Dean-Hicks, 1922.

Belknap Writings and Correspondence. Captain Charles Eugene Belknap Collection. Grand Rapids History Center, Grand Rapids, MI. 1926. https://archive.grpl.org/repositories/4/archival_objects/32386.

Bergman, Roger. "Teaching Justice after MacIntyre: Toward a Catholic Philosophy of Moral Education." *Catholic Education: A Journal of Inquiry and Practice* 12, no. 1 (2008): 7–24. https://ejournals.bc.edu/index.php/cej/article/view/829.

Bergquist, S. G. "The Glacial History and Development of Michigan." East Lansing: Department of Geology, Michigan State College, 1941. https://www.michigan.gov/documents/deq/Glacial_History_Bergquist_opt_306035_7.pdf.

Berry, Wendell. *Home Economics: Fourteen Essays.* Berkeley, CA: Counterpoint Press, 1987.

Berry, Wendell. *It All Turns on Affection: The Jefferson Lecture and Other Essays.* Berkeley, CA: Counterpoint Press, 2012.

Berry, Wendell. *A Small Porch.* Berkeley, CA: Counterpoint Press, 2016.

Berry, Wendell. "Think Little." The Berry Center. March 26, 2017. https://berrycenter.org/2017/03/26/think-little-wendell-berry/.

Berry, Wendell. "Watersheds and Commonwealth." In *Citizenship Papers*, 135. Berkeley, CA: Counterpoint Press, 2003.

Bjelland, Mark. "From Stewardship to Place-making and Place-Keeping." In *Beyond Stewardship: New Approaches to Creation Care*, edited by David Paul Warners and Matthew Kuperus Heun, 171–83. Grand Rapids, MI: Calvin University Press, 2019.

Blackbird, Andrew J. *History of the Ottawa and Chippewa Indians of Michigan: A Grammar of Their Language, and Personal and Family History of the Author.* Ypsilanti, MI: Ypsilantian Job Printing House, 1887. https://www.loc.gov/resource/lhbum.16465/?sp=2.

Blitz, J. H. "Adoption of the Bow in Prehistoric North America." *North American Archaeologist* 9, no. 2 (October 1, 1988): 123–45.

Boissoneault, Lorraine. "The Cuyahoga River Caught Fire at Least a Dozen Times, but No One Cared until 1969." *Smithsonian Magazine*, June 19, 2019. https://www.smithsonianmag.com/history/cuyahoga-river-caught-fire-least-dozen-times-no-one-cared-until-1969-180972444/.

Bonilla-Silva, Eduardo. *Racism without Racists: Color-Blind Racism and the Persistence of Racial Inequality in the United States.* Lanham, MD: Rowman and Littlefield, 2003.

Bonzo, J. Matthew, and Michael R. Stevens. *Wendell Berry and the Cultivation of Life*. Grand Rapids, MI: Brazos Press, 2008.

Boomgaard, Joe. "After 27 Years, Grand River Bands of Ottawa Indians Continues Fight for Federal Recognition." *MiBiz*. July 18, 2021. https://mibiz.com/sections/economic-development/after-27-years-grand-river-bands-of-ottawa-indians-continues-fight-for-federal-recognition.

Bouma, C., E. Huizenga, and D. Warners. "Assessing a Reconciliation Ecology Approach to Suburban Landscaping: Biodiversity on a College Campus." *Michigan Botanist* 52 (2015): 93–104.

Boyer, Ernest L. "The Scholarship of Engagement." *Journal of Public Service and Outreach* 1, no. 1 (1996): 11–20.

Brickell, Paul. "London and the River Lea." *Urban Waterways Newsletter*, no. 6 (Spring 2016), 40–41. http://anacostia.si.edu/urbanwaterways/wp-content/uploads/2020/05/Final-Urban-Waterways-Newsletter-6.pdf.

Brown, Christopher N. "The Watershed Approach: Making the Transition from Corridors to Watersheds." *River Voices* 7, no. 4 (Winter 1997): 1–6. https://www.rivernetwork.org/wp-content/uploads/2016/04/River-Voices-v7n4-1997_The-Watershed-Approach.pdf.

Brown, Rebekah, N. Keath, and T. Wong. "Transitioning to Water Sensitive Cities: Historical, Current and Future Transition States." Edinburgh: 11th International Conference on Urban Drainage, 2008.

Buchholz, Tracy, and Tamim Younos. *Urban Stream Daylighting: Case Study Evaluations*. Blacksburg, VA: Virginia Water Resources Research Center, Virginia Tech, 2007.

Bullard, Robert D. *Dumping in Dixie: Race, Class, and Environmental Quality*. 3rd ed. Boulder, CO: Westview Press, 2000.

Bullard, Robert D. "Environmental Justice in the 21st Century: Race Still Matters." *Phylon* 49, nos. 3/4 (Autumn–Winter 2001): 151–71.

Bullard, Robert D., ed. *The Quest for Environmental Justice: Human Rights and the Politics of Pollution*. San Francisco, CA: Sierra Club Books, 2005.

Bullard, Robert D., Glenn S. Johnson, and A. O. Torres. "Atlanta Megasprawl." *Forum for Applied Research and Public Policy* 14, no. 3 (Fall 1999): 17–23.

Burian, Steven J., and Findlay G. Edwards. "Historical Perspectives of Urban Drainage." In *Global Solutions for Urban Drainage: Proceedings of the Ninth International Conference on Urban Drainage*, edited by E. W. Strecker and W. C. Huber, 1–16. Reston, VA: ASCE, 2002.

Butterfield, C. W. *History of Brulé's Discoveries and Explorations, 1610–1626*. Cleveland, OH: Helman-Taylor, 1898.

Calvin University. "Historical Field Botany: A 100-Year Retrospective Assessment of

Emma Cole's Grand Rapids Flora (1901)." https://calvin.edu/academics/research-scholarship/historical-field-botany-a-100-year-retrospective-assessment-of-emma-cole-s-grand-rapids-flora-1901.

Catton, Bruce. "The Real Michigan." In *A Michigan Reader: 11,000 B.C. to A.D. 1865*, edited by George May and Herbert Brinks, 4–19. Grand Rapids, MI: William B. Eerdmans, 1974. Originally published in *Holiday*, August 1957, 26–39.

Chawla, L. "Benefits of Nature Contact for Children." *Journal of Planning Literature* 30, no. 4 (2015): 433–52. https://doi.org/10.1177/0885412215595441.

Chawla, L. "Childhood Experiences Associated with Care for the Natural World: A Theoretical Framework for Empirical Results." *Children, Youth and Environments* 17, no. 4 (2007): 144–70.

Christopherson, R. W. *Geosystems: An Introduction to Physical Geography*, 3rd ed. Upper Saddle River, NJ: Prentice Hall, 1997.

"Clean Water Act Section 303(d): Impaired Waters and Total Maximum Daily Loads (TMDLs)." U.S. Environmental Protection Agency. Updated March 30, 2023. https://www.epa.gov/tmdl.

Cleland, Charles E. *Rites of Conquest: The History and Culture of Michigan's Native Americans.* Ann Arbor: University of Michigan Press, 2001.

Clifton, J. A., G. L. Cornell, and J. M. McClurken. *People of the Three Fires: The Ottawa, Potawatomi and Ojibway of Michigan.* Grand Rapids, MI: Michigan Indian Press, Grand Rapids Inter-Tribal Council, 1986. https://files.eric.ed.gov/fulltext/ED321956.pdf.

Coffinberry, Wright L., and E. A. Strong. "Notes upon Some Explorations of Ancient Mounds in the Vicinity of Grand Rapids, Kent County, Michigan." *Proceedings of the American Association for the Advancement of Science* 24 (1876): 293–97.

Cole, Emma J. *Grand Rapids Flora: A Catalogue of the Flowering Plants and Ferns Growing without Cultivation in the Vicinity of Grand Rapids, Michigan.* Grand Rapids, MI: A. VanDort, 1901.

Collado, S., H. Staats, and J. A. Corraliza. "Experiencing Nature in Children's Summer Camps: Affective, Cognitive and Behavioral Consequences." *Journal of Environmental Psychology* 33 (2013): 37–44. https://doi.org/10.1016/j.jenvp.2012.08.002.

Commission for Racial Justice, *Toxic Wastes and Race in the United States: A National Report on the Racial and Socio-Economic Characteristics of Communities with Hazardous Waste Sites.* New York: United Church of Christ, 1987. https://www.nrc.gov/docs/ML1310/ML13109A339.pdf.

Cook, Peter. "Ontonio Gives Birth: How the French in Canada Became Fathers to Their Indigenous Allies, 1645–73." *Canadian Historical Review* 96, no. 2 (June 2015): 165–93. https://muse.jhu.edu/article/585627/pdf.

Craig, Kevin. "Rivers Run High as More Rain Lurks." WXMI-TV. April 13, 2013.

Cronon, William. *Changes in the Land: Indians, Colonists, and the Ecology of New England.* New York: Hill and Wang, 1983.

Crow, Garrett E. "Emma Cole's 1901 *Grand Rapids Flora*: Nomenclaturally Updated and Revised." *Great Lakes Botanist* 56 (2017): 98–176. https://quod.lib.umich.edu/cgi/p/pod/dod-idx/emma-coles-1901-grand-rapids-flora-nomenclaturally-updated.pdf?c=mbot;idno=0497763.0056.302;format=pdf.

Crow, Garrett E., and David P. Warners. "The Legacy of Late-19th-Century Emma Jane Cole and Her Grand Rapids Flora Lives on in the 21st Century." Biodiversity Heritage Library. March 21, 2019. https://blog.biodiversitylibrary.org/author/dr-garrett-e-crow.

Davidson-Hunt, Iain J., Phyllis Jack, Edward Mandamin, and Brennan Wapioke. "Iskatewizaagegan (Shoal Lake) Plant Knowledge: An Anishinaabe (Ojibway) Ethnobotany of Northwestern Ontario." *Journal of Ethnobiology* 25, no. 2 (2005): 189–227. https://doi.org/10.2993/0278-0771(2005)25[189:ISLPKA]2.0.CO;2.

DeJong, Randall. "Final Report: Plaster Creek Bacterial Monitoring and Source Tracking Project, March 27, 2015—March 26, 2017." Calvin College and Plaster Creek Stewards. https://calvin.edu/go/ecoli-sourcing.

Dillenback and Leavitt. "Paris." In *History and Directory of Kent County, Michigan, Containing a History of Each Township and the City of Grand Rapids*, 78–82. Grand Rapids, MI: Daily Eagle Steam Printing House, 1870.

Dillenback and Leavitt. "Wyoming." In *History and Directory of Kent County, Michigan, Containing a History of Each Township and the City of Grand Rapids*, 107–13. Grand Rapids, MI: Daily Eagle Steam Printing House, 1870.

Dorr, John A., and Donald F. Eschman. *Geology of Michigan.* Ann Arbor: University of Michigan Press, 1970.

Downtown Grand Rapids Inc. "200th Anniversary Commemoration: Treaty of Chicago (1821)." YouTube. November 8, 2021. https://www.youtube.com/watch?v=gbmJLXskC3g.

Dwyer, Dustin. "An Idea on the Land" (interview with Willie Jennings). Michigan Radio. October 18, 2018. https://www.michiganradio.org/post/hear-our-extended-interview-willie-jennings-yale-divinity-school-idea-land.

EGLE [Michigan Department of Environment, Great Lakes, and Energy]. "Michigan's *E. coli* Water Quality Standard: Fact Sheet." July 2019. https://www.michigan.gov/documents/deq/wrd-swas-ecoli_527147_7.pdf.

EJI [Equal Justice Initiative]. "Congress Creates Fund to 'Civilize' Native American People." A History of Racial Injustice. March 3. https://calendar.eji.org/racial-injustice/mar/03.

Emerson, Michael O., and Christian Smith. *Divided by Faith: Evangelical Religion and the Problem of Race in America.* New York: Oxford University Press, 2000.

Erdrich, Louise. *The Sentence.* New York: HarperCollins, 2021.

Farrand, William R. *The Glacial Lakes around Michigan*, Bulletin 4. Lansing: Michigan Department of Environmental Quality, Geological Survey Division, 1988. https://www.michigan.gov/documents/deq/GIMDL-BU04_216119_7.pdf.

Feest, Christian F. "Andrew J. Blackbird and Ottawa History." *Yumtzilob* 8 (January 1996): 114–23.

Ferrier, Kayne. "Water Resource Recovery Facility History Document." Unpublished manuscript, last modified July 8, 2019. PDF document. Grand Rapids Water Resource Recovery Facility.

"Finding Aid for the Rix Robinson Collection, Collection #295." October 2009 version. Grand Rapids History and Special Collections. Grand Rapids Public Library, Grand Rapids, MI. https://www.yumpu.com/en/document/read/19262016/295-rix-robinson-grplpedia-grand-rapids-public-library.

Fischer, William, Jr. "L'Arbre Croche (Waganakising)." Historical Marker Database. September 15, 2016. https://www.hmdb.org/m.asp?m=97815.

Floyd, M. F., J. N. Bocarro, W. R. Smith, P. K. Baran, R. C. Moore, N. G. Cosco, M. B. Edwards, L. J. Luau, and K. Fang. "Park-Based Physical Activity among Children and Adolescents." *American Journal of Preventive Medicine* 41, no. 3 (2011): 258–65. https://doi.org/10.1016/j.amepre.2011.04.013.

Francis, R. A. "Perspectives on the Potential for Reconciliation Ecology in Urban Riverscapes." *CAB Reviews: Perspectives in Agriculture and Veterinary Science Nutrition and Natural Resources* 4, no. 73 (2009): 1–20.

Francis, R. A. "Positioning Urban Rivers within Urban Ecology." *Urban Ecosystems* 15 (2012): 285–91.

Freire, Paulo. *Pedagogy of the Oppressed: 30th Anniversary Edition.* New York: Continuum International, 2003.

Frumkin, H., G. N. Bratman, S. J. Breslow, B. Cochran, P. H. Kahn Jr., J. J. Lawler, P. S. Levin, P. S. Tandon, U. Varanasi, K. L. Wolf, and S. A. Wood. "Nature Contact and Human Health: A Research Agenda." *Environmental Health Perspectives* 125, no. 7 (2017): 075001-1-07001-18. https://doi.org/10.1289/EHP1663.

Gamson, Zelda F. "Higher Education and Rebuilding Civic Life." *Change* 29, no. 1 (1997): 10–13.

Garfield, Charles W. "The Peoples Play Grounds." Fortieth Annual Report of the Secretary of the State Horticultural Society of Michigan, 1910. https://calvin.edu/

dotAsset/5c37dae9-b361-4307-8231-d70767534630.

Ghose, Tia. "Humans May Have Been Stuck on Bering Strait for 10,000 Years." LiveScience. February 27, 2014. https://www.livescience.com/43726-bering-strait-populations-lived.html.

Gilio-Whitaker, Dina. *As Long as Grass Grows: The Indigenous Fight for Environmental Justice, from Colonization to Standing Rock*. Boston: Beacon Press, 2019.

Goudzwaard, Bob. *Capitalism and Progress: A Diagnosis of Western Society*. Toronto: Wedge Publishing Foundation, 1979.

Grand Rapids Board of Trade. *Grand Rapids as It Is*. Grand Rapids: Eaton, Lyon and Allen, 1888.

Grand Rapids Historical Commission. *Glance at the Past: An Album of Grand Rapids History*. Vol. 1. Grand Rapids, MI: GRCC Print Solutions, 2011.

Grand Rapids Historical Commission. "Gypsum Mines." History Grand Rapids. http://www.historygrandrapids.org/article/2330/gypsum-mines.

Green, Otto. *Annual Report on Operation of the Waste Water Treatment Plant*. Grand Rapids, MI: Grand Rapids Michigan Department of Public Service, 1970.

Grimsley, G. P. *The Gypsum of Michigan and the Plaster Industry*. Vol. 9, pt. 2 of *Geological Survey of Michigan*, by Alfred C. Lane. Lansing: Robert Smith Printing, 1904.

Gutschick, R. C., and C. A. Sandberg. "Late Devonian History of Michigan Basin." In *Early Sedimentary Evolution of the Michigan Basin*, by Paul A. Catacosinos and Paul A. Daniels Jr., GSA Special Papers 256. Boulder, CO: Geological Society of America, 1991. https://doi.org/10.1130/SPE256-p181.

Gyasi, Yaa. *Homegoing*. New York: Knopf, 2016.

Halsey, John R. "The Converse Mounds: New Research on Michigan's Greatest Hopewell Site." *Newsletter of Hopewell Archeology in the Ohio River Valley* 4, no. 1 (June 2000): 2–14.

Hartig, Terry, Richard Mitchell, Sjerp de Vries, and Howard Frumkin. "Nature and Health." *Annual Review of Public Health* 35 (2014): 207–28. https://doi.org/10.1146/annurev-publhealth-032013-182443.

Hedeen, Stanley. *The Mill Creek: An Unnatural History of an Urban Stream*. Cincinnati: Blue Heron Press, 1994.

Hedrick, U. P. *The Land of the Crooked Tree*. New York: Oxford University Press, 1948.

Heffner, Gail Gunst. "Making Visible the Invisible: Environmental Racism." In *Beyond Stewardship: New Approaches to Creation Care*, edited by David Paul Warners and Matthew Kuperus Heun, 147–57. Grand Rapids, MI: Calvin University Press, 2019.

Heffner, Gail Gunst, and Claudia Beversluis. *Strengthening Liberal Arts Education by Embracing Place and Particularity*. A Teagle Foundation White Paper. Grand Rapids, MI: Calvin

College, 2007. https://calvin.edu/offices-services/community-engagement/teagle/.

Heffner, Gail Gunst, and Claudia DeVries Beversluis. *Commitment and Connection: Service-Learning and Christian Higher Education.* Lanham, MD: University Press of America, 2002.

Heffner, Gail Gunst, and David Warners. "Educating in Places, Not Spaces." *Christian Educators Journal*, February 2020. https://www.cejonline.com/article/educating-in-places-not-spaces/.

Herb, William R., Ben Janke, Omid Mohseni, and Heinz G. Stefan. "Thermal Pollution of Streams by Runoff Paved Surfaces." *Hydrological Processes* 22, no. 7 (March 2008): 987–99. https://doi.org/10.1002/hyp.6986.

Herman, K. D., L. A. Masters, M. R. Penskar, A. A. Reznicek, G. S. Wilhelm, W. W. Brodovich, and K. P. Gardiner. *Floristic Quality Assessment with Wetland Categories and Examples of Computer Applications for the State of Michigan.* Revised, second edition. Lansing: Michigan Department of Natural Resources, Wildlife Division, Natural Heritage Program, 2001. https://www2.dnr.state.mi.us/publications/pdfs/HuntingWildlifeHabitat/FQA.pdf.

Higgs, Eric. "What Is Good Ecological Restoration?" *Conservation Biology* 11, no. 2 (April 1997): 338–48.

Hilton, R., T. B. Church, J. Ball, W. N. Cook, R. H. Smith, and W. I. Blakely. *History of Kent County Michigan; Together with Sketches of its Cities, Villages, and Townships, Educational, Religious, Civil, Military, and Political History; Portraits of Prominent Persons and Biographies of Representative Citizens.* Chicago: Charles C. Chapman, 1881.

Hoffman, Walter James. "The Mide'wiwin or 'Grand Medicine Society' of the Ojibwa." In *The Seventh Annual Report of the Bureau of Ethnology to the Secretary of the Smithsonian Institution, 1885–1886*, 143–300. Washington, DC: Government Printing Office, 1891.

hooks, bell. *Teaching to Transgress: Education as the Practice of Freedom.* New York: Routledge, 1994.

Hopkins, W. G. *Introduction to Plant Physiology.* 2nd Edition. New York: John Wiley & Sons, 1999.

Hudson's Bay Company. "The Canoe." HBC Heritage. 2016. https://www.hbcheritage.ca/things/technology/the-canoe.

Hutchings, W. Karl. "Finding the Paleoindian Spearthrower: Quantitative Evidence for Mechanically-Assisted Propulsion of Lithic Armatures during the North American Paleoindian Period." *Journal of Archaeological Science* 55 (March 2015): 34–41. https://doi.org/10.1016/j.jas.2014.12.019.

Jackson, Andrew. "Fifth Annual Message." Edited by Gerhard Peters and John T. Woolley. The American Presidency Project. https://www.presidency.ucsb.edu/documents/

fifth-annual-message-2.

Jaffe, Eric. "This Side of Paradise: Discovering Why the Human Mind Needs Nature." *American Psychological Society Observer*, May/June 2010. https://www.psychologicalscience.org/observer/this-side-of-paradise.

Jennings, Francis. *The Founders of America: How Indians Discovered the Land, Pioneered in It, and Created Great Classical Civilizations, How They Were Plunged Into a Dark Age by Invasion and Conquest, and How They are Reviving*. New York: W. W. Norton, 1993.

Jennings, Willie James. *The Christian Imagination: Theology and the Origins of Race*. New Haven, CT: Yale University Press, 2010.

Jensen, Brad, and Jennifer Muladore. "The Grayling Stormwater Project 2007 Update." Michigan Water Environment Association. November 29, 2007. https://www.mi-wea.org/docs/Huron%20Pines.pdf.

Jensen, Erik M. "The Imaginary Connection between the Great Law of Peace and the United States Constitution: A Reply to Professor Schaaf." *American Indian Law Review* 15, no. 2 (1990): 295–308. https://doi.org/10.2307/20068679.

Jimmy, Elwood, and Vanessa Andreotti. *Towards Braiding*. Guelph, Ont.: Musagetes, 2019. https://decolonialfutures.net/towardsbraiding.

Johnston, Basil. *The Manitous: The Supernatural World of the Ojibway*. New York: HarperCollins, 1995.

Johnston, Basil. *Ojibway Heritage*. Toronto: McCleland and Steward, 1976.

Jones, Dan. "Shaking Tent." YouTube. November 29, 2012. https://www.youtube.com/watch?v=3XR_Cz-3mJE.

Kaplan, Stephen. "The Restorative Benefits of Nature: Toward an Integrative Framework." *Journal of Environmental Psychology* 15, no. 3 (1995): 169–82. https://doi.org/10.1016/0272-4944(95)90001-2.

Kaplan, S., and Marc G. Berman. "Directed Attention as a Common Resource for Executive Functioning and Self-Regulation." *Perspectives on Psychological Science* 5, no. 1 (2010): 43–57. https://doi.org/10.1177/1745691609356784.

Kimmerer, Robin Wall. *Braiding Sweetgrass: Indigenous Wisdom, Scientific Knowledge, and the Teachings of Plants*. Minneapolis: Milkweed Editions, 2013.

Koch, A., C. Brierley, M. M. Maslin, and S. L. Lewis. "Earth System Impacts of the European Arrival and Great Dying in the Americas after 1492." *Quaternary Science Reviews* 207 (March 2019): 13–36. https://doi.org/10.1016/j.quascirev.2018.12.004.

Kozol, Jonathan. *Savage Inequalities: Children in America's Schools*. New York: Crown Publishers, 1991.

Krajick, Kevin. "Defending Deadwood." *Science* 293, no. 5535 (August 31, 2001): 1579–81.

LeBeau, Patrick Russell. *Rethinking Michigan Indian History.* East Lansing: Michigan State University Press, 2005.

Lelyveld, Joseph, and Correspondents of the *New York Times. How Race Is Lived in America: Pulling Together, Pulling Apart.* New York: Times Books, 2001.

Logan, W. B. *Oak: The Frame of Civilization.* New York: W. W. Norton, 2005.

Lopez, Barry. *Embrace Fearlessly the Burning World.* New York: Penguin Random House, 2022.

Lorr, Michael J. "Defining Urban Sustainability in the Context of North American Cities." *Nature and Culture* 7, no. 1 (Spring 2012): 16–30. https://doi.org/10.3167/nc.2012.070102.

Louv, Richard. *Last Child in the Woods: Saving Our Children from Nature-Deficit Disorder.* Chapel Hill, NC: Algonquin Books, 2005.

Lydens, Z. Z. *The Story of Grand Rapids: A Narrative of Grand Rapids, Michigan.* 3rd ed. Grand Rapids, MI: Kregel Publications, 1967.

Maathai, Wangari. "Marching with Trees (interview)." On Being with Krista Tippett. April 6, 2006. https://onbeing.org/programs/wangari-maathai-marching-with-trees/.

Maguire, D. "The Feminist Turn in Social Ethics." In *Mainstreaming: Feminist Research for Teaching Religious Studies*, edited by A. Swindler and W. E. Conn, 77–83. Lanham, MD: University Press of America, 1985.

Mann, Charles C. "1491: New Revelations of the Americas before Columbus." *The Atlantic*, March 2002. https://www.theatlantic.com/magazine/archive/2002/03/1491/302445/.

Mann, Charles C. *1491: New Revelations of the Americas before Columbus.* 2nd ed. New York: Knopf, 2011.

Marr, J. S., and J. T. Cathey. "New Hypothesis for Cause of Epidemic among Native Americans, New England, 1616–1619." *Emerging Infectious Diseases* 16, no. 2 (February 2010): 281–86. https://doi.org/10.3201/eid1602.090276.

Marsh, James H. "Dekanahwideh." *The Canadian Encyclopedia.* Last updated December 15, 2013. https://thecanadianencyclopedia.ca/en/article/dekanahwideh.

Martinez, Dennis. "American Indian Cultural Models for Sustaining Biodiversity." In *Special Forest Products: Biodiversity Meets the Marketplace*, edited by Nan C. Vance and Jane Thomas, 108–21. Washington, DC: U.S. Department of Agriculture, Forest Service, 1997.

Martinez, Dennis. "Native Perspectives on Sustainability." Interview by David E. Hall. *Native Perspectives on Sustainability: Voices from Salmon Nation*, March 1, 2008. http://www.nativeperspectives.net/Leaders_D_Martinez.php. Transcript available at: http://www.nativeperspectives.net/Transcripts/Dennis_Martinez_interview.pdf.

Massey, Douglas S., and Nancy A. Denton. *American Apartheid: Segregation and the Making of the*

Underclass. Cambridge, MA: Harvard University Press, 1993.

May, George, and Herbert Brinks, eds. *A Michigan Reader: 11,000 B.C. to A.D 1865.* Grand Rapids, MI: William B. Eerdmans, 1974.

Mayer, Johann Friderich. *Lehre vom Gyps als vorzueglich guten Dung zu allen Erd-Gewaechsen auf Aeckern und Wiesen, Hopfen- und Weinbergen* [Instruction in gypsum as an ideal good manure for all things grown in soil on fields and pastures, hops yards and vineyards]. Anspach: Jacob Christoph Posch, 1768.

Mayer, F. Stephan, Cynthia McPherson Frantz, Emma Bruehlman-Senecal, and Kyffin Dolliver. "Why Is Nature Beneficial? The Role of Connectedness to Nature." *Environment and Behavior* 41, no. 5 (2009): 607–43. https://doi.org/10.1177/0013916508319745.

McMillin, Zane. "104-Year-Old April Rainfall Record Shattered in Grand Rapids, with More Downpours Likely." *MLive.* April 18, 2013.

Medina, Néstor. "You Are Me and I Am You." *Sojourners Magazine*, January 2021, 34–38.

Meeker, James E., Joan E. Elias, and John A. Heim. *Plants Used by the Great Lakes Ojibwa.* Odanah, WI: Great Lakes Indian Fish and Wildlife Commission, 1993.

Michelson, D. M., and P. M. Colgan. "The Southern Laurentide Ice Sheet." In *The Quaternary Period in the United States*, ed. by A. R. Gillespie, S. C. Porter, and B. F. Atwater, Developments in Quaternary Science 1, 1–16. Amsterdam: Elsevier, 2003.

Michigan History Center Staff. "A Short History of Treaties." Michiganology. https://michiganology.org/stories/a-short-history-of-treaties/

Milner, George R. *The Moundbuilders: Ancient Peoples of Eastern North America.* London: Thames and Hudson, 2004.

Moerman, Daniel E. *Native American Ethnobotany.* Portland, OR: Timber Press, 1998.

Moore, Charles. *The History of Michigan.* Chicago: Lewis Publishing, 1915.

Moore, Kathleen Dean, and Michael P. Nelson, eds. *Moral Ground: Ethical Action for a Planet in Peril.* San Antonio, TX: Trinity University Press, 2011.

Murphy, Jazmin. "Decolonizing Environmentalism." *Yes! Magazine*, September 15, 2020. https://www.yesmagazine.org/environment/2020/09/15/conservation-decolonize-environmentalism/.

Myers, Ched, ed. *Watershed Discipleship: Reinhabiting Bioregional Faith and Practice.* Eugene, OR: Cascade Books, 2016.

Orr, David. *Ecological Literacy: Education and the Transition to a Postmodern World.* Albany: State University of New York Press, 1992.

O'Shea, J. M., A. K. Lemke, E. P. Sonnenburg, R. G. Reynolds, and B. D. Abbot. "A 9,000-Year-Old Caribou Hunting Structure beneath Lake Huron." *Proceedings of the*

National Academy of Sciences of the United States 111, no. 19 (April 28, 2014): 6911–15. https://doi.org/10.1073/pnas.1404404111.

Parkman, F. "Some Comments on the Indians." In *A Michigan Reader: 11,000 B.C. to A.D. 1865*, edited by George May and Herbert Brinks, 42–49. Grand Rapids, MI: William B. Eerdmans, 1974. Originally published in *The Conspiracy of Pontiac and the Indian Waters after the Conquest of Canada*, 32–39. Boston: Little, Brown, 1903.

Pember, Mary Annette. "Death by Civilization." *The Atlantic*, March 8, 2019. https://www.theatlantic.com/education/archive/2019/03/traumatic-legacy-indian-boarding-schools/584293/.

Perhamus, Lisa M., and Clarence W. Joldersma. "What Might Sustain the Activism of This Moment? Dismantling White Supremacy, One Monument at a Time." *Journal of Philosophy of Education* 54, no. 5 (2020): 1314–32.

Pierotti, Raymond. *Indigenous Knowledge, Ecology, and Evolutionary Biology*. New York: Routledge, Taylor and Francis, 2011.

Pierotti, Raymond, and Daniel R. Wildcat. "The Science of Ecology and Native American Tradition." *Winds of Change* 12, no. 4 (August 1997): 94–97.

Plaster Creek Stewards. "Beautiful, Useful and Free Rain Gardens for Plaster Creek." YouTube. January 10, 2017. https://youtu.be/RZmOuVos6_I.

Pohl, Stefanie. "Michigan: The Hands that Feed You." Michigan Economic Development Corporation. March 3, 2023. https://www.michiganbusiness.org/news/2022/03/michigan-the-hands-that-feed-you/.

Proulx, Annie. "Swamps Can Protect Against Climate Change, if We Only Let Them." *New Yorker*, June 27, 2022. https://www.newyorker.com/magazine/2022/07/04/swamps-can-protect-against-climate-change-if-we-only-let-them.

Quaife, Milo. *The Western Country in the Seventeenth Century: The Memoirs of Antoine Lamothe Cadillac and Pierre Liette*. New York: Citadel Press, 1962.

Quimby, G. I. "The Hopewell Indians." In *A Michigan Reader: 11,000 B.C. to A.D 1865*, edited by George May and Herbert Brinks, 25–32. Grand Rapids, MI: William B. Eerdmans, 1974. Originally published in *Indian Life in the Upper Great Lakes, 11,000 B.C. to A.D. 1800*, 72–83. Chicago: University of Chicago Press, 1960.

Reardon, Kenneth M. "Participatory Action Research as Service Learning." In *Academic Service Learning: A Pedagogy of Action and Reflection*, edited by Robert A. Rhoads and Jeffry P. F. Howard, 57–64. San Francisco: Jossey-Bass.

Review of *Documents and Proceedings Relating to the Formation and Progress of a Board in the City of New York, for the Emigration, Preservation, and Improvement of the Aborigines of America. July 22, 1829*. *The North American Review* 30, no. 66 (January, 1830): 62–121.

Reznicek, A. A., E. G. Voss, and B. S. Walters. *Michigan Flora Online*. University of Michigan. 2022. https://michiganflora.net.

Rheault, D'Arcy Ishpeming'enzaabid. *Anishinaabe Mino-Bimaadiziwin: The Way of Good Life. An Examination of Anishinaabe Philosophy, Ethics and Traditional Knowledge*. Peterborough, Ont.: Debwewin Press, 1999. http://eaglefeather.org/series/Native%20American%20Series/Anishinaabe%20Tradition%20D%27Arcy%20Rheault.pdf.

Rienstra, Debra. *Refugia Faith: Seeking Hidden Shelters, Ordinary Wonders, and the Healing of the Earth*. Minneapolis: Fortress Press, 2022.

Rincon, Paul. "Earliest Evidence for Humans in the Americas." BBC. July 22, 2020. https://www.bbc.com/news/science-environment-53486868.

Robbins, Jim. "Native Knowledge: What Ecologists Are Learning from Indigenous People," *Yale Environment 360*, April 26, 2018. https://e360.yale.edu/features/native-knowledge-what-ecologists-are-learning-from-indigenous-people.

Roos, C. I., T. W. Swetnam, T. J. Ferguson, M. J. Liebmann, R. A. Loehman, J. R. Welch, E. Q. Margolis, C. H. Guiterman, W. C. Hockaday, M. J. Aiuvalasit, J. Battillo, J. Farella, and C. A. Kiahtipes. "Native American Fire Management at an Ancient Wildland-Urban Interface in the Southwest United States." *Proceedings of the National Academy of Sciences of the United States* 118, no. 4 (January 18, 2021): e2018733118. https://doi.org/10.1073/pnas.2018733118.

Rosenzweig, Michael L. *Win-Win Ecology: How the Earth's Species Can Survive in the Midst of Human Enterprise*. Oxford: Oxford University Press, 2003.

Samuelson, Linda, et al. *Heart and Soul: The Story of Grand Rapids Neighborhoods*. Grand Rapids Area Council for the Humanities. Grand Rapids, MI: William B. Eerdmans, 2003.

Santoro, Nicholas J. *Atlas of the Indian Tribes of North America and the Clash of Cultures*. Bloomington, IN: iUniverse, 2009.

Schaaf, Gregory. "From the Great Law of Peace to the Constitution of the United States: A Revision of America's Democratic Roots." *American Indian Law Review* 14, no. 2 (1989): 323–31. https://doi.org/10.2307/20068293.

Schaetzl, Randall J. "Gypsum." GEO 333: Geography of Michigan and the Great Lakes Region. https://project.geo.msu.edu/geogmich/gypsummining.html.

Schaetzl, Randall J. "Indian Land Cessions and Reservations." GEO 333: Geography of Michigan and the Great Lakes Region. https://project.geo.msu.edu/geogmich/images/indianreservation.jpg.

Schlender, James. Preface of *Plants Used by the Great Lakes Ojibwa* by J. E. Meeker, J. E. Elias, and J. A. Heim, iii–iv. Odana, WI: Great Lakes Indian Fish and Wildlife Commission, 1993.

Seltenrich, N. "Just What the Doctor Ordered: Using Parks to Improve Children's Health." *Environmental Health Perspectives* 123, no. 10 (2015): A254–A259. https://doi.org/10.1289/ehp.123-A254.

Singh, Ana, and David Warners. "Overview of PCS Transpiration Dataset 2018–2020." October 2, 2020. https://calvin.edu/go/CCRG-transpiration.

Singh, Ana, Rachel Warners, Jonathan Walt, Patrick Jonker, and David Warners. "Relative Success of Native Plants in Urban Curb-Cut Rain Gardens." *Ecological Restoration* 39, no. 4 (December 2021): 217–22. http://calvin.edu/go/CCRG-Plants.

Sire, James W. *The Universe Next Door: A Basic Worldview Catalog.* 6th ed. Downers Grove, IL: InterVarsity Press, 2020.

Smith, Clint. *How the Word Is Passed*, New York: Little, Brown, 2021.

Smith, Joshua. *Borderland Smuggling: Patriots, Loyalists, and Illicit Trade in the Northeast, 1783–1820.* Gainesville: University Press of Florida, 2007.

Sobel, David. *Place-Based Education: Connection Classrooms and Communities.* Great Barrington, MA: Orion Society, 2005.

Stateside Staff. "A Harbor Springs Boarding School Worked to Erase Odawa Culture until the 1980s." Michigan Radio. November 8, 2017. https://www.michiganradio.org/post/harbor-springs-boarding-school-worked-erase-odawa-culture-until-1980s.

Steinberg, Theodore. *Nature Incorporated: Industrialization and the Waters of New England.* Amherst: University of Massachusetts Press, 1991.

Stivers, Julie Christianson, and Garrett E. Crow. "Emma Jane Cole, West Michigan's Late-19th Century Botanist: A Biographical Sketch." *Great Lakes Botanist* 57 (2018): 50–99. https://quod.lib.umich.edu/cgi/p/pod/dod-idx/emma-jane-cole-west-michigans-late-19th-century-botanist.pdf?c=mbot;idno=0497763.0057.302;format=pdf.

Stoehr, Catherine. "Salvation from Empire: The Roots of Anishinabe Christianity in Upper Canada, 1650–1840." PhD diss., Queen's University, 2008. https://qspace.library.queensu.ca/bitstream/handle/1974/1324/MurtonStoehr_Catherine_E_200807_PhD.pdf?sequence=1.

Stokes Brown, Cynthia. *Big History: From the Big Bang to the Present.* New York: New Press, 2007.

Tarr, Joel A. "The Separate vs. Combined Sewer Problem: A Case Study in Urban Technology Design Choice." In *The Search for the Ultimate Sink: Urban Pollution in Historical Perspective*, 131–58. Akron, OH: University of Akron Press, 1996.

Taylor, Dorceta E. *The Environment and the People in American Cities: Disorder, Inequality, and Social Change.* Durham, NC: Duke University Press, 2009.

Taylor, Dorceta E. "The Evolution of Environmental Justice Activism, Research, and

Scholarship." *Environmental Practice* 13, no. 4 (2011): 280–301.

Taylor, Dorceta E. "The Rise of the Environmental Justice Paradigm: Injustice Framing and the Social Construction of Environmental Discourses." *American Behavioral Scientist* 43, no. 4 (2000): 508–80. https://doi.org/10.1177/0002764200043004003.

Taylor, Dorceta E. *Toxic Communities: Environmental Racism, Industrial Pollution, and Residential Mobility*. New York: New York University Press, 2014.

TetraTech. *BMP Planning to Address Urban Runoff: Plaster Creek Watershed SUSTAIN Pilot.* Cleveland, OH: TetraTech, 2012. https://calvin.edu/go/SUSTAIN.

Treuer, David. "Return the National Parks to the Tribes." *The Atlantic*, May 2021, https://www.theatlantic.com/magazine/archive/2021/05/return-the-national-parks-to-the-tribes/618395.

Tunison, John. "Flood Damage Report: $10.6 Million to Kent County Properties." *MLive.* May 16, 2013.

Tuttle, Charles Richard. *History of Grand Rapids with Biographical Sketches.* Grand Rapids, MI: Tuttle and Cooney, 1874.

Tutu, Desmond Mpilo. *No Future without Forgiveness.* New York: Doubleday Press, 1999.

Upper Midwest Water Science Center. "Evaluating the Potential Benefits of Permeable Pavement on the Quantity and Quality of Stormwater Runoff." USGS. March 17, 2019. https://www.usgs.gov/centers/upper-midwest-water-science-center/science/evaluating-potential-benefits-permeable-pavement.

Vande Bunte, Matt. "2013 Flood: Experts Describe How Close Grand Rapids Was to Crippling Floodwall Breach." *MLive.* January 5, 2014.

Vander Meer, Luke, Katherine DeHeer, Joseph Mellinger, Sarah Gibes, Bradley Paasch, Julie Wildschut, William L. Miller, Sheng-Yang He, and Kelly N. Dubois. "Indicator Species Characterization and Removal in a Detention Pond in the Plaster Creek Watershed." *Journal of Environmental Management* 298 (2021): 113503. http://calvin.edu/go/kreiserpond.

Van Wieren, Gretel. *Restored to Earth: Christianity, Environmental Ethics, and Ecological Restoration.* Washington, DC: Georgetown University Press, 2013.

Villanueva, Edgar, and Hilary Giovale, "Healing from Colonization on Thanksgiving and Beyond." *Yes! Magazine*, November 27, 2019. https://www.yesmagazine.org/opinion/2019/11/27/thanksgiving-colonial-gap-heal.

Walsh, Christopher J., Allison H. Roy, Jack W. Feminella, Peter D. Cottingham, Peter M. Groffman, and Raymond P. Morgan II. 2005. "The Urban Stream Syndrome: Current Knowledge and the Search for a Cure." *Journal of North American Benthological Society* 24, no. 3 (September 2005): 706–23. https://doi.org/10.1899/04-028.1.

Warners, David P. "Walking through a World of Gifts." In *Beyond Stewardship: New Approaches to Creation Care*, edited by David Paul Warners and Matthew Kuperus Heun, 185–94. Grand Rapids, MI: Calvin University Press, 2019.

Warners, David Paul, and Matthew Kuperus Heun, eds. *Beyond Stewardship: New Approaches to Creation Care*. Grand Rapids, MI: Calvin University Press, 2019.

Warners, David, Michael Ryskamp, and Randall Van Dragt. "Reconciliation Ecology: A New Paradigm for Advancing Creation Care." *Perspectives on Science and Christian Faith* 66, no. 4 (2014): 221–35.

Weston, Richard. "Observations on Alabaster or Gypsum as a Manure." In *The Repertory of Arts, Manufactures, and Agriculture*, 420–26. London: Nichols and Son Printers, 1804.

White, Richard. *The Middle Ground: Indians, Empires, and Republics in the Great Lakes Region, 1650–1815 (Studies in North American Indian History) 20th Anniversary Edition*. Cambridge: Cambridge University Press, 2011.

Wildcat, Daniel R. "Introduction: Climate Change and the Indigenous Peoples of the USA." In "Climate Change and Indigenous Peoples in the United States: Impacts, Experiences, and Actions," edited by J. K. Maldonado, B. J. Colombi, and R. E. Pandya, special issue, *Climatic Change* 120 (2013): 509–15. https://doi.org/10.1007/978-3-319-05266-3_1.

Wildcat, Daniel R. *Red Alert! Saving the Planet with Indigenous Knowledge*. Golden, CO: Fulcrum Publishing, 2009.

Witgen, Michael. *An Infinity of Nations*. Philadelphia: University of Pennsylvania Press, 2012.

Wynder, Ehren. "Grand Rapids Celebrates Reopening of Ken-O-Sha Park." Crain's Grand Rapids Business. August 25, 2021. https://grbj.com/news/government/grand-rapids-celebrates-reopening-of-ken-o-sha-park/.

Young, Davis A., and R. E. Stearley. *The Bible, Rocks and Time: Geological Evidence for the Age of the Earth*. Downers Grove, IL: InterVarsity Press, 2008.

Zwinger, Ann. *Into the Field: A Guide to Locally Focused Teaching*. Great Barrington, MA: Orion Society, 1996.

Index